D0891507

DATE DUE

TIJTATU99

TEJANOS AND TEXAS
UNDER THE MEXICAN FLAG

NUMBER FIFTY-FOUR:
The Centennial Series of the
Association of Former Students,
Texas A&M University

Tejanos and Texas

under the

Mexican Flag

1821–1836

Andrés Tijerina

TEXAS A&M UNIVERSITY PRESS
College Station

For my mother,
Belia

The paper used in this book meets the minimum requirements
of the American National Standard for Permanence
of Paper for Printed Library Materials, Z39.48-1984.
Binding materials have been chosen for durability.

Library of Congress Cataloging-in-Publication Data

Tijerina, Andrés.
Tejanos and Texas under the Mexican flag, 1821–1836 / Andrés
Tijerina.
    p.   cm. — (The Centennial series of the Association of Former
Students, Texas A&M University ; no. 54)
Includes bibliographical references and index.
ISBN 0-89096-585-4. — ISBN 0-89096-606-0 (pbk.)
    1. Texas—History—To 1846. 2. Mexicans—Texas—History—19th
century. 3. Texas—Ethnic relations. I. Title. II. Series.
F389.T53   1994
976.4-dc20   93-40484
                                                      CIP

Contents

List of Illustrations vi
List of Tables vii
Preface ix
Introduction 3
I. Tejano Settlements on the *Frontera* 5
II. Governing the Towns of the *Frontera* 25
III. The Tejano Community 46
IV. Tejano Justice on the *Frontera* 65
V. Military Reorganization in Texas 79
VI. Texas Statehood under Coahuila 93
VII. The Emergence of Tejano Politics 113
VIII. The Tejanos between Two Frontiers 137
Notes 145
Bibliography 161
Index 169

Illustrations

Figures

1. *Fandango,* by Theodore Gentilz 49
2. *Sobre la huella,* by Theodore Gentilz 80
3. Agustín Viesca 117

Maps

1. Tejano Population Regions 8
2. *Porciones* of Laredo in Webb County 52
3. Tomas de la Vega Land Grant 56
4. Department of Texas in 1834 106

Tables

1. Béxar-Goliad Civilian Population 12

2. Age, Sex, Status Report of Béxar, 1820 13

3. Age, Sex, Status Report of Béxar, 1831 14

4. Age, Sex, Status Report of Béxar, 1833 14

5. Age, Sex, Status Report of Victoria, 1830 16

6. Age, Sex, Status Report of Goliad, 1831 17

7. Tejano Ranches by Region 18

8. Nacogdoches Tejano Population 20

9. Age, Sex, Status Report of Nacogdoches, 1833 21

10. Tejano Composite Age, Sex, Status Report of Béxar, Goliad, and Nacogdoches, 1833 22

11. Schools of Coahuila y Texas, 1831 61

12. Tejano Headrights Patented by Region and Year 140

13. Mexican-Born Heads of Household by Occupation by Region, Texas, 1850 142

Preface

In 1893, Professor Frederick Jackson Turner delivered his famous paper on "The Significance of the Frontier in American History" to the American Historical Association. In this speech, Turner presented his thesis that in adapting to the environment, the pioneers had developed a rugged individualism integral to American democracy. Walter Prescott Webb added a variation to the Turnerian theme in 1931 in his book *The Great Plains*. Webb agreed with Turner's basic tenets, but added that the plains environment had also impressed its indelible stamp on the American character. The Indians, the land, the climate, and therefore the adaptation of the American were different on the plains. Both Turner and Webb did much to explain the historical development of the American culture as it moved westward. But the character of the Anglo American underwent a change by the mid-nineteenth century, for which neither the plains nor the early frontier could fully account.

As the great Anglo-American frontier pushed westward from the Atlantic toward the Pacific, it entered a significant phase during the 1820s and the 1830s. In its tremendous migratory thrust of this period, the Anglo-American frontier first entered the Mexican borderlands frontier. Here, Anglo Americans encountered a different kind of Indians, many of whom had European names and had intermingled among white people in a western-style civilization. The harsh environment demanded adaptation indeed, but by the time Anglo Americans arrived here, the adaptation had already taken place. European culture and institutions had already been adapted to the problems of water, industry, and the management of natural resources. This new region already had a social order befitting its particular natural environment, and both factors would affect the Anglo-American experience.

Texas played a key role in the encounter of the Anglo-American and the Mexican frontiers, geographically and chronologically. The early waves of Anglo-American settlers arrived first in Texas shortly after 1820, and the first major clash between the two frontiers was in 1836. The drama of the Alamo, an independent republic, and popular leaders like Sam Houston and Stephen F. Austin held the attention and imagination of westward-gazing Americans. Again in 1845, Texas drew the attention of Americans as the nation plunged into war with Mexico. The Mexican War ended three decades of interaction which left the United States in possession of Texas and the Mexican Cession.

So dramatic a shift in land and resources greatly affected Mexicans, but it had its effect on Anglo Americans as well. As the Anglo-American pioneers approached Texas in the 1820s, they wore buckskin clothing and walked in leather moccasins. They were hunters and trappers of the ilk of Andrew Jackson and David Crockett who wore a soft "coon skin" cap. They were also farmers who planted corn, wheat, and cotton. But after their encounter with the Mexican culture in Texas, many of the frontiersmen began to wear boots and "cowboy" hats. They used heavy Mexican saddles to ride horses taken from the wild mustang herds of Texas. They drove great herds of longhorns north and westward, spreading the grazing economy and ranch life as they went. And with the cattle ranch went many words, practices, and legal principles which had been developed long before by the native Mexicans of Texas—the Tejanos.

The term *Tejanos* refers to native Hispanic inhabitants of Texas and is used in a comparative sense in this context, as opposed to Texans of Anglo-American background. Although native Hispanic inhabitants of El Paso could also be classified as Tejanos, they are not included here because of their remoteness and the distinctiveness of their cultural influence during the period covered in this work.

This study focuses on Texas between 1821 and 1836 in an effort to provide structure for an understanding of the exchange of land, power, culture, and social institutions that took place between the two frontiers during those critical years. Historians have amply recorded the battles and the Anglo Americans' military, economic, and political domination of the Mexican lands. But few studies have documented the reverse flow in this interchange. This book represents an attempt to document the two-way cultural exchange within a limited scope. The purpose is to describe the basic institutions of Tejano life and culture and then to document their transmission to the Anglo-American frontier. The work is intended as a foundation for the study of the early Mexican-American culture in Texas and its influence on Texans of all ethnic backgrounds.

Much of the material in this book is the result of research in primary documents which too long have been ignored by historians. Much of it is simply a compendium of bits of information which have to date remained scattered in a variety of published sources. Perhaps more than anything else, the book is aimed at unifying matters that have been known intuitively by historians, but have never been conjoined and committed to formal writing. Indeed, if Texas has lived under six flags, then it is time to tell her story under the Mexican flag.

In conducting the research represented in this book, I owe gratitude to many persons. To David M. Vigness, Alwyn Barr, and Seymour V. Connor, I owe thanks for that first spark of imagination and training in historical documentation which led to my commitment to writing Texas history. To Nettie Lee Benson, I owe appreciation for my first introduction to the richness of the Béxar and Nacogdoches archives at the University of Texas. To Joe B. Frantz, I owe my fondest gratitude for his continued guidance and encouragement ever since I first wrote up the research under him as a dissertation at the University of Texas fifteen years ago. I finally took his advice, and rewrote it. I was in no small way inspired by my colleagues, such as Gilberto Hinojosa, David Montejano, and Emilio Zamora, who led a whole generation of writers in the establishment of Tejano history. Their support and advice reassured me greatly. And finally, I must formally acknowledge the total dedication of Juanita, my wife, who gave years of sacrifice and understanding in a time of emerging women's rights that I might complete this book. My thanks to her and to my three sons, Andrew, Juan-Michael, and Marcos.

Tejanos and Texas
under the Mexican Flag

Introduction

Tejanos had a significant and lasting influence in the history of Texas. They gave unique reality to the larger historical forces centering on Texas in the early nineteenth century. When international events brought changes to the political status of Texas, Tejanos provided a vital continuum. Their local laws gave meaning and movement to national legislation. Their culture, their lives, their problems, and their solutions contributed much to the historical character of Texas. For these reasons, Tejano society must be studied and understood within the context of the broader historical perspective of Texas.

One of the first major events to affect Texas in the nineteenth century occurred when she was still a province of Mexico, or New Spain. In September, 1810, New Spain felt the first tremors of a movement for freedom when a Mexican priest named Miguel Hidalgo began a movement that would lead to independence from Spain. King Ferdinand VII of Spain was in France at that time, being held prisoner of Napoleon. Ferdinand watched helplessly as the Spanish Cortes convened in 1810 to establish a constitutional monarchy during his absence. The new Spanish Constitution of 1812 allowed for many liberal reforms which Mexicans quickly began to implement. In 1814, Ferdinand returned and repudiated the constitution, reversing the liberalization movement. But in 1820, the Spanish Army rebelled against the king, and compelled his acceptance of the 1812 constitution. This action reawakened open revolt in Mexico as well.

The structure of Texas provincial government slowly evolved during these years despite many rebellions and filibustering expeditions in the province. When the Spanish Army rebelled in Spain, provinces of New

Spain resumed implementation of the provincial form of government as set forth by the Spanish Constitution of 1812. Before Texas obtained her own provincial authority, Mexico achieved formal independence in 1821 under the leadership of Agustín de Iturbide, who named himself emperor. His empire was overthrown in 1823 by Mexican republicans who thereupon created a national constituent congress. As a result of that constituent congress, Texas finally obtained her own provincial deputation which governed her until the promulgation of the federal constitution of 1824. The new constitution ended Texas' experiment as a self-governed province by making her a department of the new state of Coahuila y Texas.

Despite changes in the relationship of Texas to the Spanish or Mexican governments, however, her internal government structure maintained a high degree of integrity. The underlying reality in the government of Texas was not so much in the phase-to-phase changes which it underwent from Spanish colonial rule to Mexican federation—or even in its transition to Anglo-American republic—as in the continuum throughout these years of turmoil. While the direction of politics and economic power shifted from Spanish to Mexican and from Mexican to Anglo, the basic socioeconomic institutions and the management of resources and manpower followed a continuous evolutionary pattern during the Mexican years. As the Mexican state replaced the Spanish colony, it recognized and retained the old institutions and concepts of the frontier or *frontera*. These legislative concepts remained, in substance, under still another government. Thus continued many of the same institutions by different names, in different languages, imposed by the force of logic on whoever should claim and hold this land of the *frontera*.

The following chapters attempt to describe the pattern of continuum in the government of Texas. First, a description of Tejano society and local government lay the framework for a picture of life in the municipalities of Texas and the legacy of the Hispanic frontier concept. Then a description of the evolution of the statehood of Texas under the Mexican republic leads into the account of the legislative labor and legacy of Tejano statesmen. Such a discussion of state and local government should help to clarify the factors by which Texas is so uniquely a part of the Hispanic tradition and so distinctly apart from the Anglo-Saxon.

I

Tejano Settlements on
the *Frontera*

When Anglos first arrived in what is now Texas in 1821, Tejano settlement consisted of three distinct and separate regions—the Nacogdoches region, the Béxar-Goliad region along the San Antonio River, and the Río Grande ranching frontier between the Nueces River and the Río Grande. Each of these populations fluctuated independently from the others; and yet, all of them had certain characteristics in common.

The basic factor unifying the Tejano community was the military purpose of the settlements. All Tejanos shared a military background which had developed into a strong sense of mission to defend Mexico's northern *frontera*. Soldiers stationed on the *frontera* integrated socially into the Tejano civilian communities, reinforcing the unity of the different regions. A second factor unifying the Tejano *frontera* was the mixture of racial groups peculiar to Tejano settlements. And finally, the racial heritage of the Tejanos reinforced the contrast between them and the Anglo-American settlers daily arriving from the United States.

Spanish colonial administrators had originally settled Texas as a "buffer province" for northern New Spain. The Spaniards had learned from the Iberian peninsula centuries earlier to use a buffer zone between their own settlements and those of the Moorish invaders. They had learned to control a depopulated zone, or *despoblado*, for defensive purposes as they steadily reconquered their lands occupied by the Moors. The Spaniards had established armed municipalities, *presidios* or forts, and missions within the *despoblado*. These municipalities, presidios, and missions constituted the defensive borderland or *frontera*. In the New World, the Spaniards sought to establish a *frontera* in northern Mexico as well. Here they faced not

5

Moors, but foreign interlopers just the same. French explorers had landed on the Texas coast in the late seventeenth century, stirring Spanish fears of encroachment. In reaction, the viceroys of Mexico ordered the exploration and settlement of Texas. Thus, in its very settlement, Texas had developed a defensive governmental structure which was described by historian Herbert E. Bolton as being "almost wholly military."[1]

The role of Texas as a defensive *frontera* province was strongly reinforced by the influential statesman of Saltillo, Miguel Ramos Arizpe, in the late eighteenth century. Ramos Arizpe warned that Mexico should secure her hold (her *conservación*) of Texas, "particularly in the vicinity of the United States."[2] In his official reports to Spain, he expressed a commonly held Mexican preoccupation with Anglo-American incursions from the United States as well as with Indian depredations from the north. In order to strengthen the Mexican *frontera*, Ramos Arizpe proposed specifically to colonize the zone with new settlers from interior Mexico and from other nations as well. Ramos Arizpe's argument was reinforced by a royal inspector, the Marques de Rubí, who toured the northern provinces in 1766 and recommended that a line of presidios guard the *frontera*. In time, Texas came to represent the northern defensive line, or *frontera*.

Officials in Mexico City, greatly influenced by Ramos Arizpe's arguments, sought to strengthen the Texas *frontera* by promoting civilian settlements. But peopling of the Texas *frontera* was problematic at best for the Mexicans. The army failed to entice Mexicans to settle a buffer zone against Anglos just as the church had failed to establish a mission system among the Indians of Texas. While Mexican settlers had been willing earlier to settle the northern province of Coahuila, they became reluctant after 1700 to move farther north into Texas—home of the feared Lipan and Comanche Indians. The settlers who had come to Texas in the late eighteenth century came only as a last resort. Disease and famine in central and northern Mexico had uprooted thousands of people after 1750, and had driven some of them into Texas as an influx of immigrants. But without such compelling forces, few civilians offered themselves to the government's policy of moving north merely to serve as a buffer colony.

Between 1800 and 1830, the government in Mexico attempted to sponsor military settlements and formal colonization of armed citizens or *ciudadanos armados* in the Texas *frontera*. Neither of these programs succeeded as originally planned by Mexico. Indeed, as the years passed, other Mexicans developed a condescending attitude toward the isolated *frontera* settler, the Tejano. One report in 1833, for example, quoted a prominent citizen of Saltillo as speaking in a "tone of contempt" about "the poor, out-of-the-world" Tejanos, adding that personally, he "could not live happily in such banishment."[3] Tejanos frequently demanded reinforcements from Saltillo as late as the 1830s, but were denied these due to a lack of prospective settlers. A typical response to these demands in those years was one particular message from Saltillo which stated: "The government is lacking the funds to send the four hundred farmers requested . . . unfortunately not one Mexican has applied for an empresario contract."[4]

Attempts to establish strategic military settlements along the Trinity River and north of San Antonio encountered similar problems. In the first ten years of the century, soldiers in Texas were regularly assigned to escort, guard, and even augment (*engrosar*) several planned settlements such as Trinidad de Salcedo, San Marcos de Neve, Jesús y Jaen, and San Telésforo. Failing to establish these strategic settlements, however, the Mexican administrators then invited foreign colonization during the 1820s. The most significant of the resulting communities was the Anglo-American colony of Stephen F. Austin.

Austin had come to Coahuila y Texas in 1821 to take over the colonization contract granted earlier to his father, Moses. Thousands of Anglo-American cotton farmers had already settled in the Louisiana Territory, waiting anxiously for an opportunity to move onto the Blackland soils of Texas. With Austin's contract validated, his colony and other Anglo-American settlements quickly drew these settlers. Mexican officials witnessed a greater migration than they had ever seen from Mexico. But their nagging fear of Anglo designs on Texas prompted new orders for Mexican military settlements in 1830. In that year, the government ordered defensive establishments at Anáhuac, Tenoxtitlán, and Terán, by which Mexico again tried to foster strategic population centers in East Texas. All were failures by 1832. In fact, few of the military-sponsored settlements of this entire Mexican period ever survived more than about three years.[5]

The major pattern of Tejano settlement then was not the planned spread of strategic military settlements that the Mexican government tried so diligently to achieve. Instead, the population of Texas, particularly in the Béxar-Goliad region, increased only as the established presidio soldiers, or *presidiales*, steadily integrated or amalgamated into the neighboring communities through intermarriage or retirement. The presidial amalgamation increased the population and promoted a racial mixing as well. Most of the

7

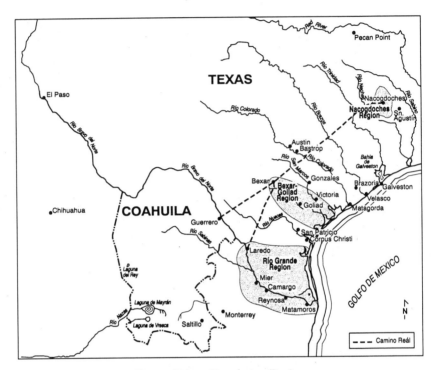

Map 1. Tejano Population Regions

Mexican settlers and soldiers who inhabited the communities and presidios of Texas had come from staging areas in northern Mexico where racial mixing had been prevalent. They were *mestizos,* a racial mixture of Spanish and native Mexican Indian. The Mexican natives in northern Mexico were largely of the Tlascalan tribe from the former Aztec empire. Thus, the original Tejano community was most likely a blend of intermarrying between Tlascalan soldiers and Spanish and mestizo settlers. *Presidiales* married into civilian communities; Tlascalans married into Spaniard families.

The merging of these different subgroups in Texas was most graphic in the very founding of the province in 1716. Captain Don Domingo Ramón established the province of Texas that year with an expedition of sixty-five civilian settlers from the Saltillo area. Two years later Don Martín de Alarcón laid the first permanent foundations on the San Antonio River by establishing the Presidio de San Antonio de Béxar and the Mission San Antonio de Valero. Alarcón's settlers were troops and mestizo settlers from

8

Monclova in the northern province of Coahuila. These founders later established four other missions near San Antonio de Béxar, along the San Antonio River. These were the missions of San José, San Juan, Concepción, and San Francisco de Espada. The missions, however, dwindled in population and importance. They were built to attract the local native Indians of Texas; to Christianize and assimilate them into Spanish society. But they were largely unsuccessful in attracting the local natives, and had little significance for Tejano society in the nineteenth century. More significant was the arrival of a group of Spanish settlers in 1731 from the Canary Islands. The Canary Islanders established their *villa*—village—and church of San Fernando de Béxar adjacent to the original San Antonio presidio and across the river from Mission Valero. Thus they developed the neighborhood pattern which prevailed in San Antonio for a century—the presidio and Spanish villa on the north side of the river and Valero as the *barrio del sur* or the "south neighborhood."[6]

Another example of the racial composition of Tejanos in the San Antonio area can be seen in the arrival of the *compañía volante* or "flying squadron." The Compañía Volante of San Carlos de Parras was originally from Alamo, a community near Parras in southern Coahuila. When the squadron reported for permanent military duty at Mission Valero around 1803, its troops were mostly Tlascalan, and numbered 241, including accompanying wives and children. Tlascalans generally found it easy to intermarry with other civilized tribes and races on the *frontera*. In the *barrio del sur* they readily mixed with the 108 Spanish and mestizo inhabitants of the old Pueblo de Valero beside the mission. The troops intermarried with some of the local Indians as well.[7]

In any consideration of the racial mixing process or *mestizaje* on the Mexican *frontera*, it is necessary to distinguish between Indians of Mexican origin such as the Tlascalan and those of Texas origin such as the Apache. The Indians of Mexico differed substantially from the Texas Comanche or Lipan Apache. In fact, the Mexican tribes possessed easily distinguishable traits even among themselves. For example, the nomadic Chichimeca "grubbers" of Tamaulipas, northern Mexico, were vastly different from the "civilized" Tlascalans and Aztecs of central Mexico—a distinction sometimes lost on nineteenth-century Anglos and modern historians as well.[8]

The Tlascalans who had come to Texas from Coahuila were civilized before the arrival of the Europeans, and had lived under the Aztec empire.

They had become allies of the Spaniards in the conquest of the Aztecs, and had later become an important factor in Spanish colonization throughout northern Mexico. In 1591, for example, four hundred Tlascalan and Aztec families came north with Spanish Captain General Francisco de Urdiñola to settle Saltillo. They later became, as Bolton said, "the mother colony from which numerous offshoots were planted at the new missions and villages further north,"—that is, in Texas. The main attributes of the Tlascalans in this process were stated in a 1698 petition, which proclaimed that they "would be a buffer against enemies and that they would always have arms and horses to resist . . . [and] because the natural Indians get along well with the Tlascaltecos and help them in everything." The Tlascaltecos or Tlascalans were able to settle permanently such important frontier towns as Monclova, Parras, Punto de Lampazos, and Boca de Leones—all in Coahuila, northern Mexico. Tlascalans and a few Otomís also settled Monterrey and its surrounding villages in 1646. Thus as José de Escandón came northward from Querétaro in 1748 to settle the Río Grande Valley, he picked up settlers at many of these Tlascalan villages along his way.[9] By the end of the eighteenth century, the northern tier of Mexican provinces—San Luis Potosí, Nuevo León, Coahuila, and Nuevo Santander—were heavily influenced by Tlascalan racial characteristics; Texas could hardly be less so.

At San Fernando de Béxar, the Canary Island Spaniards initially tried to remain aloof from the "lower" mestizo classes of Valero. As one old San Fernando resident of the 1830s recalled, "Most of the Canary Islanders who lived on this side took great pride in preventing any intermarriage with mixed races and when one did mix he lost his caste with the rest."[10] These Spaniards did avoid mixing with the Negroes, mulattoes, and Indians in San Fernando, according to the official census records prior to 1820. But the Spaniards did not avoid mixing with the "upper" mestizo castes who lived in the barrio of Valero. Eventually, the Spaniards intermarried with the mestizos of Valero. By 1820, about thirty percent of the San Fernando married couples were mixed Spanish and mestizo.

Francisco Amangual, commander of the compañía volante, was one of the "ice breakers" who first married a local woman from San Fernando. His marriage application in 1807 was one of the first of a string of applications registered in the San Fernando Chancery Archives. His marriage strengthened the pattern of amalgamation between the *presidiales* and San Fernando women. As Amangual and other *presidiales* were breaking the caste barriers into San Fernando society, military organization on the *frontera* was undergoing changes which further facilitated such intermarriages.

By the 1820s, the Mexican military began to assign troops permanently to the presidios on the Texas *frontera*. Under the previous Spanish government system, the military command had drawn troops from scattered outposts across northern Mexico, and assigned them only temporarily to the outposts in Texas. In 1805, for example, there were seven hundred troops assigned to Texas, a hodgepodge of pickets, cavalry units, and state militias taken from Coahuila, Nuevo León, and Nuevo Santander. After Mexican Independence, however, there were only 250 troops at the presidios of Béxar, La Bahía, and Alamo. But these troops were there on permanent assignment. By 1826, the Béxar and Valero garrisons were completely reorganized. They began to enlist local Bexareños into presidial duty. The troops found it easier not only to marry local women in Texas, but to retire with their families in the presidial towns on the *frontera*. Such a person was José María Balmaceda, who became a leading Tejano statesman by 1830 after having been *retirado* in Béxar. Other *presidiales* included Francisco Xavier Chaves and José Antonio Menchaca, who became important Tejanos of the 1830s.[11]

Eventually, the military and civilian neighborhoods of Béxar blended into a unified community. Local Bexareños and official visitors alike perceived Béxar as one settlement instead of as several outposts. The official census enumerator for the 1820 census, for example, listed all the barrios in a single census as the "Capital de Béxar." In 1828, another government visitor, José María Sánchez, reported in his official *Trip to Texas in 1828* that the barrios constituted a single city, the "Ciudad de San Fernando de Béjar." Béxar had become a single town, and its residents had amalgamated into one people. No single record remains of the exact number of families introduced to the Texas *frontera* by this presidial amalgamation, but obviously many of them had military origins. As one old Bexareño reminisced, "My ancestors, both on my father's and mother's side were military men and all of them engaged in the service of their country at some time."[12]

In addition to the process of the *mestizaje* and the presidial amalgamation, the Béxar community developed in this period other significant social characteristics. The population size, for example, proved to be rather erratic. Also, the mortality rates of children and adult men remained disproportionately high. All of these characteristics emerge vividly in the official census reports.

TABLE 1 Béxar-Goliad Civilian Population

Year	Béxar	Goliad	Victoria	TOTAL
1805[a]	1,998	524		2,522
1820[b]	1,814			
1825	1,562	522		2,084
1826	2,026[c]			
1828[d]	1,330	570		1,900
1831[e]	1,634	1,246	513	3,393
1833[f]	1,559	1,479	378	3,416
1834[g]	2,500	700	300	3,500

NOTE: All figures include only civilians, and exclude military troops and their families.
SOURCES: [a]*BA*, Census of Texas, Jan. 30, 1805.
[b]*BA*, Census of Texas, Jan. 1, 1820.
[c]*BA*, Béxar Statistical Report, Aug. 19, 1826; Coahuila y Texas, *Nota estadística remitida por el gobierno supremo del Estado de Coahuila y Tejas a la cámara de senadores del soberano congreso general con arreglo al artículo 161 número 8° de la Constitución Federal de los Estados Unidos Mexicanos el año de 1827*, appendix no. 14, "Población, 1825"; *NA*, La Bahía Census, Apr. 24, 1825.
[d]*AGC*, Census of Texas, June 1, 1828.
[e]*NA*, Béxar Census, Dec. 31, 1821; Goliad Census, Dec. 31, 1831.
[f]*NA*, Béxar Census, June 30, 1833; Goliad Census, June 30, 1833.
[g]Juan N. Almonte, *Nota estadística sobre Tejas*, p. 25.

The Béxar population fluctuated between roughly fifteen hundred and two thousand throughout the years 1805 to 1833 (see table 1). In 1828, when the population total dipped by over one-third in one year to 1,330, the report narrative included an explanatory note. It stated that the population appeared to decline because many civilian men and their families had been reclassified as military troops and dependents that year. The report stated as follows: "The difference seen in the census of the population for this year as compared to the one in 1826 is due to the Presidial Companies' having been reconstituted with local citizens, and because many of these military individuals have brought along their families who are not included in the general census due to their unique status."[13]

There were other causes for the decline in population after 1825. The census report for 1827 cited "the war with the Indians and the natural death rate." These two factors not only explain the post-1825 decline, but also indicate the major cause for the erratic and slow overall population growth in Béxar. The highest natural death rate was reflected mostly among the children. The casualties in the Indian wars were reflected among the adult men.

TABLE 2   Age, Sex, Status Report of Béxar, 1820

Ages	Bachelor Male	Bachelor Female	Married Male	Married Female	Widowed Male	Widowed Female
Less than 7	176	191				
7 to 16	241	218		1		
16 to 25	81	83	16	58	1	13
25 to 40	50	26	76	160	2	68
40 to 50	12	6	47	37	7	38
50 and up	10	2	68	36	7	83
TOTALS	570	526	207	292	17	202

SOURCES: *BA*, Béxar Census, Jan. 1, 1820; *AGC*, Béxar Census, Leg. 25, Oct. 1, 1831; *NA*, Béxar Census, June 30, 1833.

The men had come as armed citizens, *ciudadanos armados*, primarily to defend the *frontera*. As such, they were expected to serve in military forays. They regularly served, and they often gave their lives in the process. The highest mortality was among men in their most productive years. As an example of the stark decline in adult men, the 1820 census listed 98 men and 154 women in the age group of 16 to 25 years (see table 2). But in the age group of 25 to 40 years, there were only 128 men compared to 254 women. Of these 254 women, 68 were already widows. Many men had been killed, no doubt, in the turmoil of the Mexican Independence period after 1810. But the numbers of adult men continued to suffer high attrition even after those years, as indicated by subsequent census reports. The only figure that remained consistently high in the census reports was that of widows. It increased even more for the higher age groups. Tejanas, the females, were the oldest (and often the wealthiest) on the Texas *frontera*.

The Béxar population also reported a consistently high infant mortality rate in the official census reports. Béxar officials submitted quarterly birth/death reports which revealed that the deaths were highest in the younger age groups of children less than age seven. The high death rates among productive men and among infants combined to produce the erratic and apparently stagnant population figures for Béxar during this period. The census reports did not cite specific reasons for high infant mortality, but disease was a constant on the *frontera* (see tables 3 and 4).

Down the San Antonio River from Béxar, near the Gulf Coast, was

TABLE 3   Age, Sex, Status Report of Béxar, 1831

Ages	Bachelor		Married		Widowed	
	Male	Female	Male	Female	Male	Female
Less than 7	172	152				
7 to 16	165	160		16		
16 to 25	89	72	56	71		9
25 to 40	32	34	114	132	12	43
40 to 50	11	6	48	36	11	32
50 and up	14	3	47	29	16	52
TOTALS	483	427	265	284	39	136

SOURCE: *NA*, Census of San Fernando de Béjar, Dec. 31, 1831.

TABLE 4   Age, Sex, Status Report of Béxar, 1833

Ages	Bachelor		Married		Widowed	
	Male	Female	Male	Female	Male	Female
Less than 7	160	142				
7 to 16	162	152		20		
16 to 25	81	69	54	81	2	11
25 to 40	39	36	115	131	11	46
40 to 50	8	7	44	30	5	27
50 and up	8	1	38	14	18	48
TOTALS	458	407	251	276	36	132

SOURCE: *NA*, Béxar Census, Jan. 30, 1833.

Goliad. The Goliad community was very similar to Béxar, particularly in the founding of a presidio and its social characteristics. The Presidio La Bahía del Espíritu Santo was founded by Ramón in 1722, and moved in 1749 to its permanent site. There, it became the population base for the community later known as Goliad. The settlers, like those at Béxar, had migrated primarily from the northern provinces of New Spain such as Coahuila and Nuevo León, and therefore reflected the same racial characteristics. The La Bahía missions of Refugio, Loreto, and Rosario were in the same "deplorable" state as those at Béxar after secularization. Since none of them had ever housed many Spaniards, the effect of the missions on Tejano social patterns in La Bahía was negligible. The effect of the presidial amalgamation at La Bahía, however, was even more pronounced than at Béxar.

The *presidiales* of La Bahía augmented the civilian populace through the amalgamation process described above; moreover, they had a stronger social influence on the small villa. The presidio not only had a larger numerical advantage over its civilian counterpart in La Bahía than in Béxar, but the military retirees seem to have enjoyed a higher social status in their role as civilians. This numerical advantage was emphasized by a shift in strategic importance from Béxar to La Bahía. The military became more important at La Bahía particularly after 1830 when troubles began among the Anglo-American colonies near there. These factors tended to strengthen the military character of La Bahía and to increase its population even as that of Béxar was declining in the mid-1820s.

La Bahía appeared more dynamic than Béxar in many ways. Ironically, La Bahía had not become an official villa until 1820. Its population, which was in the villa surrounding the presidio and on neighboring ranches, had traditionally been about half that of Béxar. But within a few years, the population of the area began an upward trend (see table 1). During this time, La Bahía changed its name to Goliad. Also at this time, Goliad was joined by the new settlement of Guadalupe de Jesús Victoria, which was founded nearby. Adding substantially to the area's growth trend, Victoria had been founded in 1824 by empresario Martín de León of Tamaulipas, or Nuevo Santander. This robust, new settlement included capable men like Placido Benavides as well as fifty other founding settlers from Cruillas, Tamaulipas. Victoria grew within a few years to a population of 238, and was later augmented by the arrival of 117 new troops and their families under the Law of April 6, 1830.

Goliad presents an interesting example of the presidial amalgamation process. The *presidiales* contributed greatly to the population, and more significantly they provided outstanding leadership among the Tejano community in general. Indeed, a steady flow of distinguished Goliad citizens emanated from the presidio. Antonio Menchaca, for example, who attained fame in the Texan Revolution, was the son of Captain Menchaca of the presidio. Other distinguished names among presidio descendants were Carlos de la Garza, of the ranch community "Carlos Rancho," and Ignacio Zaragoza, who went on to become the victorious general at the famous Mexican battle of the Cinco de Mayo. Another very important Tejano, though seldom recognized in history, was the former commander of the

TABLE 5   Age, Sex, Status Report of Victoria, 1830

Ages	Bachelor		Married		Widowed	
	Male	Female	Male	Female	Male	Female
Less than 7	28	17				
7 to 16	35	13		3		
16 to 25	11	6	6	14		
25 to 40	14	3	27	29	1	1
40 to 50	3		10	6	1	1
50 and up			4	2	1	2
TOTALS	91	39	47	54	3	4

SOURCE: *BA*, Census and Statistical Report, Aug. 26, 1830.

presidio, Rafael Antonio Manchola. Manchola became one of the most successful Tejano statesmen in Coahuila y Texas politics. He had arrived at La Bahía in 1822, served as a state congressman, and became the Goliad *ayuntamiento* president in 1831. Likewise, Captain José de Jesús Aldrete had retired as the presidio commander, and established a ranch in 1821 near the presidio. The Aldrete family later went on to settle in a new village known as San Patricio. They were followed by other noted *presidiales* like Lieutenant José María Cobián and Captain Enrique Pobedano. These and other military retirees would be regularly enumerated on the civilian census reports of Goliad. After retirement, the *presidiales* retained their military privileges, known as the *fuero*. The Goliad census report for 1833, for example, listed sixteen "military men retired with privileges" (*militares ret.ˢ con fuero*).[14]

The Goliad area had a more dynamic and youthful population group than did Béxar. Goliad's total population was already approaching that of Béxar by 1831, and actually surpassed it, counting the 513 souls at neighboring Victoria (see tables 5 and 6). Male adults had a high death rate around the age of forty at Goliad just at they did at Béxar, but there were more adolescents in Goliad than in Béxar by 1831. In fact, Goliad had a greater number of young men (age sixteen to twenty-five years), giving Goliad a younger median age. The Goliad census did, however, reflect the same *frontera* pattern of young brides and few old bachelors or widowers.

Ranches represented a significant social element in the Béxar-Goliad region. A belt of ranches extended along much of the San Antonio River

TABLE 6 Age, Sex, Status Report of Goliad, 1831

Ages	Bachelor Male	Female	Married Male	Female	Widowed Male	Female
Less than 7	156	164				
7 to 16	117	112		2		
16 to 25	78	47	43	60	5	
25 to 40	47	34	92	96	7	13
40 to 50	6		37	25	2	12
50 and up	2		32	21	7	29
TOTALS	406	357	204	204	21	54

SOURCE: *NA*, Goliad Census, Dec. 31, 1831.

between Béxar and Goliad. Although the ranch inhabitants were not regularly counted in official censuses, the ranches were known to house some of the most powerful and wealthiest (*pudientes*) citizens in the municipality. The number of ranches, however, fluctuated erratically throughout the early years of the nineteenth century. Indian raids and the turmoil of the Mexican independence movement in 1813 and 1819 virtually eliminated the region's ranches in those periods.[15]

Bexareños and Goliad *rancheros* began in the 1820s to reestablish the ranch belt along both sides of the San Antonio River and its tributaries. Indeed, former *presidiales* from both towns began to move onto the ranches, reflecting an extension of the presidial amalgamation (see table 7). By 1830, rancheros with the names of Balmaceda, Manchola, De la Garza, and Menchaca had moved onto new ranches. These new Tejano leaders brought with them a shift in wealth and status. The De León families—the wealthiest in Victoria—lived on their ranches, not in town. The Seguins, formerly of Béxar, reestablished their old ranch on the river in 1832. Built as a veritable fortress, the Seguin ranch housed several families and was described as a "beautiful place" by contemporary travelers. The De la Garza ranch near Goliad, "established and flourishing by 1830," included the related families of Cavasos, Ybarbo, and Tijerina. They were said to have "lived in the grandee style with many servants and retainers."[16]

The ranchero move onto ranches indicates the Tejano value for the land and ranching lifestyle as opposed to living in town. This pattern of outmigration by the wealthy tended to confuse census enumerators and visitors

17

TABLE 7   Tejano Ranches by Region

Year	Béxar-Goliad	Nacogdoches	Río Grande
1825	11[a]		
1830[b]	16	49	241
1831	73		
1833[c]	80	50	356

[a]O'Connor, *Presidio La Bahía*, p. 249; Béxar-Goliad region includes Béxar, Goliad, and Victoria settlements.
[b]*BA*, Victoria Census, Aug. 26, 1830; *BA*, Nacogdoches Census, June 30, 1830; *GLO, Spanish Archives*, James R. Miller and W. H. Bourland, "Report of James R. Miller and W. H. Bourland, Commissioners to Investigate Land Titles West of the Nueces"; *GLO, Maps of All Texas Counties*.
[c]*NA*, Béxar Censuses, Dec. 31, 1831, and June 30, 1833, and Goliad Census, Dec. 31, 1831; *GLO*, Miller and Bourland, "Land Titles West of the Nueces"; *GLO, Maps of All Texas Counties*.

alike. Census enumerators rarely accounted for the ranch inhabitants; visitors often described the Tejano towns as "wretched," failing to understand that many of the wealthier Tejanos preferred to live away from town. Many rural Tejanos crested the social hierarchy much as did plantation owners in the contemporary rural South of the United States.

The northern region of Tejano settlements in this period was Nacogdoches. Removed in physical distance from the Béxar-Goliad region, Nacogdoches was also distinct in character. Unlike Béxar, Nacogdoches had no major presidio to feed its bloodlines. Instead, the Nacogdoches racial and cultural structure drew as much from its French and Anglo neighbors in Louisiana as it did from Mexico far to the south. Located on a well-established trade route between Mexico and the United States, Nacogdoches lacked the comfortable inertia of Bexareño society. And Nacogdoches developed more than any other Tejano settlement the ability to remove its entire populace in time of attack and return when conditions permitted. Throughout its existence, the population of Nacogdoches ebbed and flowed, evacuated but never abandoned its frontier homeland.

Don Domingo Ramón had established Nacogdoches in 1716 with the same stock of Coahuilans who settled Béxar and Goliad. Nacogdoches was the principal Tejano settlement of the eastern frontier, near the Adaes Indians. For a while after its establishment it even served as the capital of Texas. In 1772, however, the New Regulations of Presidios inspired by

Marques de Rubí ordered the elimination of Nacogdoches. The settlers, known as Adaesaños, were ordered to remove to Béxar. Reluctantly the families moved in 1774. Nacogdoches, according to one historian, was "never wholly abandoned," however, and the displaced Adaesaños soon returned to their beloved ranches led by the stalwart Antonio Gil Ybarbo. By 1800 the approximately six hundred settlers at Nacogdoches were grudgingly "accepted" by the Mexican government officials as the northernmost salient of the Texas *frontera*.[17]

Nacogdoches led an uneasy existence during the independence movement after 1810. In 1811, roving bands of the Gutiérrez-Magee expedition forced the settlers to withdraw from Nacogdoches. Two years later the Spanish counterattack reportedly left the area "temporarily depopulated" as the royalist forces "swept eastward to Nacogdoches, murdering, plundering, and destroying."[18] Resurgence of revolutionary disturbances in the 1819-to-1822 period sent the ravaged settlers fleeing for the relative safety of Louisiana and Béxar. Throughout this constant state of upheaval, however, Nacogdoches was still not abandoned, but was held tenaciously by at least a few brave souls. Old settlers such as Luis Procela, Manuel Hernández, James Dill, and José Antonio Sepúlveda remained in the area and were among the first to solicit permission from the government to rebuild their town. By 1822 Don Pedro Procela enumerated nineteen families in the area. June of the next year saw 136 persons returning as the harbingers of what one historian has called a "steady flow of the Mexican population back to Nacogdoches and the surrounding district" (see table 8).[19]

Nacogdoches had always been a small, decentralized settlement. Its defense had been provided primarily by the settlers brought in by Gil Ybarbo. With the exception of the strategic settlement attempts on the Trinity and Brazos rivers, East Texas experienced no direct military augmentation. The one possible exception to this came when eighteen hundred Mexican troops and their families occupied the posts at Anáhuac, Terán, Tenoxtitlán, and Nacogdoches after the Law of April 6, 1830. But these left shortly afterwards, during the liberal revolts of 1832.[20] As a result, East Texas lacked the concentration of settlers evident around the presidios of Béxar, Valero, or La Bahía. Nacogdoches consisted of a small town surrounded by its approximately fifty founding ranches situated roughly between the Angelina and Attoyac Rivers (see table 7).

The Nacogdoches social and racial mixture had always drawn from a variety of sources. Originally founded by the same families of Béxar and

TABLE 8 · Nacogdoches Tejano Population

Year	Population[a]
1805[b]	670
1823[c]	136
1825[d]	500
1828	576
1829[e]	513
1830[f]	582
1831	596
1832	608
1833	647
1834	659
1835[g]	537
1850[h]	171

[a]All figures include only Spanish-surnamed or persons married with Spanish-surnamed in Nacogdoches jurisdiction.
[b]*BA*, Nacogdoches Census, Jan. 1, 1805.
[c]Lester G. Bugbee, "The Texas Frontier, 1820–1845," pp. 111, 112.
[d]Coahuila y Tejas, *Nota estadística, 1927*, appendix no. 14, "Población, 1825."
[e]*BLAKE*, vol. 18, pp. 315, 344.
[f]*BA*, Nacogdoches Census, June 30, 1830.
[g]*BLAKE*, vol. 19, pp. 9, 32, 69, 108, 149.
[h] U.S. Census, 1850 *MS*, Nacogdoches County.

Goliad, it continued to draw primarily from those communities. Continuous interchange occurred however, between Tejano towns, especially during the population dispersals prior to 1822. Some Adaesaños remained in Béxar, and some Béxar residents such as the family of Don Vicente Michelí moved to Nacogdoches. Many of the Nacogdoches residents, however, were natives of Louisiana and reflected the area's racial composition as well. Antonio Gil Ybarbo himself was believed to have been mulatto, and several of the other Tejano families had Anglo or creole ancestry. The Simms family, for example, were fully intermixed with Mexican families by the nineteenth century. Other families such as the Eldee, O'Connor, Córdova, López, and Fontán were complete mixtures of French, Irish, Spanish, Indian, and Negro.[21] The racial and geographical mobility of Nacogdoches surely affected its cultural attitudes, but it evidently had no peculiar effect on its sex and mortality structures as compared with the Béxar-Goliad region (see table 9).

TABLE 9   Age, Sex, Status Report of Nacogdoches, 1833

Ages	Bachelor Male	Female	Married Male	Female	Widowed Male	Female
Less than 7	91	101				
7 to 16	92	90		2		
16 to 25	50	29	9	60		2
25 to 40	59	21	61	96	4	8
40 to 50	14	15	26	25	1	6
50 and up	13	5	26	21	4	18
TOTALS	319	261	122	204	9	34

SOURCE: *NA*, Census and Statistical Report, June 30, 1833.

The Béxar-Goliad and Nacogdoches regions were not substantially dissimilar. Each had its own racial mixing experience, but the differences were only in degree and chronology. All heavily reflected the north Mexican *mestizaje*. All had a strongly rural dispersal of wealth by 1835. And all of them retained a traditional *frontera* character. In general, life was as precarious for the child as it was arduous for the producing male Tejano (see table 10). All of them—male and female—would know the rigors of disease, war, and privation at one time or another.

To the south of the original Tejano settlements lived a third population which at the turn of the century was just on the threshold of an upward thrust from the Río Grande toward the Nueces. Formerly citizens of Tamaulipas and northern Mexico, these southern rancheros became citizens of Texas by virtue of the boundary claims by Texas to the Río Grande after the Texas Revolution. More significantly, they became Tejanos by settling lands under the new headright programs of the Republic of Texas. With these headright settlers came a wave of other immigrants from Mexico. All of these people, strongly Mexican, probably thought of themselves as "Mejicanos" rather than as "Texans." Nevertheless they were closer to the Béxar-Goliad region than Nacogdoches was. All three groups had descended from the same families and bloodlines. And in any case, they all stood across the same cultural and racial lines from the Anglo Texans after 1836.

The northern settlement of Tamaulipas included Laredo, Camargo, Reynosa, Dolores, and Mier along the Río Grande. These were all part of the

TABLE 10   Tejano Composite Age, Sex, Status Report of Béxar, Goliad, and Nacogdoches, 1833

Ages	Bachelor Male	Female	Married Male	Female	Widowed Male	Female
Less than 7	458	443				
7 to 16	375	349	8	20		
16 to 25	274	162	123	128	2	13
25 to 40	169	100	326	319	24	59
40 to 50	35	24	112	58	8	41
50 and up	24	6	87	40	34	89
TOTALS	1,335	1,084	656	565	68	202
TOTALS BY STATUS		2,419		1,221		270

Statistics	Male	Female
Mean Age	23	22
Median Age	23	20
SEX TOTAL	2,059	1,851
TOTAL OF BOTH SEXES		3,910

SOURCE: *NA*, Census and Statistical Reports, June 30, 1833.

Escandón group that had come north from Querétaro in 1748, reflected the same mixture of Spaniard and Tlascalan. The population figures in this region were similar to those in Béxar and Goliad. Laredo, for example, had a population of 1,418 in 1819 and only 1,402 in 1823. Its male-female and age statistics were strikingly similar to those of Béxar. Here also, Mexico had tried in vain to settle strategic outposts with soldiers during the 1800-to-1830 period. The most notable example of this military colonization is the village of Palafox near Laredo. After several expeditions of civilian and troop reinforcements, Palafox finally succumbed to Indian attacks and lack of irrigation in the late 1820s. Government efforts to attract foreign colonization also failed in this area for the same reasons.[22] The only successful population growth was from expansion of the original communities, as in the case of the Béxar-Goliad region. The expansion in the Río Grande region, however, involved ranches more than presidios.

The Río Grande ranching frontier can best be described as a wedge based along the present counties of Webb, Zapata, Starr, Hidalgo, and

Cameron—that is, the original Escandón frontier line along the river. Although many of these first settlers had established *porción* holdings (elongated land units) along the north bank of the Río Grande, few of them had ever extended beyond this first tier before 1820. In the mid-1820s, however, the descendants of the founding families flowed in a northward thrust covering the present counties of Willacy, Kenedy, Brooks, Jim Hogg, Duval, Jim Wells, and Kleberg with its northern point at Nueces County. Laredo experienced a population growth in this period, which was accompanied by a pronounced spread of ranching, specifically sheep grazing. By 1835 approximately 350 ranches existed in this region, many of which provided the foundation for future Texas towns. The major ranches included San Diego, San Juan, Palo Blanco, Agua Dulce, El Sauz, Los Olmos, San Luis, Pansacol, Zapata, San Ignacio, and Los Saenz. Although few of the *rancheros* were soldiers, most of them had come as armed citizens, *ciudadanos armados.* Claiming lands under the state of Tamaulipas, they were commissioned to defend the territorial integrity of the state and to provide a frontier line against Indian incursion.[23] Thus it seems quite natural to see these same families applying for frontier grants on the same lands after 1836—this time under the Republic of Texas—as discussed in a later chapter.

The defensive and presidial nature of the frontier tended to unify Tejanos socially as well as militarily, with the presidio as an integral institution in this unity. The presidio provided a veritable complex of social functions in Tejano society, as well as military protection for the settlers. It introduced new blood and distinguished leadership. As the mission did in other provinces of New Spain, this presidial complex served as a major institution in Tejano society.

Perhaps the most important racial trait of the Tejanos lies in their Tlascalan and mestizo background. Tejano society was a composite of many cultures and races which produced a complex *mestizaje.* Tlascalan and native Texas Indian, Spanish and European—the Tejanos were culturally receptive to persons of various racial origins. The facility of the Mexican to assimilate is also reflected in the names of foreigners holding responsible government positions in this period. Such surnames as Bean, Austin, Gritten, Bastrop, Tisequima, Bradburn, Woll, and Filisola represented a variety of ethnic backgrounds. In fact, the colonization laws of Coahuila y Texas included provisions encouraging the *mestizaje* by granting one-fourth more land to colonists who married Mexican women. This racial attitude contrasted sharply with that of the Anglo colonists.

The Anglos, as one historian has noted, "did not blend or assimilate with the opposite race, but kept themselves apart."[24] Anglo Americans were not only racially distinct from the mestizo Tejanos, but also a more racially homogeneous group representative of the southern United States. Propelled by a dynamic rate of natural population growth in the United States, Anglo-American settlers continued to pour into Texas. Austin's colony reported a population of eighteen hundred by 1825, including 443 slaves. By 1831, he had divided his colony into seven districts. Other Anglo-American empresarios had settled other colonies as well. Most were between the Brazos and the Colorado rivers, although Green DeWitt Colony was uncomfortably close to Martín de León's Victoria. By 1834, the estimated number of Anglo-American immigrants in Texas was in excess of twenty thousand—legal and illegal, including thousands of blacks who were brought in as slaves.

Thus, in their very colonization, Anglos and Tejanos were worlds apart in racial attitude as well as in the philosophy of government and law. Although Anglos were quite firm in their racial attitude, however, they were to become more generally receptive to many of the liberal provisions of Tejano local government.

II

Governing the Towns of the *Frontera*

One of the most important facets of Tejano life was the Mexican form of local government that prevailed in the years between the consummation of Mexican independence in 1821 and the Texas Revolution in 1836. That government was an essential part of Tejano life because, based as it was in the Roman tradition, it set forth a "code" for society. From this code emerged the basic political principles to which Tejanos strove to adhere in the daily governance of their community. A survey of Tejano government, then, provides not only a study of that political philosophy, but a structural framework of Tejano life as well.

Local government during these years had an added significance in the specific rôle which Texas played in the Mexican federation. As a frontier province, Texas acquired a sense of function or mission which Tejano culture eventually internalized. As a *frontera* province, Texas was a "frontier" in the English sense of the word—that is, it was that austere region which functioned as the frontrunner of society. But in Spanish, *frontera* is defined as a fixed border.[1] Forming the outlying buffer line was more than a temporary phase in Tejano life, as explained earlier. It was an integral function of Tejano government as well. The primary function of the communities and their governments was defense. And just as Tejanos struggled beneath its taxing burden, so did they develop institutions and principles which became hallmarks of Tejano life. Anglo Americans would initially react against the differences between their own legal experience and that of the Tejano municipality; but in time, they accommodated and adopted some of the codes of the Tejano municipality.

The basic unit of Mexican government was the municipality, *municipio,*

25

its jurisdiction encompassing the city. But unlike in a modern city, the municipal jurisdiction included the surrounding area as well, more like in a modern American county. Based on the ancient Roman *municipium*, the system had continued most strongly on the Iberian Peninsula from which the Spaniards transmitted the concept to the New World. With a centralized government for the city and its surrounding region, the municipality was well suited for protection of settlers grouped around a presidio in remote areas subject to hostile attack. And just as it had served Spaniards against Moorish invasions on the Iberian Peninsula, so did the municipality find particular applicability on the remote *frontera* of New Spain where Indians replaced the Moorish menace.[2]

The concept of the municipality was reinforced by the presidial complex so integral to Tejano life by the nineteenth century. It became especially vital to survival as Texas came under constant attack from all sides in the early federation period. The independence movement had brought destruction and chaos before 1823 in Texas. The 1820s brought renewed attacks by Spanish naval fleets along the Gulf Coast, and ever-worsening clashes with Anglos and Indians from the Brazos River to the Sabine. At a time when Tejanos dearly needed external security and the luxury of peace to initiate a republican government, they drew inward instead for mutual protection—back to the ancient concept of the *municipio*.

Tejanos relied on their municipality for defense as their Spanish forebears had done centuries earlier. They perceived themselves ever more as a remote *frontera* entity. In their frequent *memorias* from Béxar, Goliad, and Nacogdoches to the federal government during these years, Tejanos demanded acknowledgement of their sacrifices on the *frontera*. They continually asked the government for special consideration as frontier settlers who had for so long shed their blood to defend the *frontera* for Mexico. Laredo residents demanded special legislation "for their worthy status as inhabitants of the frontier, who have undergone sacrifices and risks unknown to the people of the interior, and for which the latter are indebted to the former."[3] As landed Tejanos moved onto their ranches around 1830, the municipality strengthened its outward grasp on the surrounding region. In time, the hostile environment solidified the concept of the municipality in the mind of the Tejano. It became their defensive entity, their community fortress.

The geographical concept of the municipality became entrenched in the Tejano mind; and with it came the Spanish *ayuntamiento* government which had traditionally run the municipality. Instituted by the kings of Spain to curb the usurpation of power by provincial nobles in the eleventh and twelfth centuries, the ayuntamiento traditionally held civil and criminal jurisdiction over the municipality. It had been authorized by the court to consist of a specified number of councilors and an *alcalde* as president. Any appeals were made directly to the royal court. By the time this concept was transmitted to the New World, it was formally codified into a series of royal books of law commonly called the *Recopilación*.[4] These were the codes that had governed Spanish municipalities around the world, and they set out the structural framework for Tejano town governance.

Shortly after the discovery of the New World, Spain issued the first of a series of regulations intended to guide and direct the government of her new colonies. Initially issued in 1512, the *Recopilación* instituted the mercantilistic principle of channeling wealth and resources to the seat of empire. The first comprehensive book defining the standard ayuntamiento arrangement was issued in 1680. This code was a compilation of Spanish laws entitled *Recopilación de las leyes de los reinos de las Indias*, or "Compilation of the Laws of the Kingdom of the Indies." Revised editions of the *Recopilación* appeared in 1772, 1791, and in 1805, but the later editions represented mere supplements to the original. The codes specified in explicit terms the activities of all government bureaus and bureaucrats, their duties, procedures, and values—one even detailed the procedure for a city official to set the town clock. Such was the Spanish legal tradition that laid the basis for Tejano legal thought as people set about establishing their municipal and state government under the new Mexican federation in 1821.[5]

According to the dictates of the original *Recopilación*, a Spanish municipality should be governed by an ayuntamiento or city council, composed of its own citizens. The size of the ayuntamiento was a function of the community's designation as a *ciudad* (city) or *villa* (town). A community designated as a ciudad could have two alcaldes, as many as twelve *regidores*, and a commensurate augmentation of junior officials. A villa should have four regidores or councilors, each taking specified geographical and departmental responsibilities. One alcalde would preside over the regidores, the five members serving as the legislative and administrative council for the municipality. The alcalde served also as the local magistrate or judge of the first instance. In addition to these voting members, the ayuntamiento also included two *escribanos* or clerks who served as secretary and notary public. To complete the municipal government the ayuntamiento could appoint one *alguacil* or chief of police, and one *mayordomo* to supervise town functions such as public works, irrigation, or use of the common lands.[6]

Ayuntamiento government came into Texas with the Spanish and mestizo settlers in the early eighteenth century. Although they were often illiterate, these settlers had all lived under ayuntamiento government and were familiar with the procedures of the institution. The first ayuntamiento in Texas was established in 1731 by the Canary Island settlers of San Fernando de Béxar. Because of the sparse population in this villa, the Spanish viceroy authorized certain deviations from the instructions of the *Recopilación*. Instead of standard elections, the ayuntamiento members were appointed by the commander of the Béxar presidio. The first ayuntamiento consisted of six regidores. Two served coterminously as alcaldes, one as alguacil, one as escribano, and one as the mayordomo. Succeeding ayuntamientos in Béxar were elected by the former ayuntamiento members. Because of frontier conditions, these differences existed between the *Recopilación* and actual practice, but at least one historian has concluded that "those conversant with the actual local government of the Spanish colonies will be struck by the identity of the two rather than by their differences."[7]

Tlascalan and mestizo families also strengthened the traditional concept of ayuntamiento as they steadily migrated to Texas communities. These particular settlers functioned well under the system. Mexican Indians had formerly lived under a tribal *calpulli* unit under a tribal chief, for which the Spaniards merely substituted the ayuntamiento and alcalde. As Tlascalan and other Aztec tribes moved northward, therefore, they smoothly incorporated Spanish systems. In northern Coahuila, for example, the Tlascalan communities of Parras and San Esteben adjacent to Saltillo had maintained their ayuntamientos since the early 1600s. Their municipalities retained a stubborn control over their own jurisdictions until the Mexican federation period despite constant encroachment by Saltillo. By the 1820s, these settlers had a well-defined sense of municipal government.[8] These were the residents of the emerging Tejano communities which sought their own ayuntamiento government.

In time, the communities along the Texas frontier obtained their own municipal charters. Laredo, originally a part of the state of Tamaulipas, received her first charter in 1767. That year, the royal "General Visit to the Town of San Agustín of Laredo" officially recognized the villa and authorized an ayuntamiento election. The new ayuntamiento was duly installed the following year with Don José Martínez de Soto as alcalde and Don

Salvador Hidalgo and Don Nicolás Castellanos as the two regidores. Laredo was officially part of the Department of the North of Tamaulipas along with Cruillas, San Fernando, Burgos, Matamoros, Reynosa, Camargo, Mier, and Guerrero. Laredo, however, enjoyed a greater relative importance than the other communities on the Río Grande frontier because of her strategic location and population. Also, Laredo was at the end of the chain of official city-to-city correspondence which greatly enriched her municipal archives.[9]

Other remote communities in Texas lacked sufficient population to warrant an ayuntamiento in accordance with the *Recopilación*. These smaller settlements like the old missions of San José, San Juan, and San Francisco near Béxar annually elected administrative officials similar to a constable and a city attorney. Each mission had its own *comisario* to conduct official correspondence with provincial government, and a *syndico* to perform legal functions for the citizenry. These junior officials were in effect a liaison with the ayuntamiento of the nearest municipality such as Béxar. When the population of the remote community grew enough to be designated as a villa under the *Recopilación*, it obtained its own ayuntamiento.

In some cases, a remote community was granted a modified pre-ayuntamiento government. In the villa of Palafox which occupied a strategic location north of Laredo, the municipal authority was vested in a single alcalde. Such an official undoubtedly served the multiple functions of alcalde, comisario, and syndico. Indeed, the Palafox alcalde seems to have served as something of a defense leader as well, as indicated by his correspondence in the 1820s.[10]

Nacogdoches also had a pre-ayuntamiento government which proved to be as irregular as the population of that settlement. Officially recognized as a civil settlement in 1779, the Nacogdoches jurisdiction included the smaller settlements of Bayou Pierre and the eastern frontier. The civil administration of Nacogdoches had traditionally consisted of a single alcalde like that of Palafox. But the racial heterogeneity of Nacogdoches complicated matters somewhat. In the summer of 1821, Erasmo Seguin appointed James Dill, an Anglo-American settler, as alcalde and commander of the militia. During his tenure, Dill struggled with the administrative problems of continued illegal immigration from the United States and the resulting population growth of the Nacogdoches region. In 1824, Nacogdoches held its first election of an alcalde, electing Juan Seguin, a long-time resident of that region. Anglo residents protested that Seguin had won over Dill only because of the "prejudice" of native Tejanos. Seguin remained in office, and was succeeded by Pedro Procela, who died just after taking office. Procela's son, Luis, arbitrarily assumed the office and served the term as "interim" alcalde. The next year, Samuel Norris, an Anglo American representing Tejano interests, defeated another Anglo who represented a new group of Anglo immigrants. This election also stirred dissent which eventually led to the historic Fredonian Rebellion. And thus continued the political instability of Nacogdoches until the new state government finally authorized the community to elect its own ayuntamiento in 1827.[11]

There were some changes in ayuntamiento jurisdiction while Mexico adjusted to independence between 1810 and 1824. Even during this period of transition, however, the ayuntamiento held firm over local government. Each phase in the political transition contributed minor modifications to the ayuntamiento; but the changes were more in degree and size than in substance and structure.

The first major shift in political organization in colonial Mexico was in the new Spanish Constitution of 1812. Among other liberties, this constitution allowed elective ayuntamientos and provincial deputations. The number of regidores was set as a function of the municipality's population vis-à-vis its designation arbitrarily as a ciudad or a villa. The elections were to be annual, and no municipal official could succeed himself in office. The constitution also created the office of *jefe político* or political chief of provincial districts. These changes were incorporated by the ayuntamientos of Béxar and La Bahía despite the fact that King Ferdinand repudiated the new constitution of 1814. The ayuntamientos maintained the new structure, and in March, 1820, Ferdinand was again forced to swear allegiance to the 1812 constitution. A decree issued on July 4, 1820, reaffirmed the ayuntamiento structure. At that time, Béxar's ayuntamiento consisted of the provincial jefe político, Don Antonio Martínez, Alcalde Don José Erasmo Seguin, four regidores, and a *syndico procurador.* La Bahía's ayuntamiento consisted of Alcalde Encarnación Vásquez, only two regidores, and one syndico procurador commensurate with the smaller population. The political shifts of the Iturbide interim and the federal constitution of 1824 did little to alter the ayuntamiento structure. The La Bahía ayuntamiento did augment its membership during Iturbide's reign by adding two more regidores, but the change was merely an adjustment in accordance with the provisions of the Spanish Constitution of 1812.[12]

The transition to the state government of Coahuila y Texas did not radically affect local government. One facet of the transition from colonial province to federal state was the official separation of civil and military powers. The Texas ayuntamientos had a civil structure, but there had always been an overlap between the civil authority and the military. In fact, provincial commandants and presidial commanders exercised limited authority over governors and alcaldes, respectively, in matters of security and defense. This jurisdictional overlap came to an end by a national executive order on July 26, 1823, stating "that in all provinces the political government be separated from the military."

The early phases of state government under federalism brought one unwelcome decree in 1824 from the constituent congress of Coahuila y Texas. The Béxar ayuntamiento was to be reduced to half its original size. Bexareños greatly resented this order, which emanated from Saltillo. The Saltillo legislators reasoned that Béxar was no longer a provincial capital and thus deserved no better. The Bexareños were extremely slow in implementing this order. Indeed, they delayed until November, 1826, when Tejano delegates to the legislature succeeded in passing Decree No. 27 authorizing the delay. The decree authorized all existing ayuntamientos to continue in office according to the former structure until the forthcoming state constitution should issue a new set of rules. Although this decree pitted Béxar against Saltillo, it nevertheless represented a major link in the continuation of the traditional ayuntamiento structure in Texas.[13]

The promulgation of the Coahuila y Texas state constitution in March, 1827, formally recognized the ancient ayuntamiento as the form of government to rule over the municipality. Article 156 of the constitution stated that all communities with populations over one thousand should immediately proceed to establish ayuntamientos. The new ayuntamientos should consist generally of alcaldes, syndicos, and regidores in proportion to the specifications decreed by the state legislature. On 14 April, Decree No. 33 detailed the procedures for elections and composition of the new ayuntamientos. The municipalities were to hold ayuntamiento elections immediately after the publication of the new state constitution. The decree also stated in Article 3 that towns with less than 2,500 population should elect one alcalde, two regidores, and one syndico procurador; populations from 2,500 to 5,000 should elect two additional regidores; and communities of more than 5,000 should elect three alcaldes, six regidores, and two syndicos.

Although Decree No. 33 clarified some of the ambiguities of the Spanish system, it came as an unwelcome rule in some of the older municipalities. Béxar and Monclova, which had traditionally enjoyed special privileges because of their status as provincial capitals, again found themselves challenged by the new state capital of Saltillo. For years they complained about this issue in the state legislature. In 1829 for example, the Béxar ayuntamiento submitted a *memoria* demanding an additional alcalde. Béxar had traditionally been a provincial capital, they argued, and now needed a second alcalde to meet the work overload and the new population growth. Bexareños finally obtained relief in 1834 when Monclova and Béxar deputies dominated the state legislature and passed a full slate of liberal reforms. Decree No. 262 of this liberal body stated that cities with five thousand inhabitants should have one alcalde, two regidores, and one syndico procurador. The decree did not add a new alcalde to the Béxar ayuntamiento, but it created a new judicial position which effectively reduced the work load of the traditional alcalde. It also offered clearer definitions of his municipal duties.[14] Thus, even in the radical reforms introduced by the Coahuila y Texas liberals in 1834, the old ayuntamiento remained very similar in structure to the ayuntamiento of seventeenth-century Spain.

The Mexican government of Texas continued the full implementation and development of the ayuntamiento form of government. Béxar and La Bahía were fully developed ayuntamientos with full membership by the time the state constitution was published in 1827. As mentioned earlier, La Bahía changed its name in February, 1829, to Goliad in honor of Father Hidalgo. Goliad was intended as an anagram of the name Hidalgo, who was supposed to be remembered as the "heroic giant" (Goliath) of Mexican independence. Except for the name change, however, Goliad city government remained relatively stable throughout this period. Nacogdoches finally obtained its full-fledged ayuntamiento in June, 1827. Samuel Norris was the first constitutional alcalde and president of the first official ayuntamiento. His ayuntamiento included Regidores José Ignacio Ibarvo, Patricio de Torres, and Syndico Procurador Juan Ysidro Acosta. The new ayuntamiento was duly installed in the home of the new alcalde, who proudly reported the installation to the state authorities and the local military garrison.[15]

After allowing for the establishment of ayuntamientos in the older municipalities, the state government of Coahuila y Texas decreed in June, 1827, that each ayuntamiento should draw up and submit its municipal ordinances for approval in Saltillo. In December, a general guide was distributed to aid in the expeditious preparation of these ordinances. The guide described the general topics to be addressed by each ayuntamiento: municipal election meetings, municipal funds, sanitation, and so forth. Within each section, the guide stated the specific objectives and the philosophical reasoning for that section. For example, the section on *comodidad*, or public facilities, explained that "*comodidad* is nothing more than the prompt and smooth satisfaction of the needs which man has while he exists which require him to unite with others in society."[16]

The Texas ayuntamientos were slow in submitting their ordinance proposals to Saltillo. Because of this, Governor José María Viesca issued a harsh reminder threatening punishment for unreasonable delay. Finally, Béxar submitted its draft in August, followed by Goliad and San Felipe de Austin. All of these were received, approved, and issued by the state government as official decrees the next year. Nacogdoches was the only one of the major settlements which still had not submitted its ordinance proposal by this time.

The Nacogdoches Ayuntamiento requested more time to draw up its proposal which, members said, was complicated by peculiarities of their municipality. Nacogdoches had just recently obtained its regular ayuntamiento government, and the old town had never been surveyed in accordance with the standard requirements of the *Recopilación*. The new state constitution had continued the old requirements for each town to have a square plaza and perpendicular streets, which seemed too much to ask of the old irregular homesteads of Nacogdoches. Straightened streets would cut through the middle of established lots and would cut new ones short, complained the ayuntamiento. Pleading delay after delay, the Nacogdoches ayuntamiento finally accommodated the new state requirements to their old settlement. On May 6, 1831, Ramón Músquiz received the Nacogdoches proposal and relayed it to Saltillo—with amendments.[17]

By 1834, all of the old Tejano municipalities had established a formal government. Each had a constitutional alcalde and the specified number of regidores. As previously mentioned, the actual government structure was more like than unlike the standard form. The town plat was actually a square. The principal town square or plaza was in the center with perpendicular streets oriented to the four ordinal directions. Each city street as well as the plaza itself was set to standard measurements, so many *varas* or yards (approximately) in length and width. The east side of the plaza was designated for ecclesiastical structures such as the cathedral, chapel, or chancery. On the west side were the government and public buildings such as the *casa capitular* or state house, the customs house, and the governor's palace. Each town had its own *ejido* or commons, its own *tierra de pasto* or common pasture, and its own *propios* or rented lands for municipal revenue. All of this was detailed in the new state law, but it was little different from the instructions in the old *Recopilación*.[18]

A basic principle in the colonization of settlers in Texas was that the new colonies should move as early as possible into equal status with the older Tejano municipalities. The state colonization law of 1825 included this principle in Article 40, which stated that whenever a colony should include a total of forty families, the settlement should "proceed to the formal establishment of the new town." When the population reached two hundred, the settlers should elect an ayuntamiento from their own citizenry in accordance with the existing regulations. These regulations included the state constitution and the aforementioned decrees, No. 33 and No. 262. The most important regulations regarding the new colonies appeared in September of 1827 as the official "Instructions to Commissioners" by which state land commissioners brought new towns into official status. By means of these regulated procedures, Texas obtained a total of thirteen ayuntamientos by 1834.

The "Instructions to Commissioners" represent a most revealing method of accommodating Anglo Americans and other settlers to the Hispanic municipality tradition. The land commissioner, usually a Tejano, was responsible for registering the colonists and sponsoring their municipal organization. He was the official responsible for receiving the colonists' certificates, ordering surveys, and issuing titles. This agent was to select the official town site and lay it out according to the ancient Spanish tradition with perpendicular streets and a plaza. He would designate the land to be used for commons, for municipal revenue, and for ferries and roads. And most important, the land commissioner was to preside over the election of the town's first ayuntamiento in accordance with the colonization law of 1825.[19]

One by one the budding colonies became full-fledged municipalities. The villa of San Felipe de Austin was one of the first municipalities chartered under the new state government, as mentioned above. Along with San Felipe, the other new towns of this Mexican period obtained their charters which were later recognized by the Republic of Texas. Modern Texas towns like Gonzales and Victoria still have their municipal and ecclesiastical buildings on opposite sides of the town plaza. The traditional commons and *propios* of such towns were ruled valid even in the twentieth century by the Texas Supreme Court. Such lands are still property of the town's inhabitants and not taxable by state government.[20]

The Hispanic system of formal settlement contrasted somewhat with the system employed in the United States. For all its faults, the Hispanic administrative system paid close attention to new settlements. Important officials such as the Baron de Bastrop, the elder Tejano statesman Erasmo Seguin, or the governor personally commissioned a new municipality in Texas. This contrasted with what historian Earl S. Pomeroy has called a "weak" territorial system of absentee officials in the United States. And while Anglo-American settlers may have been unaccustomed to the strict Roman codes of the *Recopilación*, they could not fault the clarity and applicability of the codes. Many of the principles of the English common law had been developed in Europe, and contained what another historian labeled "traditional defects and peculiarly inappropriate provisions" in the semiarid environment of Texas. On the other hand, Hispanic codes had originally been written to sponsor settlements in that type of environment on the Iberian Peninsula. They were later transmitted through the *Recopilación* specifically for that purpose into New Spain.[21] Indeed, Anglo Americans might have developed similar legal adaptations in Texas, but the Hispanic codes facilitated the adaptations.

Election procedures for the new ayuntamientos were detailed in the state decrees and constitution. The first step in an election was the public announcement, which was to be posted throughout the town and on the most distant ranches of the municipality. The two-day process was to be held on the first Sunday and the following Monday in December in a convenient location, usually a public building of the town plaza. On that Sunday, the outgoing alcalde would assemble and preside over all the voters of the municipality. Voters were defined as "citizens enjoying their rights, domiciliated and resident within the limits of the respective Ayuntamiento." Colonists were specifically included in a decree which specified that "those who have acquired letters of citizenship provided they combine the conditions required by this law, shall have the right of suffrage in popular juntas." In extending suffrage, Decree No. 31 stated: "No person of this class can decline attending the same." Many citizens undoubtedly violated this last clause because of the lack of time and the difficulties of transportation, but the responsibility and the right of suffrage were quite clear nonetheless.[22]

On the first day, the citizens would elect one literate person as secretary and two others as tellers for the recording and tallying of the votes. The voters were to cast their votes in an audible voice for the candidates in different categories for alcalde, regidor, and syndico procurador. Candidates were usually nominated by the senior regidor of the outgoing ayuntamiento. As the voters filed in, during the two days of voting hours, the alguacil assisted them in an orderly flow. There was to be no coercion by election officials during the entire process. Article 58 of the state constitution specifically stated, "Municipal assemblies shall be holden with open doors, without any guards and no persons, of whatever class, shall appear armed therein." At the end of the second day, the results were tallied and announced by the presiding alcalde and the secretary and tellers. One copy of the election results was then submitted to the governor, one copy was posted in a public place, and a third was retained for the archives. As with suffrage, state law dictated unequivocally, "Ayuntamiento offices shall be municipal charges, which no one can decline."

Constitutional prerequisites for ayuntamiento membership required that the candidate be a citizen with three years' residency in the municipality, one of those years being the year prior to taking office; that he be twenty-five years old if single or twenty-one if married; that he be able to read and write; and that he possess some capital or a trade by which to subsist while performing his duties. Members of the clergy and the military were expressly forbidden to hold municipal office. Alcaldes were elected annually, regidores rotated on a two-year basis, and no official could succeed himself in office without a two-year interim period.[23]

The duties and operations of the Texas ayuntamiento under Mexican federalism represented a continuation of those of the earlier Spanish colonial government. The municipal ordinances which the state issued for each ayuntamiento were merely modern codifications of the old traditional practices. The major advantage in the new ordinances was that they had originated in the respective municipalities and not in a far-away capital city. In these ordinances is seen the traditional rôle of the ayuntamiento in a Tejano municipality.

One of the primary functions of the ayuntamiento, which ordinarily assembled one morning per week, was to formulate and manage the town's fiscal operations. Each ayuntamiento prepared its own revenue plan, *plan de arbitrios*, on an annual basis, regulating the administration of the town *propios* and listing the fees on any activities subject to local taxation. These included taxes on the transportation and sale of goods, round-up and sale of livestock, and entertainment. The plan was submitted to the state government where it received a perfunctory perusal and approval.

One particularly instructive plan submitted by the Béxar Ayuntamiento deserves close attention. The Béxar "Plan de Advitrios" *(sic)* of October 20, 1823, was addressed to the provincial deputation—the provincial assembly that governed Texas as an independent province after the downfall of Iturbide. This plan vividly illustrates the inherent stability of local government during the uneasy period of transition.

The original plan included taxes on many items and activities which the plan said were to be taxed *como está acostumbrado* or "as is the custom." Such taxes included stated amounts of *pesos* and *reales* or bits per head of livestock being driven to the United States. Each cart driver or mule driver paid taxes of one peso per load on entry into the municipality. Musicians paid one peso for a dance, and shopkeepers paid monthly taxes for their permits. This same plan appeared again in March, 1825, under the new state government. The 1825 plan merely duplicated most of the 1823 duties bit by bit. It included one fee which it assessed, as it stated, "in accordance with Article 7 of the Plan de Advitrios of the Provincial Deputation of October 24, 1823"—the original plan dated and approved under the former provincial deputation.

The final phase in the transition appeared in the municipal ordinances of Béxar, issued as Coahuila y Texas State Decree No. 98 on June 6, 1829. Chapter Nine of the Béxar ordinances, "On the Creation of Municipal Funds," bore great resemblance to the earlier plans. The tax for a mule driver was still one *real* per load. Other items included similar fees for shopkeepers and musicians. The *propios* were retained as a major source of municipal revenue. The same continuity appears also in Decree No. 99, the Municipal Ordinances of Goliad, 1829.[24]

The ayuntamiento was required to compile and to submit quarterly reports to the governor on economic conditions, vital statistics, and social conditions. Quarterly statistics included births, deaths, and marriages. Accompanying these statistics was a report on the state of the public order. Economic reports included the value of goods sold or purchased and the number of merchants in the town. Also included in the economic reports were any special matters such as smuggling activities or seasonal records such as the regulation of fruit vendors during the spring.[25]

Another major responsibility of the ayuntamiento was to maintain the public order. Here also, the new municipal ordinances drew heavily on the *Recopilación*. The ayuntamiento prohibited and strictly guarded against such activities as gambling, vagrancy, and public disorder. Regulations permitted billiards and ball games, but like the *Recopilación*, the new ordinances strictly forbade gambling in these games. Dice and card games were forbidden, and debts resulting from any of these games were not recognized by law. The highest crimes were murder, theft, robbery, personal injury, and usury. Vagrants and habitual drunkards were to be arrested, reported in the quarterly reports, and prosecuted. Although jails were unimproved, they were closely monitored by the ayuntamiento through weekly visits. The visiting member of the ayuntamiento reported on the number of persons in jail, their offenses, and the length of their terms in the jail. It was for vagrants to leave town either by order of the ayuntamiento or simply by choice to avoid prosecution.[26]

The ayuntamiento was responsible for licensing professional practitioners and for conducting relations with the Indians. Licensing involved the granting of franchises to promoters of cockfights, public dances, and raffles. The ayuntamiento also had to regulate the licensing of doctors and lawyers within the municipality. For its relations with the Indian tribes, the ayuntamiento relied on an Indian agent, usually a man of status who knew the Indians well, who was responsible for distributing gifts to them, treating with them, and for keeping a vigil on their activities. He also submitted regular reports as a liaison to the state government.[27]

To maintain public health and order, the ayuntamiento appointed permanent committees. The *junta de sanidad* or sanitation committee managed the community's sanitation efforts. To be composed of one doctor (if one were available), one alcalde, one regidor, one syndico procurador, one priest, and two citizens, the sanitation committee was authorized to inspect public services such as the *acequias* or irrigation canals, the streets, and the market place. The ayuntamiento also appointed a committee of six to ten men called a *ronda* to patrol the streets twice a week for security purposes as well as for public order. The *ronda* was presided over by the alcalde, and patrolled between the hours of 9:00 P.M. and 3:00 A.M. The *ronda* and the *junta de sanidad* were authorized to fine violators of municipal ordinances, such fees limited to fifty pesos or fifteen days in jail, and the revenues went to the *propios* fund.[28]

The status and duties of the municipal officers obtained formal definition during the federalist period. The local government hierarchy represented a strong line of authority from the alcalde down to the comisario, with increasingly specific responsibilities and duties. The alcalde, as mentioned above, served as the ayuntamiento president and as the local *juez* or judge. Thus, he held a highly responsible and respected position, much like that of a modern mayor. But as historian Eugene C. Barker has noted, "the alcalde's part in the State administration was much more direct than that of our mayors."[29] Indeed, the alcalde was immediately responsible to the political chief or to the governor.

The alcalde had primary responsibility for all of the functions of the ayuntamiento and of the lower ranking officials as well. He collected the regular municipal fees for taxable activities like dances, market sales, and rental of the *propios*. The syndico procurador prosecuted major violators of city ordinances much as a modern attorney would. A regidor, though elected at large, was responsible for a geographic area, usually a specific *barrio* or neighborhood. Each regidor had under him a comisario who conducted regular duties in the barrio and reported any violation of law to his respective regidor. The comisario, then, was the actual enumerator of the census for the quarterly reports. He was often the first man to arrive at a public disturbance or to apprehend violators. Thus, the comisario was the closest public official to the daily lives of the people in the barrio. Some towns employed a person called a syndico at the barrio level, but this syndico (as differentiated from the syndico procurador) had the same function and status as the comisario. Neither the comisario nor the syndico held a seat on the ayuntamiento, although both attended *ex officio*. On the remote ranches and uninhabited regions, the *juez de campo* or field judge performed all of these functions with modified authority, as discussed in a following chapter.[30]

The alcalde's most important function of all was perhaps that of magistrate. In the age-old tradition granted him by the Spanish *Recopilación*, the alcalde had primary jurisdiction in civil and criminal cases in his municipality. The alcaldes of Goliad, Béxar, Nacogdoches, and Laredo all tried many civil cases as well as criminal cases. The cases ranged from violations of sanitation ordinances to murder. The most common criminal cases were perhaps those involving illegal slaughter or sale of livestock. Usual civil cases involved law suits for payment of debt, although recovery of damage caused by stray livestock was also common in these towns.[31]

The alcalde's judicial functions, as other ayuntamiento positions, underwent a formal codification under the state government of Coahuila y Texas.

The first state law to affect the alcalde was Decree No. 37, which did nothing more than limit the alcalde's fines to twenty-five pesos or eight days in jail or public works. Most of the other judicial procedures of the alcalde were left intact as stated in the *Recopilación*, or they were simply continued locally as customary practices.

In 1829, the state issued Decree No. 39 which represented a refinement of the *Recopilación* and local custom as well. This decree, "The Code of Laws for the Administration of Justice," detailed the limits and procedures of the alcalde as magistrate. The alcalde had somewhat summary authority in cases involving less than ten pesos. In cases involving between ten and one hundred pesos, the alcalde had each party in the suit appoint a disinterested person as a representative in the case. The alcalde would then decide the verdict through conciliation by plurality of his own vote and those of the representatives. In cases of over one hundred pesos, the alcalde followed the same procedures with the representatives, but such cases had to be legally set forth in a writ in case of referral or appeal to higher authority.

The Spanish tradition of trial by conciliation had been transmitted to the New World by the *Recopilación*, which stated that *hombres buenos* or reputable citizens should assist the alcalde in civil suits between persons of equal station in society, or, as they said in Béxar, "*de ygual clase.*" The practice found particular applicability in Tejano society. It helped to discourage arbitrary decisions by alcaldes in remote areas, and it helped to preclude long trips to the capital for judgment. In continuing the tradition, Coahuila y Texas Decree No. 39 set specific monetary limits to the cases tried by conciliation. It went on to state that "attempts at conciliation shall take place in the presence of the alcalde, and to that end each of the parties to the suit shall name a competent representative, who will consider the case in company with the alcalde." All such cases were to be recorded in the annual register entitled *Libro de juicios conciliarios* or the "Book of judgment by arbitration."[32]

The procedures which the alcalde followed in formal cases were standard throughout Texas, notwithstanding the fact that many were unwritten, customary practices. In major cases, the alcalde followed procedures which he recorded in a formal *sumaria* or written report of the investigation. The *sumaria* included the formal complaint, the subpoenas, and any formal statements made by either party. Many of these procedures involved fees which the alcalde charged in accordance with a standard fee bill called an *arancel*, such as the one published by Coahuila y Texas in 1828. The *arancel* was another Spanish tradition with obvious advantages. More complicated cases involved the posting of bonds, formal inventories of goods in question, public auctions, and often translations by bonded translators. Typical cases lasted from several days to two weeks, but some cases involving appeals and transfers might last four months or longer.[33]

As mentioned above, Tejano officials complained of the heavy work load and the wide responsibility falling upon a single alcalde. State Decree No. 26 of 1834 was a partial solution to that problem. For the first time in centuries of Hispanic law, the decree separated the judicial responsibilities from the administrative duties of the alcalde. It created a new judge's position, elective annually. The judge had to meet the same requirements as an alcalde, but the new judge was to be independent of the former administrative position. In enabling the new position, the decree stated, "The respective Alcalde shall pass to the aforementioned primary judges, as fast as they are established, the business they might have pending, and that is within the sphere of their attributes." There was to be one judge for municipalities of less than five thousand inhabitants, two judges for those of five to ten thousand, and three judges for populations over ten thousand.

Tejanos also began to demand modernization of the old *hombres buenos* system of trial by conciliation. The state constitution of 1827 had included an article authorizing trial by jury in criminal cases, and stated that it should be extended to civil cases "as the advantages of this valuable institution become practically known." But more than five years later, the state had not yet implemented the provisions of the article. One *memoria* submitted to the legislature by the Goliad Ayuntamiento in 1833 complained of the maladministration of justice resulting from the inadequate system of courts in the Texas department. The ayuntamiento urged the state legislature to implement the jury system as a "fundamental part of the law." Unfortunately, the law would be passed in 1834, only as an appeasement to a political crisis which would negate its effect.

By far the weakest link in the administration of justice was the appeals procedure. Any appeal of an alcalde's decision went to the state's *asesor general* or attorney general, which caused a delay of at least four months. The *asesor general*, who resided in Saltillo hundreds of miles away, reviewed the case and returned it with his *dictamen* or recommendation. Appeals in cases of corporal punishment were referred to the state supreme court, also in Saltillo. There the judges heard the arguments of the *hombres buenos* and issued a final decision.[34]

These cumbersome appeals procedures did not seem entirely prohibitive to Texas citizens, however. Tejanos appealed cases involving excessive fines, derogation of honor, or violation of civil rights. One case in 1825 illustrates a typical situation in Texas local courts. José Salvador Díaz of Mission San José appealed the fine of two *fanegas* (approximately two bushels) of corn for damages caused by his oxen. Citizen Díaz appealed the decision on several counts. First, he said, there was no proof that the oxen were his since no one actually witnessed the incident. Next, he challenged the alcalde's right to collect fees in excess of the standard *arancel*. And finally, the alcalde failed to seek the assistance of two *hombres buenos*, which Díaz claimed, "is my right." This case was referred to the state level where it undoubtedly remained for months. If this case reveals the inadequate and sometimes arbitrary procedures of Tejano justice, it also offers an insight into the stirrings that later led Tejanos to demand rectification of these problems.[35]

Tejanos suffered under the inadequate administration of justice on the frontier, and undoubtedly the Anglo settlers suffered or complained as much if not more. Actually, the rumblings were as much the characteristic of a frontier region as they were of the Mexican system. Anglo-American statesmen at around the same time harshly criticized similar conditions on the Anglo-American frontier. U.S. Senator Thomas Hart Benton of Tennessee cited the long delays due to "trifling errors" and "magistrates without legal knowledge." Tennesseeans, as Tejanos, also had to "travel a hundred miles across poor roads to Supreme Court sittings, and then wait for their cases." While many complained, however, one Missouri settler in Texas praised the Mexican system. J. F. Perry wrote to Stephen F. Austin in 1832, "[I] . . . beleave [*sic*] the laws here are as well administered as they are in Arkansas and perhaps better, and equally as well as they were when I first went to Missouri."[36]

Early Anglo-American empresarios let it be known that they felt paralyzed by the vagueness of their judiciary authority in the Mexican domain. The state colonization law of 1825 had authorized empresarios to administer justice, mediate disputes, and maintain order, but it neglected to expound upon this authority. The provincial governor of Texas and the provincial deputation had granted Austin absolute judicial power over his colony, but they also left Austin in a quandary over the details of the Mexican system of administration of justice. After much research on the topic, Austin produced his own civil regulations in January of 1824. Austin's code, although cited by historians as "the first fee bill ever in operation in

Anglo-American Texas," was Austin's own codified version of the code which Tejanos had long referred to as an *arancel*. It also contained many Mexican *sumaria* procedures. Like the Mexican procedures, Austin's code contained an article allowing for judgment by conciliation through the good offices of "arbitrators"—Austin's term for the *hombres buenos*. Austin's *arancel* listed the exact fees to be charged by the Anglo-American alcaldes, stated in bits—the equivalent to a Mexican *real*.

Austin's code deviated in some details from the standard Tejano procedures. For example, Austin allowed his alcaldes a limit of two hundred "dollars." Nevertheless, Texas Political Chief José Antonio Saucedo approved the code, adding only two amendments. Anglo alcaldes undoubtedly deviated from Hispanic traditions, but there is evidence that their deviation was not substantially greater than their compliance. By 1826, Anglo settlers were already registering cases of "judgment by arbitration." And in February, 1834, the legislature appointed Thomas Jefferson Chambers as *asesor general* of the state of Coahuila y Texas.[37]

In March, 1834, the liberal legislature of Coahuila y Texas finally created the long-promised trial by jury. In creating the Superioridad Judicial de Texas, the legislature allowed for trial by jury and for the creation of three circuit courts in Texas. Each circuit court was to have one judge, one *srion*, and one *cherif (sic)*. As mentioned above, however, these reforms represented as much a political device of the liberal legislature as they did a sincere response to the needs of the citizens who had so long demanded them.

The Anglo citizens of Texas responded with appreciation. Thomas Jefferson Chambers commented on the judicial reforms that "the mere passing of these laws had a political effect which nothing but their repeal could ever destroy." But these reforms were only laws to the Mexicans in 1834. They were not deeply rooted institutions like the *arancel* or the tradition of the *hombres buenos*. And by 1835, a stronger Mexican power did in fact repeal the reforms, as if to spite Chambers' own optimism. In 1835, the centralist government of Mexico created the *Código de las Siete Leyes constitucionales*, which restructured local government and made departments of all of the former states of Mexico. This, of course, was a major factor leading to the Texas revolution.

The revolution obviously brought changes to the local government structure in Texas, but the changes in the structure of local government were hardly more radical than those proposed by the *Código de las Siete*

Leyes. Although there were radical changes under Anglo-American law, many elements of the old structure remained. Indeed, the revolutionary provisional government and its Organic Law were, in the words of Seymour V. Connor, "an amalgamation of the Anglo-American experience and the tradition with the existing Mexican institutions."[38] The delegates to the 1835 Consultation which drew up the Organic Law for the government of Texas by the General Council went to San Felipe representing their old municipalities. Their militia units also represented the traditional Mexican divisions and districts for local defense. One important provision of Anglo-American law was the elimination of primogeniture and entail by the Texas Constitution. This alone did not alter Mexican law significantly because the Spanish Cortes and the Mexican Congress had already abolished those ancient institutions in 1820 and 1823 respectively. It did have the effect of facilitating the exchange of private lands from Tejano families to Anglo Americans after the revolution, but that was the result of economic and social events rather than any radical changes to the Hispanic governmental structure.

Many changes during this transitional phase—name changes, for example—often left the functional aspects of local government intact. Perhaps the most illustrative example of such superficial transition in local government was in Section VI of the Organic Law for the creation of local government. The constables and prosecuting attorneys had functions very similar to those of the old comisario and syndico procurador of Tejano government, respectively. To simplify the transition, one clause stated, "alcaldes and commissarios [*sic*] shall have the same jurisdiction . . . as the Justice of the Peace." Other names changed more informally. The municipality, for example, remained fixed in the Anglo mind at least long enough for Governor Smith of the General Council to create, as he did, the new municipality of Jackson. In time, the Anglo term "county" replaced the Mexican term, but most of the old municipalities retained their established boundaries.[39]

As the provisional government gave way to the Republic of Texas, the transition and continuum went into more permanent status. In December, 1836, the congress of the republic created district courts and added a clause formally transferring local jurisdiction. It stated that "all processes heretofore issued for an amount of $100.00 and upwards returnable to the court of the first instance created by the law of 1834 [this referred to Decree No. 262 mentioned in text above] shall by the judge of the court of each county be returned to the first term of the District Court of their counties, respectively." In so doing, the law kept alive the age-old function of the Spanish alcalde in Texas. One twentieth-century lawyer told the courts, "It will thus be seen that the District Court of the Republic is by legislative succession the evolution of the Alcalde and primary courts."[40]

While in the remainder of Texas the alcalde function smoothly evolved into the district court, in Laredo it survived through an acting alcalde. Laredo, because of its location in the disputed region south of the Nueces River, retained its Mexican government until the Mexican War. In 1846, Mirabeau B. Lamar became the military governor of this region. While in Laredo, Lamar acted through the existing ayuntamiento. The alcalde, Andrés Martínez, continued to function in his elected capacity, treating with Lamar, issuing decrees, and officially endorsing documents issued by Lamar. In July, 1847, Lamar finally brought Laredo into the Anglo-American government. He authorized the election of two justices of the peace, one constable, and one county commissioner. This was the first election for Laredo as a part of the North American United States. Former Mexican citizens actively participated in voting and in running for office. Their participation was reassuring to Lamar according to historian Gilberto Hinojosa, although the old Tejanos were beginning to feel "apprehensive" at losing to the newer Anglo-American residents. The Tejanos were more worried, however, about preserving their land titles, and the Anglos immediately focused their attention on control of the new county government structure. The Laredo alcalde nevertheless survived, and by doing so until 1847, the Tejano alcalde actually outlived the Republic of Texas.[41]

III

The Tejano Community

As the conditions of the *frontera* imposed their influence on Tejano government, they manifested themselves on Tejano social structure. Lulled by tradition, constantly threatened by attack, the Tejanos retained many vestiges of communal life in their municipality. These were the peculiar characteristics which Anglo visitors often failed to appreciate in the Tejano. These characteristics, anachronistic as they were, represented a concession to the rugged environment of the Texas frontier. As such, they were practical adaptations. Many of them survived as unique characteristics of the Mexican culture in Texas; others became distinguishing characteristics of the Anglos in Texas as well.

The single most distinctive characteristic of Tejano culture was the strong sense of community. The early Spaniards had brought with them a strong neighborhood concept of the barrio. When this was superimposed over the Mexican Indian's traditional concept, the *calpulli*, the result was a reinforced sense of social unity. Then as the early expeditions came in to settle Texas, the people came as whole families or communities. Some of these families grouped themselves around the early missions where they remained for decades. Others huddled around the presidio or in distant communities like Nacogdoches, where even the different races tended to be drawn together.[1]

To the nineteenth-century Tejano the barrio was home, and the *vecindario*, or neighboring populace, was family. It was not enough for municipal government to provide an alcalde as the leader of the town. Each barrio had to have its own resident comisario or "judge of the barrio." The comisarios, who saw to the social welfare and administrative matters in their respective barrios, were seen officially as the heads of these extended families. One Béxar ordinance described the comisarios as "the true Fathers of the *vecindario* in their respective territories."[2]

An element of this concept of community was imposed on the Anglo Americans who first colonized under Tejano management. Just as the Tejano land commissioner was instructed to introduce settlers to the municipality and ayuntamiento, so was the empresario to function as a transitional introduction to the community and alcalde. The settlers would encounter formidable hardships on the Texas frontier, but the empresario should mold them into a community much as the comisarios and alcaldes had done for over a century in the Tejano barrios.

The empresario *par excellence* was, of course, Stephen F. Austin. In a graphic description of Austin's function as empresario, Guy M. Bryan offered: "Nobly did they perform their mission under the direction of their leader, empresario, lawgiver, judge, and military commander, whose wisdom and forecast, justice and prudence, patience and forbearance, tempered with firmness and decision, united to great tact and fidelity to obligations, enabled them and him to succeed in their objects, where so many other similar enterprises had failed in this and other countries, even when supported by the strong arm of government and wealthy corporations and capitalists." Indeed, Austin conscientiously shouldered these many responsibilities. When Governor José Felix Trespalacios granted him civil, judicial, and military authority as empresario, Austin accepted and added, "in fact, I look upon them as one great family who are under my care." The good empresario was, indeed, a true father of his *vecindario*.[3]

Another important aspect of Tejano community life lay in the common lands and *propios* which were a part of the municipality. As mentioned above, all municipalities, including San Felipe, had title to this type of land. This communal ownership enhanced the sense of unity within the *vecindario*. It offered a common source of timber, communal or *pueblo* water rights, and common pasture or woodlands. The revenue from the *propios* made the community a fiscal entity as well. Thus, the programs supported by ayuntamiento expenditures were, in effect, community ventures which demanded the concern and contribution of all of the citizenry.[4] And the management of the town's social functions—whether in recreation, in social services, or in crisis—lay almost exclusively in the hands of the *vecindario*.

Standard procedure in the management of a municipality's social functions called for the appointment of quasiofficial committees, or municipal commissions. These commissions were composed of local government officials, professionals in the respective endeavor, and ordinary citizens. They were responsible for collecting funds, making necessary arrangements, and conducting the operations of the social function. One such municipal commission was the *junta patriotica*, or patriotic committee, responsible for conducting patriotic or civic endeavors. Patriotic committees, for example, held a fund-raising drive among citizens and soldiers of Texas to contribute to a national collection for repairs on the warship *Guerrero* in 1828. Their most common activities involved official celebrations, however, of such events as Constitution Day, the Feast of Corpus Christi, Christmas, Easter Thursday and Good Friday, the Feast of San Felipe de Jesús, the Feast of the Virgin of Guadalupe, and Independence Day. Preparations for these events sent the city officials busily buying refreshments, renting a dance hall, and contracting for musicians.

Mexican Independence Day was one of the major themes of the year. By 1825, it had been officially ordered that the sixteenth of September would be a national feast of "the first *grito* [proclamation] of independence." This celebration was a highlight of the year in Béxar. The junta patriotica membership included the most distinguished men in Tejano society, each heading a different subcommittee. Festivities involved a three-day celebration starting on September 15 with a torchlight parade, a cannonade, and the ringing of church bells. The next day began with a solemn Te Deum mass, a day parade, speeches, and the official reenactment of the *grito*. Prisoners were released, troops paraded, and señoritas were officially invited to the *gran baile* or grand ball, sometimes called a *fandango*. At the fandango, a señorita Tejana could dance and display her fine dress. The Tejana wore one of the most distinctive, though seldom recognized, of Mexico's regional costumes *(trajes típicos)*. The formal announcement to the fandango was a colorful affair, much like a parade, called a *convite* or invitation. The young men of the city rode through the streets in a group on gaily decorated horses, playing the guitar and singing as they went. The third day terminated the activities with all the citizens dressed in mourning to attend a "mass for the departed." Throughout all of these events, the junta patriotica was responsible for refreshments, music, and official speeches.[5]

Another commission, the *junta de sanidad*, ordinarily supervised sanitation ordinances, and served as a vital coordinating committee in times of epidemic. In the smallpox epidemic of 1831, for example, the Béxar Junta de Sanidad played such a rôle. The state government of Coahuila y Texas had

Fig. 1 *Fandango,* by Theodore Gentilz. The Tejana wore one of the most distinctive of Mexico's regional costumes *(trajes típicos). Courtesy Daughters of the Republic of Texas Library, San Antonio.*

decreed in May of 1830 that immunization procedures should begin at once for the spreading epidemic. Jefe Político Ramón Músquiz of Béxar relayed the order to Goliad, Nacogdoches, and to the Anglo colonies, setting forth the time and place for vaccination of the public. By the end of the year, the disease had reached Béxar. On January 22, 1831, the town fathers met to discuss measures to combat the epidemic. They decided that the junta de sanidad should be fully activated and authorized to direct such measures in accordance with the law.

The Béxar Junta de Sanidad met on January 23 to develop a plan of action. As jefe político, Músquiz was the president of the junta. Official members included Juan Martín de Veramendi as vice president, Alcalde José María Salinas, and parish priests Refugio de la Garza and Francisco Maynes. Other members were appointed from among the citizenry. The first act of the junta was to assign *cuarteles* (headquarters) for each barrio of the municipality with a leader in each *cuartel.* They drew up a set of instructions for public procedures during the crisis, and administered medicine free to indigents and at a reasonable price to others. As the community of Béxar weathered the epidemic, the junta continued to meet regularly, to administer aid, and to keep official count of the cases.[6]

The cholera epidemic that struck Texas in 1834 illustrates the effects epidemics had on Tejano communities. This particular scourge struck most heavily in the Goliad region, killing ninety-one in Goliad and twenty-five in Victoria. Its effects cast an aura of xenophobia on the bewildered communities. Townspeople evacuated the barrios and camped in the countryside. Goliad was said to have looked as if it had been "wiped out." Béxar declared a general quarantine and posted guards to intercept and bar travelers from the direction of Goliad.

Authorities issued instructions for combating the epidemics, but ignorance of the nature of diseases resulted in speculative reasoning and desperate measures. The Laredo authorities prohibited dances, and had the streets watered down regularly. The Goliad ayuntamiento took pork and fruit off the market as suspected bearers of the disease. They filtered the cistern water before using it for drinking purposes. They buried immediately any victims of the disease in a new cemetery located downwind from the town. With the the evacuation of towns and prohibitions against intercity travel, Tejano society went into a state of suspended animation until the disease slowly died out on its own. If these procedures seem futile to the modern reader, they were no less justifiable to the nineteenth-century Tejanos, for if they survived such a scourge on the frontier, it was through one of the many desperate actions of their families and the *vecindario*. Therein, they saw the means and their only hope for survival.[7]

Tejano water law also amply illustrates the Tejanos' development of local self-government. Their Hispanic background had given the Tejanos a highly developed philosophy on water management. Drawing on this tradition, the Tejanos created local water systems which they governed by basic principles of ancient law. In so doing, the Tejanos instituted the first adaptation of European civilization to the semiarid environment of Texas. More than a century later, Anglos would add the advantages of technology to the acquisition and control of water. The result was a combination that would become one of the many distinctive traits of Texas. Few institutions demonstrate as vividly as water law the historical genius of Texas for combining Mexican traditional culture with Anglo technology.

In the Hispanic mind, the consideration of water was a natural function in the valuation of land. Betty Eakle Dobkins states in her classic study *The*

Spanish Element in Texas Water Law that the Spaniards of Texas "recognized, as Anglo Americans have not always done, that water is the life blood of the land, a precious commodity to be carefully and wisely husbanded." As knowledgeable a person as Manuel de Mier y Terán had made a similar comparison in the early nineteenth century. In a letter to Lucas Alamán, Mier y Terán recommended colonizing central Mexicans in Texas, for they could use their knowledge of irrigation to make semiarid land produce while Anglos who had technology let it go to waste.[8]

The Hispanic land-water concept was introduced into Texas on the earliest Spanish explorations. In their reconnaissance of a region for new settlement, Spanish officials always mentioned the potential for irrigation, which they called *reigo*, and the possibility of drawing water from stream beds, a process they called *saca de agua*. This concept is also reflected in nineteenth-century statistical reports in which Tejano officials regularly listed *saca de agua* and the number of natural springs or *ojos de agua* in the municipality.

The Spanish land unit was one of the most visible examples of this land-water concept. The land unit revealed, in its size and shape, the philosophy embodied in the Hispanic land grant. As a concession to aridity and sparse vegetation, land grants allowed for large, often vast, expanses; hence the characteristic size of the *rancho*. The shape of land units was a function of their size and number, based on the principle that all units should share a *porción* or portion of the available stream. The land unit, then, represented the right of each landowner to an equal share of the area's water. In order to optimize the number of such beneficiaries, the *porción* took its characteristic shape which has been called a "prolonged quadrangle" with an extended depth and a narrow river front. One has but to look at a map of Tejano land grants to appreciate the influence of the *porción* principle on the Mexican mind (see map 2 showing *porción* grants in Webb County).[9]

The public nature of water ownership is probably the most pervasive of the Hispanic traditions in Texas water law. The ancient codes of the Spanish *Recopilación* stated unequivocally that all waters in New Spain would belong to all inhabitants thereof; that such waters should be governed and used by local bodies such as ayuntamientos; and that the preexisting native water systems and practices should enjoy the same privileges. The *Recopilación* allowed for common law to prevail in all cases or situations not covered by the standard Spanish codes. In such cases, the alcalde was to ascertain the traditional common practices of a region, and to avoid insti-

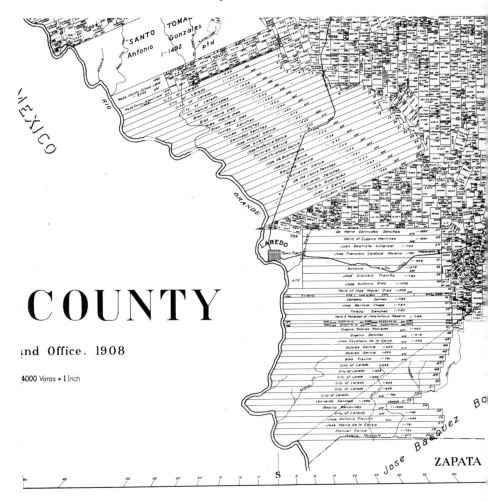

Map 2 *Porciones* of Lardeo in Webb County. *Courtesy*
Texas General Land Office, Austin.

tuting innovative procedures. In effect, a local area such as Béxar was
authorized to use procedures suited to its peculiar situation. Thus, in
time, local management developed as a major characteristic in Tejano
water law.

To begin with, the very construction of *acequias* was a local, communal
effort in Texas. In other parts of New Spain, the acequias and dams were
built by Indian labor supervised by missionaries. In Texas communities,

52

which had never experienced substantial neophyte populations, the eighteenth-century Tejano citizens had to provide for the construction and management of water works. Organizing themselves as shareholders in a communal enterprise, the participating *vecinos* (local citizens) contributed tools, materials, and labor. They jointly secured the services of an experienced canal builder, and petitioned the government for permission with respect to the prior rights of earlier users of the stream's flow. They were then authorized to proceed in the construction of the several components of the system in accordance with the standard specifications of width, depth, and proportion.[10]

The actual construction of the system components was done by *vecinos* under the supervision of the hired professional. Some wealthier shareholders like the Seguin of Béxar hired peons to do their share of the labor. They constructed the dams by placing large, flat "flag stones laid one on the other," according to one study of such irrigation sites. The acequia they dug, leading from the dam along the contours of the land toward their fields or *labores*. Where the acequia traversed an arroyo, they constructed aqueducts with arches of classic Roman proportions. These structures consisted of stone masonry and a mortar which, according to tradition, was made of "the whites of thousands of eggs and much goat milk."

Acequia systems were scattered across the Spanish frontier of Texas. Some of the early efforts were at Missions Espíritu Santo, Rosario, San Sabá, Candelaria, San Lorenzo, and San Xavier—all of which formed a wide semicircle around the northern and western quadrants of Béxar. The acequias which served Tejanos most were those built in and near Béxar. The San Pedro Acequia, tapping the waters of the San Pedro Creek, served the villa and *labores* of San Fernando. The Alamo Madre or Acequia Madre was six miles long, and watered nine hundred acres in and around the Alamo barrio. The four missions down the river from Béxar also had highly useful acequias. Those of Concepción and San José flowed until the 1860s, and those of San Juan and Espada were used until the twentieth century.[11]

The local nature of water systems management was reflected in laws from the *Recopilación* to the state decrees and, of course, to the city ordinance level. As mentioned above, the *Recopilación* delegated such authority to the ayuntamiento. The state of Coahuila y Texas issued Decree No. 190 on April 28, 1832 placing shareholders under the authority of the ayuntamiento as well. Article 6 of that decree stated the following: "In towns which admit of irrigation canals, said canals shall be made at the expense of the person interested. The commissioner shall divide them into channels or drains, procuring to have them made half a vara in width at least, and the same in depth, assigning one for the use of the town, and the rest for that of the fields in cultivation."[12] This authority was fully accepted and detailed in municipal ordinances.

Sanitation was one of the most important principles of acequia management. By municipal ordinance, the ayuntamiento was responsible for the cleanliness of acequias. The ayuntamiento then delegated the authority on to the junta de sanidad for annual inspection. The junta, acting unilaterally or through the syndico procurador, could fine anyone for putting dead animals or refuse into the water. The junta also meted out fines for persons washing clothes in the water or otherwise polluting it. The actual cleaning was done, of course, by the *vecinos*. Even so, the alcalde was required by law to arrange for military escort for this exercise, which they called the *limpia de acequias*.

Sharing the life-giving waters of the acequia represented a noteworthy tradition in itself. This process was, by law, the duty of the comisario; but by practice, implicit in the very design of the project. The basic unit of an equal share was determined by the volume of water flow of a particular acequia. Each shareholder was entitled to one day's flow of the acequia's water. The shareholders drew straws to determine the order in which they would partake of the acequia's flow; thus, the term *suerte*, meaning "luck," was used as the generic designation for the size of land unit which the acequia could water in one full day. So fully developed was this concept that special terms existed for different types of *suertes* depending on their size, soil fertility, topography, or crop assignment. A certain field might be a *surco de agua*, a *buey de agua*, a *naranja de agua*, or a *manzana de agua*. Many of these terms derived from Moorish words; most remained as common expressions to later nineteenth-century Tejanos.

Decree No. 37 of June 15, 1827, included a section which provides a most illustrative example of the complete integration of land and water concepts in the Tejano mind. The provisions of the section allowed for secularized mission lands to be divided among the families of the mission *vecindario*. Each family that had lived on such lands was to receive absolute property rights in one *porción* per family. The decree added that each *porción* should have "as absolute dominion and property, the days or hours of water which belong to the aforementioned pueblo and likewise the water." It thereby preserved the individual property rights as well as those of the pueblo or community.[13]

The influence of Hispanic water philosophy is ubiquitous in Texas. Common vocabulary as well as law books include such words as *suerte, porción, acequia, surco* (row), *agostadero* (pasture), *labor, arroyo,* and *canoa* (watering trough). Some of the first companies to utilize Texas land and water legislation were the irrigation and ditch (acequia) companies. The presence of such companies is most evident in the Texas counties where Tejanos had previously laid their acequia systems. The very landscape of many modern Texas cities also testifies to their Hispanic background. Although crossed and crisscrossed by more recent subdivisions, the old *porción* pattern has predetermined the major contours of many such cities. As one historian has indicated, "The Tomas de la Vega Eleven League Grant on the Brazos" has played a significant rôle in the historic development of modern Waco, Texas (see map of Waco). In the south of Texas, whole counties magnify the same effect.[14] These are only the most obvious effects, though certainly not the most important.

The most important influence of Tejano water systems is in Texas water law. As previous Hispanic principles held that the water belonged to all the inhabitants even though *porciones* owned use of the water, Texas retained such ownership of water in all perennial streams and beds. According to modern law, the state "has reserved title to it in trust for the whole people." Early Texas law moreover preserved control over water at the local level by, in effect, transferring ayuntamiento authority to county courts.

Wording in the 1852 Act Concerning Irrigated Property left little doubt as to its origin. It stated as follows: "That the County Courts be . . . authorized to order, regulate and control the time, mode, and erecting, repairing, cleaning, guarding and protecting the dams, ditches, roads and bridges belonging to any irrigation farms and property . . . owned cojointly by two or more different persons." The act recognized the "ancient usage" of equal daily assignment of waters by the commissioner, and authorized the courts to fine, as the procurador had done, "any owner of a suerte or subdivision lot" for using water excessively or out of turn.

Authorship of this 1852 law further illustrated the transition from Mexican to Anglo. The major supporters were Robert S. Neighbors of Medina County and Samuel A. Maverick of Béxar. The rôle of such men in this transition was acknowledged in a detailed study of the law: "This law was authored and sponsored by legislators familiar with such early Texas sys-

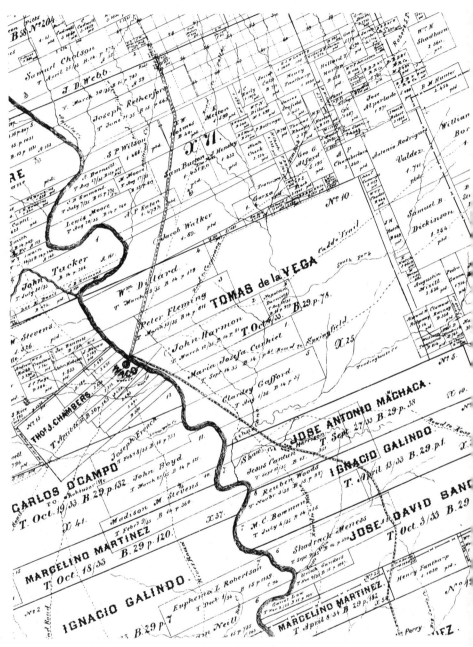

Map 3 Tomas de la Vega Land Grant in Waco, Texas. McLennan County
Survey Map, 1878. *Courtesy of the Texas General Land Office, Austin.*

tems and was passed by a legislature consisting of a substantial number of men, all of whom, who were as much as forty years of age, could have had first hand knowledge of irrigation practices throughout the most active period of Texas colonization . . ."

Indeed, Samuel A. Maverick had been mayor of San Antonio in 1840 when his Tejano city council members revalidated the provisions of Decree No. 190 in a new ordinance entitled "Ordinance for the Better Regulation of the Water Devoted to the Irrigation of the City of San Antonio and Its Vicinity." Even the Texas Supreme Court in 1868 reaffirmed in *Tolle v. Correth* that in the Irrigation Act of 1852, the Texas Legislature had "intended to carry out the principles of the Mexican laws."[15] By transferring the water law administration to the county courts, of course, the Anglo government also handed the control over the Tejano communal system to Anglo business interests such as those of Neighbors and Maverick.

In 1872, the Texas Supreme Court recommended that the state officially adopt the doctrine of prior appropriation embodying the Hispanic philosophy which was better suited to the arid and semiarid parts of the state. The legislature responded in 1889 and in 1895 by making unappropriated waters the property of the public and adopting the arid-region doctrine. Later laws modified Texas water codes to create a state-level Board of Water Engineers and to adopt elements of the Riparian Doctrine from Anglo-Saxon common law. As a result, Texas has acquired a dual set of codes. As mentioned, even the *Recopilación* had allowed for necessary elements of common law. The only significant disadvantage for Texas has been the loss of *pueblo* rights by cities. While cities in California and New Mexico still enjoy the full Mexican *pueblo* rights to waters flowing through their city limits (the municipality), Texas cities forfeited all rights to water except for private use such as gardening, sewage, and fire fighting.[16]

With regard to water rights, the Hispanic heritage of Texas lies in the remaining local authority over water and in her smooth transition to workable water codes. Dobkins explains that the transition was not so natural for other Anglo Americans coming into the Mexican borderlands: "In the arid West the riparian system, with its emphasis on land, proved unworkable. It cut off all but a few persons from the life-giving water." Some groups such as the California miners in 1849 found it natural to employ the doctrine of prior appropriation. Nine of the western states, however, were forced by the arid environment to abrogate the common law of riparian rights "entirely" and to adopt the prior appropriation system. Referring to such adoptions, a former water commissioner of Texas stated that "the early American legislators in the Southwest did little more than crystallize and adopt an amalgamation of long-established Moorish, Spanish, and Indian customs." The United States Congress eventually passed a statute that recognized the doctrine of prior appropriation in those states where it was already instituted by local law or custom.[17] But while other state laws borrowed and experimented, Texas water law rested on the firm foundation of her Mexican systems. And the benefits of those laws were the legacy of the local Tejano community, at which level the systems and principles were conserved and ultimately transmitted to the incoming order.

Education was another major area of concern to the Tejano community. No other facet of life was so exclusively dependent on local support. Nor does any other illustrate so vividly as education the sacrifice and unfaltering dedication of the *vecindario*. Through a local public education commission or the *comisión de escuelas*, Tejanos continually strove to erect a viable education system. Too often their efforts were frustrated, however, by the insecurity of a foundling political system: too many resources had to be spent resisting enemy attack. Ultimately, their efforts were overshadowed by a revolution which shattered many of their hard-earned achievements. Nevertheless, their objectives guided the educational efforts of later Tejano generations; and their ideals created a prototype for the system that Texas uses today.

A basic premise in education at the beginning of the Mexican federal period was that the ayuntamiento had sole responsibility for education in its *vecindario*. All government levels—from federal to municipal—cast responsibility onto the local body. Article 215 of the Coahuila y Texas Constitution and Articles 128 through 131 of the *Reglamento* (regulations for economic and political government of the state) placed all responsibility and management in the hands of the ayuntamiento. Municipal ordinances simply reiterated these clauses. The ordinances of the Béxar Junta de Instrucción Pública accepted and proudly claimed the responsibilities of management, inspection, and reporting of education exclusively for the ayuntamiento. "The Illustrious Ayuntamiento," it said, "shall always be the immediate administrator of the funds destined and collected for this object."[18] Little was mentioned about the source of school funding, but as to their management, there was no question.

Funding, indeed, was the major obstacle to Tejano education. This heavy burden fell exclusively on the shoulders of the *vecindario*. People employed different local funding techniques, but ultimately the support came from their own pockets. According to State Decree No. 37, funding was to come from ayuntamiento revenues. This source was hardly enough for defense against the Indians. José Antonio Saucedo discovered this in 1825 when he became jefe político. The ayuntamiento wrote congratulating him on his appointment to the office and promised faithful cooperation. It added that it could not comply with his order to establish a new school, however, because of the total lack of funds. Occasionally, the school fund received money from a local tax on slaughtered cattle, but such appropriations were of dubious legality and even less regularity. There were provisions for aid from state government as a last resort, but Tejanos learned that the state had even less money for their schools.[19]

The major source of funds for schools in Texas during these years was from fund-raising drives among the *vecindario*. Different committees conducted the drives. Sometimes the junta patriotica collected the money; other times, contributors simply handed in the money to a public school fund. In Nacogdoches the most successful collecting agency was the *junta piadosa*, or committee of piety, which served charity as well as patriotic, religious, and educational fund drives. In any mission fortunate enough to have its own educational facilities such as Mission Espada, *vecinos* contributed cooperatively to the alcalde. Usually they contributed money, but particularly in the earlier years, they often contributed in kind. Thus, a parent might donate approximately four pesos to the teacher, or a Tejana might contribute a parcel of meat, lard, or salt. Tejanas were also among the most generous contributers. As mentioned, Tejana widows not only lived the longest, but they were often the wealthiest in the Tejano community. Many schools and chapels owed their existence to the generosity and dedication of Tejanas.[20]

Attracting good teachers was a major expense in education; maintaining them was a preoccupation for the *vecindario*. In some cases a community was fortunate enough to find a soldier in the local garrison or one of its own *vecinos* who could teach. Usually they had to advertise far and wide by circular. Teachers of various nationalities commonly moved from town to town. Living in private homes, they remained for as long as the contract salary sufficed. When income became inadequate, they moved on. In 1828, Béxar hired José Antonio Gama y Fonseca for a two-year contract. Other teachers during the 1830s included Victoriano Zepeda and Bruno Huizar.[21]

Other Tejano communities also established schools despite limited resources. Goliad had a small school which served intermittently until 1821, employing soldiers from the presidio and at least one *vecino*. Laredo established its school in 1825 after repeated admonitions and threats from the governor to comply with state law of Tamaulipas which, as in Coahuila y Texas, placed the responsibility on the ayuntamiento. Juan José Salinas was the teacher in Laredo where he received twenty pesos per month from local contributors. One of the commendable efforts was that of Nacogdoches, where in 1828, the junta piadosa began a determined effort in the community and in the state legislature to establish a school. Their proposals stimulated the legislature to initiate a new program of land grants for education. At home the junta accepted contributions of money and labor which by 1831 finally rewarded the *vecindario* with their own school building and teacher, an Anglo American. Quickly, Nacogdoches joined Béxar as a leader in the education of youth. The school systems in both towns boasted the highest proportion of students per population in the state despite the fact that they were, according to one historian, "supported by a population even poorer than the Anglo-Americans" (see table 11). All of these schools, unfortunately, declined with the onset of revolutionary troubles in 1835.[22]

Tejanos placed great emphasis on pedagogy. They perceived their schools as playing an integral function in the community; therefore, they closely guarded the teacher's instruction as well as the student's performance. Teachers had to satisfy the requirements of the *comisión de escuelas* which set forth a detailed policy of instruction. Competition was to be the mode of instruction as well as of evaluation. Students would be divided into teams, each challenging the others in contests of academic skill. Students and teacher would participate in civic activities together. For example, they would attend mass together or march as a group in a parade. During this period, Mexican educators began to experiment with newer pedagogical methods such as the McClure method of Indiana. In 1829, Coahuila y Texas issued Decree No. 92 authorizing the Lancastrian mutual instruction plan throughout the state, a plan by which students would teach fellow students.

As Tejanos struggled for a system that would allow state aid without sacrificing local control, they offered imaginative proposals which the legislature converted into beneficial laws. In April, 1826, Béxar submitted a proposal for state grants of land for education. The legislature responded favorably, and asked for a more detailed plan. Béxar and Saltillo jointly

TABLE 11   Schools of Coahuila y Texas, 1831

City	Population	Schools	Students
Saltillo	23,520	4 (incl. 1 college)	428
Parras	10,347	4	146
Béxar	1,634	1	114
Austin	5,665	4	77
Nacogdoches	767	1	50

Source: Alessio Robles, *Coahuila y Texas*, vol. 1, pp. 329–31.

sponsored a second proposal by which the state would donate land for the creation of two schools *(colegios)* or academies of grammar *(cátedra de gramática)*. The bill went to the public education committee for final preparation.

While the bill for two *colegios* was being proposed by Béxar, Nacogdoches introduced its own plan for primary education. On April 6, 1832, Nacogdoches proposed that the state set aside four *sitios* or leagues (17,712 acres) of land in that municipality "in order that with the product of these it may form a permanent fund [*fondo de arbitrios*] with the exclusive object being to establish a school of primary letters."[23] Six months later, on October 5 of that year, the Anglo settlers at their first San Felipe Convention drew up a similar *memoria* in what mistakenly has been considered the first such request.[24]

Implicit in all of these proposals was the principle that education should be free, at least for the poor. This principle was an integral part of Decree No. 92 in 1829. Béxar had instituted this principle in its own school system as early as 1828. In fact, free education was one of the major provisions of Béxar's school ordinance, entitled "Ordinance Which Shall Be Observed in the Public Free Primary School Dedicated to the Instruction of the Youth of the Vicinity of Béxar." The Coahuila y Texas legislature finally accepted and decreed in 1833 all of these Tejano proposals—for two *colegios*, for four *sitios* to provide a permanent fund in each municipality, and for free public education. Nacogdoches was granted its four *sitios*, as requested, on May 8, 1833. Béxar received a similar grant for its primary schools a week later in Decree No. 244. And the legislature promulgated a general education plan for the state in Decree No. 299 in April of the same year.

Decree No. 299 was the most valuable of all the decrees of this period, for it encompassed the philosophy as well as the provisions of the several

Tejano proposals. Article 1 stated that the municipalities should sell all municipal lands except *propios* to private individuals in order to provide initial capital. All capital towns were to establish schools within six months; other towns should do so as soon as possible. The decree further ordered the creation of a permanent fund as a so-called mandatory "object" of the plan. Article 24 stated, "Besides the private revenue there may have been established for the support thereof, one half the annual product of the municipal funds of the respective towns until said product reaches to two thousand dollars shall be appropriated to the same object." Additionally, state lands were to be sold with such revenue to be "collected annually . . . and appropriated to the support of the schools." With revenue from state lands, the permanent fund would continue to grow and to support future educational needs as well. The state public education committee was to administer and manage state school funds so acquired.[25] In general, this law constituted an original plan which would allow the residents of Texas to convert the state's greatest resource—land—into a viable system of education at all levels. As such, it served as a precedent and precursor for many other such Texas education laws in that century to use public lands for the same end.

As in water law, education law made a definite transition from Tejano legislation to the modern system in Texas. In 1839 and 1840, Texas President Mirabeau B. Lamar signed bills which are generally credited with having laid the foundation for education in Texas. The provisions allowed for four leagues (17,712 acres) in each county to be set aside for establishment of a county primary school. Provisions further allowed for a state "board of school commissioners" to supervise and inspect such use of the lands. Another important facet of this program was the granting of land to establish two colleges. While Lamar's legislation was unquestionably vital to the young republic (Houston's interest in education was "not at all pronounced"), it was patterned after the structure laid by Tejano legislation between 1826 and 1833. One early Texas historian made the following intuitive observation in regard to Coahuila y Texas Decree No. 92, for example:

"This is the initiative in a long line of public laws in the interest of free public education, which have secured to Texas today a munificent public-school endowment in land and a most liberal and efficient system of popular instruction."[26]

A more direct link between Lamar's program and the Mexican laws is evident in the legislative development of the 1839 and 1840 bills. Actually, Lamar's greatest service was in sponsoring the law. Other men had drawn it up—men like the Wharton brothers who were involved in the Texas House of Representatives Committee on Education in 1839 as well as in the San Felipe Convention of 1832. The long-term efforts of these men were an obvious contribution to the 1840 law, but most vividly apparent in the final product were the efforts of the Tejanos even before 1832. For example, the Lamar provision for four leagues in 1840 was obviously derived from the four *sitios* requested by Nacogdoches or the four *sitios* granted in Decree No. 240 of Coahuila y Texas; the San Felipe Convention considered requesting from twenty-five to one hundred fifty leagues, and finally omitted any mention of leagues entirely.[27]

Anglo Americans were slow to appreciate the educational philosophy of Tejanos. The modern student is constantly reminded, for example, that this was one of the grievances listed in the Texas Declaration of Independence. The Anglos scarcely understood or considered the Tejano concept of local full responsibility for financing and managing schools. Anglos were accustomed to private, home education or "old field" schools, which were private schools operated in the community by an itinerant teacher. States in the Old South had long since accepted full responsibility for financing school systems through land grants. They failed to take into account, however, the categorical difference between the federalist state of Coahuila y Texas and an Anglo-American state such as Georgia. Georgia could tap her limited state lands for education as she had done since 1783, but Coahuila y Texas had access and title to her seemingly boundless public domain as a Mexican state. It was this tremendous domain which would eventually manifest the "munificent public-school endowment in land" for later generations.[28]

Tejanos, in contrast, continued to develop their local concept of education. The *vecindario* of Béxar used their land grant to establish a school which, after the revolutionary turmoil had subsided, was recognized as "the first real public school in Texas." This Béxar school was later able to sue a modern railway company for lands which the school had received by virtue of the Mexican law. Throughout the south of Texas in the second half of the nineteenth century, Tejano descendants continued to maintain their own local, private schools. These schools received no funds from the state of Texas. They were supported by a board of directors which hired the teachers and supervised the pedagogy. Indeed, these schools and this philosophy served later generations of Tejanos in the development of private Hispanic schools during the turbulent decades after the Texas revolution.[29]

In the final analysis, the educational effort in early Texas was greatly influenced by frontier conditions. The Tejanos were unable to implement fully their program because of the revolution of 1836. The Anglo Americans who later duplicated the Tejano system in Texas struggled with the problem for years after the revolution. Frederick Eby, an education historian, attempted to explain the Anglo Americans' long delay in improving upon the situation which they had so decried in their Declaration. He said, "Other concerns, really more fundamental to human welfare in such primitive social conditions, absorbed attention." Among these concerns, he cites the organization of a civil government, public defense against Indian wars, and financial instability of a new government.[30] In effect, the Anglo Americans had exchanged positions with the Tejanos who, one decade earlier, had offered exactly the same apology.

In so many ways, the Tejano community served its own. It served them faithfully in sickness, in health, in crisis, in feast, and in daily life. Ironically, history has neglected and often spoken poorly of the early Mexican community of Texas. The laws, the vocabulary, and the principles which reflect Tejano community life have rarely been acknowledged by Texas society. But time has been more magnanimous in its own peculiar way to the old Tejano community, for it has chosen to preserve among all other aspects of historical evidence, those of the community. Indeed, the only physical imprints left by Tejanos upon the face of Texas soil—the acequia, the *porción*, the plaza—are those which attest to the earlier presence of a Tejano community.

IV
Tejano Justice on the *Frontera*

In addition to the semiarid climate and sparce vegetation, the rural environment forced Tejanos to make adjustments for the great distances on the *frontera*. Distance was a major factor in communications between villa and capital city. As Tejano society expanded onto ranches, distance became a major factor in communications between home and villa as well. The vast, sparsely populated hinterland—the *despoblado*—was a daily reality to Tejanos.

The nature of the *despoblado* only compounded the challenge of life on the *frontera*. This hinterland held valuable resources, some of which were peculiar to Texas. To exploit these, Tejanos employed the Hispanic institution of the *rancho*. In their efforts to incorporate the *despoblado* economically, however, the Tejanos confronted all of its hostile elements. Tejanos therefore had to extend their authority outward from the municipality and onto the *despoblado*. By incorporating it, Tejanos tended then to combine their livelihood with their defense. Thus, as they extended the ranch into the Texas *despoblado*, Tejanos provided for the emergence of a rural "policeman" with the authority of a rural judge. He was called the *juez de campo*. In all of its uniquely Mexican forms, this institution was to survive with ranching as an archetype in the defense of the Texas back country.

American ranch life is generally acknowledged to have originated in Hispanic Texas. It must, therefore, be considered in a discussion of Tejano life; however, the discussion herein is not intended as a mere repetition of the colorful contributions of the *vaquero* to the American cattle industry. The object instead is to depict the socioeconomic principles and techniques of the ranch as important elements of the Tejano livelihood. Tejanos made lasting contributions to the American cattle industry, to be sure, but these were only a function of their more noteworthy legacy in range resource management and defense.

Ranching grew almost naturally from the earliest *entradas* or Spanish settlement expeditions. Don Alonzo de León, on one of the first *entradas* into Texas in 1689, brought two hundred cattle, four hundred horses, and 150 mules expressly for propagation in Texas. On his return trip to Coahuila, De León left a male and a female of each species on the bank of every stream he crossed from the Neches River to the Río Grande. Later expeditions continued to import hundreds of livestock. As Tejano settlements grew toward the mid-eighteenth century, they perceived livestock production as a most logical industry. When José de Escandón reconnoitered the Río Grande region for settlement in 1747, for example, he was impressed by what he reported to be "numerous wild horses, wild cattle, and wild burros." From this discovery, he determined that the region was best suited for the establishment of ranches and livestock grazing. In 1774, the mission herds of La Bahía reported fifteen thousand branded cattle, giving La Bahía the title of "greatest cattle-raising country in the world." By that time, privately owned ranches had spread around Nacogdoches, along the San Antonio river, and across the Río Grande frontier to become what one historian of Spanish Texas has called "the largest single industry in the province."[1]

Besides being suited to the Texas environment, the ranch was highly compatible with the Tejano concept of frontier settlement. Indeed, some historians have viewed ranching as one of the most significant institutions on the Spanish frontier. Along with the mission and the presidio, it allowed for expansion and maintenance of the frontier line. The very concept of grazing was entirely compatible with the defensive nature of the Iberian *municipium*. The Spaniards who grouped around the presidio could simply move their stock to preserve their livelihood in time of attack. Such mobility, of course, would not have been possible with agricultural crops. Another natural advantage which weighed heavily in the Tejano's consideration was the minimal labor force required in ranching as compared to farming. Texas climate allowed for the cultivation of agricultural crops, but other conditions on the frontier made farming unprofitable if not unsafe. This disadvantage was underscored in one statistical report for Béxar in 1826 which affirmed the abundance of fruit in the surrounding fields. Unfortunately, the report added that the labor scarcity or *escazes de brazos* and the Indian attacks prohibited cultivation and harvest of those fields.[2]

Even in their early land unit designations, Tejanos revealed their strong predilection for a grazing economy. In and near the towns, land units had names such as *solar* for a town lot, *labor* (177.1 acres) for a small field of cultivation, and *caballería* (100 acres) for grazing. These smaller units were the ones often served by town acequias, as mentioned. The early Béxar residents, for example, received some grants of land for use as *suertes* as well as *caballerías* for grazing. Larger land unit designations were even more explicit in their grazing functions. These included the 4,336-acre *sitio de ganado mayor* for large animals such as horses, cattle, and burros (sometimes a 4,428-acre league was granted as a *sitio*); the 1,920-acre *sitio de ganado menor* for smaller animals like sheep, goats, and hogs; and the *sitio de criadero de ganado mayor*, which was intended exclusively as a cattle-breeding ranch.[3] Another major consideration in land use on the Texas ranch was the underlying reality of the open range. Openness was assumed. It had an obvious disadvantage in the insecurity of a widely scattered herd of branded stock. In the "greatest cattle-raising country in the world," however, the open range had its compensation.

No other place in the world had as many wild mustangs as South Texas by the mid-eighteenth century. They roamed the prairies south of Béxar in herds of fifteen hundred to two thousand head. Traveler Agustín Morfí in 1777 described them as majestic, wild horses, "so copious, that they have the countryside full of pathways." Few travelers in this region failed to note the herds, or to marvel at their striking appearance.[4]

The Tejanos called them *mesteñas*. The etymology of the word itself reveals the uniqueness of the animal. Based on the Spanish word *mesta* which referred to the round-up of stray animals which were "mixed," the word *mesteña* originally meant "stray" or "unclaimed." In that context, it referred to any kind of stray animal. It was often used interchangeably with the word *mostrenco*, which could refer to any other kind of unclaimed resource as well.[5] As visitors to Texas wrote home, however, they promulgated the specialized Tejano meaning for the word which eventually gained formal usage. Thus in 1806, Spanish Bishop Marín de Porras reported that he admired seeing the great herds of wild horses "which here are called *mesteñadas*." In 1810, Miguel Ramos Arizpe also spoke of the great herds of wild horses in Texas, "or *mesteño* as they call them here." In 1835, a Mexican officer, Juan N. Almonte, noted the abundance of the "*mesteñas*," and added, "That is what they call the horses in Texas which are gathered, and which inhabit the countryside."[6] Eventually, visitors who wrote in English reported to the United States of the "mustangs, or wild horses" in Texas. Or they revealed the slow transition in pronunciation from *mesteña* to "mestango," as Elias Wrightman did in a letter in 1832. Whichever language or spelling they used, visitors noted the same Tejano meaning of the word, the uniqueness of the great herds, and the apparent lack of claim or ownership of any kind over these animals.[7]

The great abundance of wild and domesticated animals offered an obvious resource potential which Tejanos regularly exploited. The most common means of exploitation, besides personal consumption, was the round-up, drive, and market of the animals. By the late eighteenth century, Tejanos had established this three-phase pattern of marketing the animals to the United States through Louisiana and Natchez. The Tejano *vaqueros* or cowboys first rode into the countryside, where they surrounded the stock and drove them into a makeshift pen or *corral*. This round-up or *rodeo* involved such necessary stock operations as separating, counting, branding, or marking. The next phase was the hazardous drive or *corredería*. The vaqueros, employing a ratio of approximately twenty men for each one thousand head of stock, drove the herds up the Camino Real from Béxar or Goliad to Nacogdoches and on to the United States. Local ranchers or traders added their herds to the drives, which sometimes departed every month with as many as two thousand head in a single drive. In this way, up to twenty thousand cattle annually left Texas for the United States, where they were marketed in the final phase of the enterprise. Horses, mules, and burros were also driven to the United States in somewhat smaller numbers by the same process.[8]

As Tejanos began to realize profits from the loose stock, government officials also perceived a need to regulate and tax the industry. The 1772 edition of the Spanish *Recopilación* had declared all unclaimed minerals or resources found in the royal domain *(cosas halladas mostrencas)* to belong to the Crown. This decree was interpreted by Teodoro de Croix, the commandant general of the Eastern Interior Provinces, to include wild livestock on the Texas prairies. Initially, De Croix attempted to make Tejanos pay for the livestock which they captured, but the resulting protests forced him to require only a head tax on the animals. As the king's hold over Tejano government officials gradually weakened by 1800, they appropriated these tax receipts to their local *arbitrios* funds.[9]

Tejanos developed their own set of procedures to regulate the round-ups of livestock in Texas. The Béxar Ayuntamiento in 1823, for example, published a standard set of regulations which were accepted by other ayunta-mientos in Texas. The tax rate established by Béxar was one *real* for each horse, two for each mule, and four for each head of cattle. Anyone wishing to round up and drive the livestock was ordinarily required to register with government officials. The governor officially appointed one applicant to head the round-up, stating the time and route of the drive. All of these procedures were included in a bill by Miguel Arciniega of Béxar in the state legislature in 1827. Arciniega specifically requested the period from Octo-ber to February as the official season for round-ups or *corredurías de mes-teñas*. His bill was officially accepted as Decree No. 8 in August, 1827. The law established the season specified in Arciniega's bill and placed a state tax on livestock exports to the United States. The state tax rates were identical to the rates set earlier by Béxar.[10]

Just as Commandant General De Croix had earlier encountered resistance, the new state governor found it difficult to collect taxes on livestock exports in Texas. Béxar officials were accustomed to using the receipts for local expenditures, and many "mustangers" were reluctant to pay any tax at all. The state government regularly prosecuted Tejanos and foreigners appre-hended for illegal mustanging. At one point, Governor José María Viesca severely admonished the Béxar Ayuntamiento itself for not passing *mesteña* revenues on to the state treasury in accordance with Decree No. 8.[11]

Another regulatory system Tejanos employed was that of the *circulación de mercader*. The *mercader* was a professional livestock trader who contracted to procure stock for town markets. Although stock raisers were exempt from taxes in Coahuila y Texas, the trade in livestock was taxed and strictly regulated in all phases from purchase to slaughter. The abundance of live-stock combined with the open range in Texas to encourage cattle rustling and illegal trading in the *despoblado*. Ranch employees found it profitable to sell the ranch owner's stock to unscrupulous traders at prices below market value. For this reason, the sixteenth-century regulations of *mercader* were gradually implemented in the frontier provinces of Texas, Nuevo León, Tamaulipas, and Coahuila during the eighteenth century.

To control the trading of livestock, state regulations prohibited any free trade or slaughter whatsoever in the *despoblado*. The *mercader* was required to register any sale or purchase of stock with an alcalde, indicating the number of head, the species, and their brands. The *mercader* was also required to present a certificate with these and other details to all alcaldes along his drive routes. The brand was critical, of course, in the positive identification and regulation of livestock trading. Besides the seller's permanent, hot brand, the *mercader* used his own temporary "sale" brand *(para ventear)*, which was applied with pitch for identification along the drive.

On arrival in town, the *mercader* rendered the standard tax to the alcalde and sold the stock at the marketplace or slaughterhouse. Every town had an official place for sale or slaughter of livestock. Just as animal slaughter was prohibited in the *despoblado*, so was it forbidden anywhere in the city except in the official slaughterhouse. The industry was thus more closely regulated. According to one study of Hispanic institutions, "investigation reveals that the Spaniards made considerable progress in coping with problems of sanitation, supply, and fair regulation in food production." So strict was the system, in fact, that it required that the branded hides of slaughtered animals be exhibited for weeks outside the slaughterhouse.

Tejanos observed a strict control over the *mercader*. As with mustangers, the alcaldes were preoccupied with the prosecution of violators—foreign and Tejano—of the *circulación de mercader*. Illegal trading and slaughter constituted a sizeable enterprise in the early 1800s. Nevertheless, Tejano officials were as reluctant to release *mercader* revenues to the state government as they were the *mesteña* funds. Indeed, such revenues were often the only dependable source of external funds for frontier communities. Tejano statesmen continued to assert bitterly their claims to these tax revenues, despite the unsympathetic attitude of state authorities.[12]

Tejanos had many types of range animals which they husbanded with great care and expertise. Besides cattle, every Tejano municipality regularly kept sheep and goats, mules and burros. Some were used for meat, others for transportation. All Tejano municipalities raised swine, but Nacogdoches seems to have had the largest herds (approximately five thousand in 1833). And they all had smaller numbers of oxen, which were commonly enumerated as "yokes" of oxen or *lluntas de bueyes*, suggesting their use by Tejanos.

The ubiquitous and continuous practice of livestock handling in Texas naturally affected the cultural characteristics of Tejano life. Constantly in the field handling such large and often untamed animals, the Tejanos developed an expertise rarely equaled in the techniques of the livestock industry: branding, round-ups, driving, open-range grazing, expert horsemanship, and a broad knowledge of animal husbandry.

Tejano livestock husbandry developed as a combination of traditional practices and a few characteristics peculiar to Texas. The concept of unique brands, for example, was brought to the New World from Spain. In Texas the Spaniards also continued the highly specialized identification of animals. Tejanos rarely referred to horses with the generic term *caballo*. More commonly, they spoke of a horse more descriptively to include its sex, special color characteristics, and its brand, in that order. Horses were commonly identified by such descriptive names as *llegüa tordilla picada* (speckled, dapple gray mare), *garañon prieto sereno* (misty black stallion), *llegüa alazana tuerta* (one-eyed sorrel mare), and *potro quatralbo* (a colt with white "socks" above all four hooves).[13]

Whereas the Spanish codes strictly regulated equine husbandry in Spain, conditions in Texas led to deviations from traditional practices. The *Recopilación* limited breeding in Spain strictly to Andalusian studs, but in Texas the *mesteñas* rendered this rule inapplicable. This condition led to other deviations as well. The use of the horse as a work platform, for example, was another well-regulated Hispanic tradition that underwent changes in Texas. The heavy, large saddle with the leather *quadralpas* which extended over the horse's rump was legally restricted for use only by Spanish nobility. Tejanos did not ride the fine Andalusians of the aristocracy, but the rugged, "sharp-backed Mexican horse," recently broken from the *mesteña* wilds. They therefore used the large saddle not entirely as a luxury, but as a necessity as well. *Recopilación* notwithstanding, Tejanos commonly used the *quadralpas*.[14]

Visitors in nineteenth-century Texas frequently marveled at the horsemanship skills of the Tejanos. "The ranchero never walks," said Abbé Emmanuel Domenech on a trip through early Texas. "Had he only half a mile to go, he does so on horseback. His horse, of which he is very proud, is his inseparable companion." One of the most conspicuous skills was the use of the *reata* or lariat. Tejanos as easily roped a running animal by the neck as by the forehooves. If attacked on the open range, the vaqueros unhesitatingly converted the *reata* into an effective weapon for defense as well. In several documented cases, Tejanos used the *reata* against Indians in surprise attack or against Anglo-American troops in heated combat. Other skills were directed more toward recreation and exhibition than strictly for work. After the work of a rodeo, for example, the vaqueros often engaged in several days of contests of skill with livestock. They called these celebrations "days of the bulls" or *días de toros*. Besides the ordinary racing and roping skills, they had other contests such as the *carrera del gallo*. In this game the vaqueros, racing at full speed on horseback, reached down to grasp the head of a cock which had been buried to the neck in the dirt. Another game, the *coleada*, involved riding beside a running bull, grasping the bull's tail, and throwing the animal off balance by expert use of the rider's horse and saddle horn.[15]

Many other Tejano skills and principles of husbandry survived primarily through transmission to the incoming Anglo-American culture in Texas. Although Anglo Americans were probably acquainted with most of these methods, it is highly doubtful that the Anglos had the breadth, specialization, and rich tradition of skills Tejanos boasted by the nineteenth century. For the most part, the Anglos learned skills from the Tejanos as well as resource management and regulation. One Anglo rancher in 1850s Texas wrote about his livestock management, using terms that revealed the transmission of practices and terminology, saying, "Once a week or oftener we would make a rodeo or round-up of the cattle."[16]

Breeding of mules and wide use of pack mules are two endeavors which Tejanos employed to a much greater extent than did Anglo Americans. One Anglo colonist described a Mexican mule caravan in 1823, reporting that "the mules were managed by Mexican muleteers, who were very expert packers." During the early phases of the Mexican War, Anglo Texan Ben McCulloch, observing a team of Mexican muleteers at work, said, "Two Mexicans will load 25 mules in less time than my Co. will saddle each his own horse and get on parade."[17]

Another skill Tejanos enjoyed was training oxen. Besides using pack mules, Tejanos employed burros and oxen to pull carts, *carretas*, for freight. The Tejanos captured wild range bulls and trained them by tying them to domesticated oxen. The rope used for this was a strong rope or *cabresto*, made by spinning horse hair on a *tarabilla* or whirligig. Lewis Birdsall Harris described the training process which he learned from two "Mexicans" who helped him build his home. These men, he said, were "quite handy with cattle and we broke in with the help of a yoke of gentle oxen enough others to haul our hewn logs to the place." This rich tradition, among others, enabled Tejanos to dominate the carting trade in Texas until the 1850s.[18]

Tejanos, who had long regulated the livestock industry, also passed much of this experience on to the Anglos. As Stephen F. Austin addressed himself to the administration of local government in his colony, he received noteworthy advice from Governor José Antonio Saucedo. As mentioned above, the two articles which Saucedo added to Austin's civil code in 1823 dealt with regulation of livestock. Article 31 incorporated the Tejano practice of posting for six months the brands of any stray animals found on a hunt, before disposal. And he added Article 32, which involved official registration of brands to be used by Anglo colonists. In time, the Anglo colonists began to incorporate not only these principles but those of the *mercader* as well, as witnessed by the Nacogdoches County Court proceedings after the Texas Revolution. Indeed, as late as 1840, the Tejanos on the San Antonio City Council passed these provisions in "An Ordinance Which Provides a Market *(Mercado)* for Meat, &c." And one historian familiar with the *mercader* principle in the Tejano experience has stated that "the system itself, in substance, was imported by Texas, and used through the hey-day of the cattle drives after the Civil War."[19]

The most important aspect of government in the *despoblado* was the special arrangement which Hispanic tradition had developed for the inhabitants of that part of a municipality. As mentioned before, Tejano homesteads were characterized by remoteness. This characteristic greatly impressed visitors or newcomers, who usually reacted unfavorably. Two Mexican visitors in 1828 and 1835 noted the inherent weaknesses in such wide population dispersal on the Texas *frontera*. Indeed, certain laws encouraged government officials to reduce to town life those individuals who lived "dispersed in the country" or *dispersos en el campo*. One Anglo-American visitor pitied the "miserable Mexicans" whom he described almost incredulously as living "far apart, at distances of ten or even twenty miles from each other."[20] Such wide population dispersal became quite standard to Tejanos as they expanded their ranches further into the *despoblado* during the nineteenth century. Even Anglo ranchers later became accustomed to—and, ironically, would learn to prize—such remoteness.

Tejanos employed a special constabulary to extend their governmental authority to the legal inhabitants in all parts of the *despoblado*. According to state law, each remote ranching community had at least one *syndico de rancho*, just as the urban barrios had their own *comisarios*. The syndico de rancho performed the same basic functions as his urban counterpart with the addition, of course, of special, rural regulations. The rural counterpart of the alcalde in Texas was the *juez de campo*. In general, the juez de campo supervised the syndicos in the regulation of round-ups, control of strays, and in settling any damage or other disputes. He was also responsible for the orderly behavior of citizens in dealings concerning timber, crops, roads or bridges in the *despoblado*.

The juez de campo in Texas proved to be a most significant position in Tejano government by the early nineteenth century. Indeed, this was the person in whom the Tejano ranching livelihood on the *despoblado* and the defense of the *frontera* eventually came together under a single unified authority. In reference to this evolutionary trend, one Texas historian stated that the juez de campo became a "rural policeman as well as brand inspector and roundup boss and thus represented a concession to frontier conditions."[21] The juez de campo in Texas was the critical link between the ancient Hispanic principles of royal privilege and control and the modern agencies for special enforcement among peripheral or unassimilated population groups. The attributes of the juez de campo clearly manifested the basic characteristics of this peculiar evolutionary trend. His was a broad authority as primary judge with civil and criminal jurisdiction in the city as well as in the *despoblado*. He was empowered to pursue, to deputize, and to prosecute. He provided law in the range industry and enforcement in the *despoblado*. The juez de campo in Texas was the product, and indeed the patron of the *despoblado*.

The concept of a juez de campo had originated in the outlying regions of the twelfth-century Spanish countryside, where local brotherhoods or *hermandades* offered a precious measure of security against Moorish attack. Queen Isabella of Castilla expanded these councils in 1474 as the formal Santa Hermandad by which she centralized her control over the cities as well as the countryside. Alcaldes of the Santa Hermandad enjoyed independent judicial authority by which they checked the local nobles who might otherwise usurp the power of the Crown. These alcaldes held special privileges such as the right to enter a private estate in search of fugitives or incriminating evidence. Thus, the Hermandad combined special privilege and law enforcement in one agency.

As the generations passed, the Santa Hermandad continued to expand its jurisdiction and to augment its privilege. In 1631, the *alcalde de hermandad* became a regular member of the town ayuntamiento. His new administrative duties tended to "submerge" his special function, but he enjoyed compensating factors as well. The alcalde de hermandad had "voice and vote" (*voz y voto*) on the town council. The Hermandad was expanded to include a vast network of agents called *quadrilleros* (crossbowmen) in every village. The alcalde de hermandad was authorized to commission the *quadrilleros* and even ordinary alcaldes in the pursuit and prosecution of fugitives across the land. He had the right to try, sentence, and punish offenders, although

74

the codes of the *Recopilación* explicitly warned him to avoid exceeding his special authority.

Through the *Recopilación*, the Hermandad was transmitted to Las Indias, the New World. For the *alcalde provincial*, as the Hermandad official was called in Mexico, the *Recopilación* offered a descriptive statement on the philosophy, privilege, and authority residing in this person:

> Having consideration of the benefit, which results in this our Kingdom of Castilla of the foundation and exercise of the Hermandad, and having recognized how necessary it is that it be conserved and expanded to the Provinces of the Indias, because of the distances that exist from some settlements to others, and in order to curb the excesses committed in deserted, uninhabited places, by the many idle, vagabond, and desperate persons, who live in them, with grave detriment to the travelers, and persons, who inhabit the remote parts, without neighboring populace, nor even communication with any who could help them in their needs, or the robberies and injuries which they suffer: We have seen fit that in the Cities and Villages of the Indias there should be Alcaldes de Hermandad, or at least one, as permitted by the number of *vecinos* . . . who may be perpetually a Provincial de la Hermandad in the City, and his land, with staff and sword, voice and vote, seat and position of a major Alcalde on the city council.

Later editions of the codes conferred additional privileges on the alcalde provincial. He was to carry his staff "in deserted regions or in the *despoblado*, or in any other populated places if the evildoers should escape into the country."[22]

In eighteenth-century New Spain, the alcalde provincial underwent a specialization which seemed to epitomize all of the privileges and attributes of the institution. In 1710, the viceroy, Marqués de Valero, appointed Miguel Velásquez as alcalde provincial in Querétaro, a particularly crime-ridden province. Velásquez, a very capable officer, agreed to accept the commission on the condition that he be fully authorized to pursue, try, and execute any bandits that he apprehended. The viceroy agreed, granting Velásquez independent jurisdiction and final authority with automatic approval or *acordada* of the viceroy. So armed, Velásquez and his small corps of officers were very effective in eradicating bandits in Querétaro. Thus developed an important strain in law enforcement as the *frontera* moved toward Texas in the eighteenth century.[23]

In the same manner as the Hermandad, another Hispanic institution, the Mesta, evolved contemporaneously and expanded to the Indias. The Spanish Mesta was a guild of sheep and goat ranchers. Inasmuch as these animals were considered property of a "specially dignified type" by Spaniards, the Mesta enjoyed special privileges in Spanish society. The codes of the *Recopilación* also transmitted this institution to Mexico where it expanded and became much more detailed and important than in Spain. The Mexican Mesta came to include all other livestock as well as sheep. Branding regulations became more highly specialized. The *alcalde de mesta* was more than simply a field judge. His authority was augmented to include primary jurisdiction in all cases involving violation of Mesta regulations of theft of livestock. He was authorized to fine violators and to collect the fines. As his jurisdiction gradually extended to include criminal cases in and around the city, his function became what one historian has labeled "a sort of police court." Eventually the jurisdiction of the alcalde de mesta and that of the alcalde provincial began to overlap in Mexico.[24]

As the institutions of the alcalde provincial and the alcalde de mesta evolved along convergent paths, their progress was cut short during the Mexican independence period. The liberal principles of the era began to challenge the right of special privilege and the disregard for "natural" rights. The liberal Spanish Constitution of 1812, for example, dealt a severe blow to many of these old institutions by placing all civil and criminal jurisdiction in Mexico under a single authority. Without judicial authority, these institutions were reduced to little more than administrative agencies. They did not disappear forever, however. Historian Paul Vanderwood, among others, has demonstrated rather lucidly that the specter of special privilege of the Hermandad and the Mesta was resurrected by President Benito Juárez in the 1850s to become the basis for the notorious Rurales of late nineteenth-century Mexico. Under dictator Porfirio Díaz, the Rurales patrolled the countryside until 1910, terrorizing political dissidents and suppressing dissimulated population groups (mustangers, filibusters, thieves, robbers) in outlying areas of Mexico.[25]

While the rest of Mexico experienced a hiatus of the Hermandad and the Mesta after 1800, however, Tejanos were not so willing to set aside such essential functions of government on the northern frontier. The *despoblado*, the *frontera*, and the *rancho* still demanded special concessions in Texas. Thus, the traditional functions, special privileges, and indeed much of the jurisdiction of these two institutions lived on. Their peculiar traits can be traced as they were diffused, redirected, and renamed by Tejanos and eventually by the Anglo-American immigrants as well.

Just before the promulgation of the Spanish Constitution of 1812, Tejanos had granted the juez de campo of Texas all of the special attributes and privileges of the alcalde provincial. Although they changed the title of the position, they retained its functions, as evident in the 1810 appointment of the Juez de Campo of Texas. Vicente Travieso took the position in San Fernando de Béxar in an appointment which clearly revealed this continuity, as seen in the following orders.

Instructions for the Jueces de Campo
of the Province of Texas

As it is necessary to repress the transgressions and crimes which are committed in the unsettled districts by runaways, vagabonds, and delinquents who escape to the woods in order to commit their crimes freely, with great injury to the haciendas or ranches and even to the settlements themselves, I have determined to appoint a juez de campo, who, with authority over the sindics of ranches, shall watch and see to the fulfillment of the duties of these, and observe and follow, on his own part the following rules:

He shall have cognizance of thefts, robberies, carrying away of properties by force, and rape, as well as of murders, inflictions of wounds which may be through malice or treachery, and also of the burning of houses, grain, or other things, whenever the said crimes may be committed in unsettled districts—by this is meant every place not a villa or *lugar* [place]—unless the government shall have had previous knowledge of the crimes and shall commission some other person [as judge thereof].

He shall see that the roads and ranches are kept free from the said class of people, pursuing them with spirit until he shall either arrest them, or put them to flight. I, therefore, order all the sindics of ranches and every other person of any class whatsoever to obey and help him every way necessary for this purpose.

The fees which he is to receive for these arrests will be fixed by this government according to the distances and circumstances.

He shall make frequent expeditions from this capital, visiting the district under his jurisdiction with the object of carrying out whatever may be ordered; and to recompense him in part for his work, he shall be exempt from all other municipal and public duties, and shall be given the preference in matters of privileges and grants that may be made to him, to his children and his descendants, provided that faithful service in favor of his country make him worthy of this distinction.

Persons who do not respect or who insult the person of the juez de campo shall incur the same penalties established in the case of all other judges; and persons who shall be injured or ill-treated by him shall come before this government, where they will be heard with the proofs they shall present—it being understood that if the complaint brought be proved to be without foundation and made only to calumniate the juez, the complainant shall be punished with all rigor, since the reputation of one exercising similar duties should never be compromised.

All syndics of ranches shall be obliged to give information to the juez de campo of occurrences worthy of mention and of offences that may have been committed, every time the juez may present himself in, or pass through their respective jurisdictions. If they do not do this, they shall be responsible for the result and shall be subject to the penalty that shall be imposed.[26]

After the liberalization of the Mexican independence years, the juez de campo reemerged in Texas as something of a combination of the former alcalde de mesta and the alcalde provincial. His primary duties were ostensibly in the regulation of the grazing industry, but the special authority granted to him bore the significant earmarks of his former jurisdictional powers. Article 31 of the Béxar Municipal Ordinances (Decree No. 98) in 1829, for example, ordered the appointment of two jueces de campo for "the conservation of the cultivated fields, as well as the forests and other trees of this town, and no less for the security of the herds which graze therein." The next article enumerated the other duties such as protection of fences, orchards, and bridges. Article 32, however, granted the juez de campo the responsibility for the actual pursuit and apprehension of thieves and other violators in his jurisdiction. The Béxar ordinances transferred all primary jurisdiction to the ordinary town alcalde. In the Goliad ordinances (Decree No. 99) the juez de campo still enjoyed original jurisdiction, but the reviewing authority had been transferred to the ordinary alcalde. In both cases, nevertheless, the juez de campo retained the authority to deputize comisarios to assist him in the enforcement of his special regulations.

The net effect of the independence period was to modify, and in some cases to combine, the special attributes of the alcalde provincial and the alcalde de mesta. But the concept of the juez de campo survived as an enduring institution in nineteenth-century Texas. Indeed, it was not long before court cases in the Anglo colonies began to reflect the registration of brands, the regulation of strays, and other tenets of this important institution. And historians have long since acknowledged the evolution of the juez de campo in the Anglo-American cattlemen's associations of later nineteenth century in Texas, California, Arizona, and Wyoming. William H. Dusenberry, for example, noted that "modern stock laws are but variations and adaptations of legislation which controlled ranching in colonial Mexico."[27] But the most important influence of the juez de campo was on the Tejano mind in the early nineteenth century. Even though the juez de campo system in Texas lost much of the power of its parent institutions after 1810, it succeeded in implanting in the Tejano mind the concept of a unified agency for the regulation and security of life and property on the *despoblado*. In various forms this concept remained a hallmark of Tejano society.

V

Military Reorganization in Texas

The *juez de campo* lost some basic attributes during the liberalization of the independence years in Mexico. Among the most important were the authority for extended pursuit and the authority to enlist the aid of comisarios. Tejanos contributed most generously to these principles. Effective long-range pursuit was essential on the Texas *despoblado*, and it was a common method used by Tejanos. Their skill with horses lent them a natural mobility. Their experience with Indians and their knowledge of the *despoblado* made them formidable stalkers and scouts. And finally, their military ancestry and background had nurtured in them a familiarity with military organization, cavalry tactics, and particularly, a predilection for the offensive campaign.

The Tejanos acquired their special knowledge of offensive cavalry tactics from the military squadrons of the *frontera*. The most important of these units was the flying squadron or *compañía volante* which defended Texas and the surrounding provinces. This unique type of military squadron structure originated in 1713 when Viceroy Duque de Linares ordered landowners in the *frontera* to organize "flying companies" to resist Indian incursions. These highly mobile units of approximately seventy mounted men became the established pattern of military structure for the militia in this region. In the Regulations of Presidios of 1772, Teodoro de Croix, commandant general of these northern provinces, ordered a more formal organization of the flying squadrons. The units were still composed of local volunteers, but they were trained by professional officers. They served longer terms of duty as they engaged in extensive campaigns throughout the frontera. In short, the compañía volante was designed to

Fig. 2. *Sobre la huella,* by Theodore Gentilz. The *compañia volante,* or Tejano flying squadron, predated the Texas Rangers. *Courtesy Witte Museum and San Antonio Museum Association.*

maintain the offensive against intruders as opposed to simply defending the home front.[1]

The Tlascalan settlers of Coahuila played an integral rôle in the refinement of the compañía volante and in its introduction to Texas. The most important squadron was the Compañía Volante of San Carlos de Parras. The Tlascalans of Parras and San Esteban added to the mobility of the compañía volante with the introduction of the *caballada* principle. The caballada was the herd of approximately ten spare horses or remounts per man, which accompanied the squadron on campaigns. The caballada became an essential element of effective pursuit and extended patrols.

Originally the entire squadron moved from presidio to presidio along the *frontera,* remaining for several months at each one. In 1803, however, the Compañía Volante of San Carlos de Parras was assigned to Béxar where it became a permanent part of Valero. As mentioned earlier, these were the men who renamed the mission "Alamo" after their hometown near Parras. From the Alamo, the squadron sent out regular sorties to patrol the coun-

tryside in all directions. The size and duration of the patrols varied. Usually the patrols consisted of one officer and two enlisted men, but one-man
patrols were common. Patrols scouted the paths and river crossings, camping at different sites every night for about a week. In one large patrol in
1808, Captain Francisco Amangual, commander of the Compañía Volante
of San Carlos de Parras, led a 202-man cavalry squadron to Santa Fe, New
Mexico, in the first major military expedition to traverse that direct route.[2]

Until the late 1820s, the major principles of the compañía volante remained unchanged. Periodic regulations reaffirmed the squadron's responsibility for incessant, offensive patrols or *cortadas* across the *despoblado*.
Through the years they retained their special status. They received special
consideration because of the isolation, the continuous fatigue, and the
trying conditions under which they served. Though their pay was continually delayed, they remained responsible for all of their special equipment.
By regulation, each man was required to possess a carbine, two pistols, a
saddle, blanket, spurs, hat, and several horses.[3] Although often their sup-
plies were low, this did not detract from the reputation of the compañía
volante on the frontier.

The compañía volante became popular among the settlers, particularly
as it expanded its responsibilities beyond the strictly military realm. The
citizens of Laredo, for example, specifically requested that a flying squadron and not a regular company be assigned to their municipality. The
obvious potential of a compañía volante made its wider use on the *frontera*
almost inevitable. Besides resisting Indian incursions it controlled against
illegal aliens in the *despoblado* and also served as a guard against encroachment from the United States. More than one illegal party of travelers in
Texas looked up from their campfire to find themselves surrounded by a
cavalry unit of the compañía volante. And by the close of the eighteenth
century, the flying squadrons of Béxar and Laredo were responsible for
pursuit of fugitives from civil jurisdiction as well.[4]

By the 1820s, it was not uncommon for civilian authorities to solicit the
assistance of flying squadrons to pursue and apprehend criminals who had
fled into the *despoblado*. The compañía volante response usually involved the
principle of the small, mobile troops with a caballada. In one such request
from the governor, for example, the military commander ordered a pursuing party of reportedly "twenty-five mounted men with two horses each,
under the command of one officer." Another such incident in 1825 demonstrated the reliable performance of these experienced riders. When it was

reported that an immigrant named James Stuart had murdered a traveler on the road between Laredo and Goliad, the commander of the Third Flying Squadron of Laredo, Nemesio Sánchez, ordered a four-man troop to catch Stuart, who had fled toward Goliad. Three of the men remained at the scene of the crime while José Antonio García effected sustained pursuit. By the time García overtook Stuart, the fugitive was tired and asleep at Tajaso Pass. The trooper arrested Stuart and, after a struggle, presented him to the Laredo alcalde for trial.[5]

The compañía volante was a natural agent for pursuit on the Texas *despoblado*. In effect, the compañía volante gradually assumed this function as the juez de campo began steadily to lose the powers of effective pursuit during the Mexican independence years. This almost natural transfer of the responsibility for pursuit revealed the absolute necessity of a unified agency for the pursuit of civilian criminals as well as external enemies. Effective as the compañía volante had proven, however, other events coincided with the close of the Mexican independence period to cause a decline in this and other formal units on the *frontera*.

As part of the transition to a federal government structure, Mexican statesmen began to draw a definite delineation between the general responsibilities of the national military forces and the more locally oriented responsibilities of the state militias. In effect, the states became increasingly dependent on their own resources at a time of increased Indian activity. And this was at a time of growing casualty figures resulting from Indian attacks in Texas between 1813 and 1820. In 1818, Laredo reported "the largest Indian invasions the river jurisdictions had faced." Four years later, many Laredo rancheros were forced to move into town. Provincial officials acknowledged the detrimental effects that such raids had on commerce and production, but provincial commanders repeatedly denied requests for aid. In 1823, for example, the Béxar Ayuntamiento appealed for a supplement of three hundred or four hundred cavalry troops to protect Texas from Indian assaults and foreigners. This appeal was denied.[6]

After 1824, the military structure of the *frontera* underwent a formal reorganization to reflect the philosophy of the new commanders. In 1824, Rafael González became the commandant general of the Texas, Coahuila, and Nuevo León frontera. Appointing Mateo Ahumada as the new commander in Texas, González began to implement his policies for the separation of national and state military responsibilities. In September, 1825, González ordered that Tejanos respond to Indian attack by forming local militia squadrons with training in cavalry tactics to be ready to confront the attacks. Even as this policy was being implemented locally, the national government issued a major set of regulations for presidios in March, 1826. The new regulations represented the culmination of González's philosophy.[7]

The Regulations for Presidios of 1826 must be carefully read and understood in context in order to avoid misinterpretation and consequent misrepresentation of the pertinent facts. The new regulations transferred the responsibility for local defense and security from the national government to the states and municipalities themselves. The state government and the ayuntamientos were required to recruit local citizens to replace the traditional cavalry companies of the presidios. The citizen militia was, moreover, to form new cavalry units under local command for local service. This militia was distinct and apart from the regular army. A curious clause in the decree provided for regular garrison forces to be composed of "vagrants and disorderly persons" recruited by levees and "by entrapment and decoy." But these men were intended for the regular army forces under the command of the national government for national service. Thus, the national government hoped to create and to employ productive individuals from otherwise idle vagrants. The local militia, on the other hand, was directed to "strike and pursue" or *vatir y perseguir,* and to have sufficient arms and horses to do so in case of an attack on their community. The regulations expressly distinguished the militia from the regular levies, stating that "those belonging to the civic militia shall, for that reason alone, be exempt from the said service."[8]

Providing for their own defense had been a customary duty for Tejanos long before it became a formal responsibility through the Regulations for Presidios of 1826. As mentioned above, Tejano settlers had originally settled in Texas as "armed citizens," reflecting a presidial complex by the late eighteenth century. The government policy for an armed citizenry continued into the nineteenth century. State decrees explicitly asserted the responsibility of settlers to be armed and to maintain several horses for defense at all times. In the 1820s, Tejanos offered strong testimony of their military background. In the state legislature, for example, Rafael Antonio Manchola proposed a land bill for Texas, reminding his colleagues that many Tejanos were descendants of the earliest founders and residents of the presidios. In another, more specific reference in 1825, the Béxar Ayuntamiento requested that their civilian caballada be maintained by the regular army since it could not be denied, they argued, "that these vecinos since the first years of the founding of this City, have been soldiers of the motherland proceeding as required to pursue without delay the barbarous Indians who have continually harassed this unfortunate land."[9]

Three months after the Béxar Ayuntamiento request in 1825, the Laredo alcalde, Pedro García Dávila, submitted a similarly demonstrative exposition on Tejano military experience. This memorial proposed a plan for controlling Comanche raids. Inasmuch as the Comanche were always mounted, García proposed that the government take the offensive by forming a company of mounted men led by "a carefully selected leader." The leader and the men should be frontier settlers, as they were the most familiar with the Comanche Indians and their camping and fighting techniques. García's proposal came at the time when the military was reorganizing on the *frontera*. The new commandant general, Don Anastacio Bustamante, was preoccupied with bringing his new command against the Haden Edwards Rebellion in Nacogdoches. Nevertheless, the Laredo citizens continued to provide the initiative against Indian problems. Indeed, J. B. Wilkinson, a historian of the Laredo area, has said that "Laredo had a company of civic militia that took to the field about as often as the soldiers of the regular army."[10] Thus, when the order came to transfer formal responsibility for defense from the presidial companies to the militia, the Tejanos effected a rather smooth transition.

The Tejano militia squadrons were already formed and active long before the Regulations for Presidios of 1826. Their numbers were reported in the official troop censuses for the garrison of Texas, along with civilian reserves as well. The most significant effect of the 1826 reorganization, therefore, was in legitimizing the militia structure and civilian leaders as integrated elements of the formal military structure. For example, the new regulations officially sanctioned the pre-1826 militia practice of electing local officers. Local civic leaders such as Carlos de la Garza, José Miguel Aldrete, José Antonio Sepúlveda, and other elected commanders likewise obtained official recognition which later proved to be invaluable in the revolutionary events of the 1830s. The Béxar militia raised a cavalry squadron of one hundred riders to deter a reported Indian advance in July, 1826—just three months after publication of the regulations in Texas.[11]

Just as Tejanos smoothly accepted responsibility for local defense, they readily adopted an offensive strategy which strongly reflected the influence of the compañía volante. In an official report to the national congress in

1826, Tejanos emphasized the importance of an offensive st
would conduct the campaign into the Indians' own camping ¡
fense was asserted to be the only hope for Texas. "To be on th
the report maintained, "is nothing less than to perpetuate a ¹
tion." In October, 1826, the ayuntamiento of Río Grande set forth a strategic plan for a cooperative effort by the several communities of the Texas
frontera. The plan called for a network of cavalry *cortadas* or patrols to
crisscross between Béxar, La Bahía, Laredo, Mier, Revilla, and Río Grande.
The ten-man *cortadas* were to rotate among the several stations which
included a new intermediate outpost called San Bartolo between Béxar and
La Bahía. Within a year, the plan was implemented with the direct support
of the alcaldes.¹²

The alcaldes and ayuntamientos assumed full command and responsibilities of their respective militia squadrons. Within a few years of the
1826 regulations, the civic militia had quite obviously replaced the compañía volante in function and in practice. After the repeated failure of
formal treaties during the 1820s, Tejanos began to launch regular forays
into the Indian camping grounds according to their previous plans. These
raids clearly demonstrated a definite transition of knowledge from the
compañía volante. In a highly successful campaign into Tawakoni territory
in 1830, for example, 150 mounted Bexareños were led by Alcalde Gaspar
Flores and former compañía volante commander Nicasio Sánchez of Laredo.
This campaign and others also demonstrated the effectiveness of Tejano
civilians being led by their own locally elected officials. In the Victoria area,
Don Martín de León was the undisputed leader of the mounted militia.
The Victoria squadron cleared the area of hostile Karankawas in February,
1831. Later that year, an alcalde and a syndico procurador reportedly led a
Béxar squadron of sixty-six riders in a campaign of "admirable enthusiasm
and valor."¹³

By 1830, local militia squadrons had completely replaced the presidial
companies in local defense responsibilities. In 1829, the Tejanos had actually endorsed a popular proclamation, the Plan de Jalapa, claiming their
local forces as "protectors" of their own state's sovereignty and not for use
by the national government. The 1830 militia census of Texas reported 289
armed troops in the "flying cavalry company" and infantry reserves of 642
men. This census did not report the garrison of Alamo because it had been
transferred to Fort Tenoxtitlán on the Brazos River. All national forces
were transferred to other new outposts like Tenoxtitlán by General Mier y

Terán to enforce the Law of April 6, 1830. The national army troops exhibited the "criminal" behavior which left an unsavory impression on Anglo settlers in the disturbances of 1832 at Anáhuac. Later that year, all of these troops abandoned the new stations in a liberal revolt which left Texas nearly devoid of national troops.[14]

The militia squadrons of Texas after 1832 developed as a highly efficient and formidable type of ranging cavalry. Despite their exemplary performance in the Texas *despoblado*, however, their influence and their very existence has scarcely been acknowledged. In every region of Texas where Tejanos had gained experience in the militia, civilian flying squadrons emerged to provide for the defense of the *vecindario* during the rebellious 1830s. In Victoria, Carlos de la Garza assumed command of the Guardia Victoriana or "Victorian Guards," who were described by a contemporary Anglo observer as constantly "patrolling everywhere." In Béxar, Mariano Rodriguez, a descendant of the founding settlers of Béxar, organized the "San Fernando Rangers." Other Béxar squadrons were led by Juan N. Seguin and Salvador Flores. In Nacogdoches, Vicente Córdova led the squadron. And south of the Nueces, another squadron of sixty men was led by Enrique Villareal, a former military commander. Villareal's riders, who had fought Indians since the 1820s, were the same Tejanos who formed the wide-ranging "ranchero cavalry" of the Republic of the Río Grande in 1838—the same vaqueros who defeated an Anglo force at Mier in 1842 by lassoing a cannon in the midst of battle.[15]

The Tejano flying squadrons presented quite a distinct threat to Anglo forces during the Texas Revolution and the early years of the Texas Republic. Probably this fact tended to delegitimize these militia squadrons as "guerrillas" or "raiders" in Anglo-American historical accounts of the era.[16] In perfecting and preserving the basic principles of the old compañía volante, the militia flying squadrons had as their objective the security and protection of their own *vecindario* from any harmful threat. Thus while Carlos de la Garza was recognized by his own Anglo adversaries as courageous and dignified, he also represented the last stubborn bulwark of recalcitrant Tejanos in the Victoria region. Similarly, Vicente Córdova and 120 Tejanos perceived themselves to be resisting "unjust treatment" and "usurpation of their rights" as they harassed Anglos in the Nacogdoches region, yet history has labeled Córdova's men as "Mexican Guerrillas."[17] Historical interpretation aside, the Tejano flying squadrons represented the culmination of the Hispanic phase in the development of the ancient principles of the *alcalde provincial* and the *juez de campo* in Texas. The evolutionary process continued, but it was handed over to the Anglo Americans who succeeded the Tejanos in governing the *despoblado*.

The transmission of the *compañía* volante and militia cavalry principles actually began when the Spanish authorities of Texas first treated with Stephen F. Austin on the establishment of the Anglo-American colonies. One of Austin's strongest assets in his colonization enterprise was his adoption of the Mexican philosophy of peopling the *frontera*. He openly stated his familiarity with Spanish laws and customs as a result of having lived in upper Louisiana for many years. Part of this familiarity was his stated belief that "without population in Texas the frontiers of the Eastern Interior Provinces are worse than nothing." These, undoubtedly by no great coincidence, were the exact sentiments of Governor Antonio Martínez, from whom Austin successfully obtained preliminary approval and arrangements for colonization in Texas.

In his proposals for colonial administration Austin reflected compatibility with Hispanic philosophy on the frontier as well as great insight and perhaps as much diplomatic acumen. In a *memoria* to Emperor Agustín Iturbide in 1822, for example, Austin proposed a "rigid and active police" to constitute a defense against Indians and criminals from the United States. His letter describes attributes similar to those of the alcalde provincial. ". . . if it be compatible with existing laws it would be very conducive to the happiness of the country, to give power to some person not only to arrest, but also to establish a tribunal of justice with enough power which would enable him to impose corporal punishment for robbery, illegal assaults, injuries, etc. and to punish under pain of death in case of homicide."[18]

If Austin were referring to the authority of the alcalde provincial or the juez de campo, his requests certainly did not fall on unappreciative ears. Tejano officials granted him sufficient powers to create a solid base of authority in his colonies. A basic concession in all of the titles conferred upon Austin as empresario was that he should organize his colonists into a national militia force. Austin was commissioned lieutenant colonel given responsibility for "the good order prosperity and defense" of his colonies. And for the first two years, Governor Trespalacios personally guided Austin's defense arrangements. All of these instructions were transmitted through the Baron de Bastrop and Austin to the colonists.

In December, 1823, Austin finally implemented the instructions in his first military order to organize the militia. He established militia districts in the Anglo colonies and ordered election of militia officers. Robert Kuykendall and James Ross were elected captains of their respective districts. Commissioning the officers, Austin allowed for the independent authority of a militia officer to conduct a campaign against hostile Indians. He ordered that a militia officer "shall act according to his discretion without waiting for orders from his superior officer." In the order, Austin phrased the standard instructions including authority to "strike and pursue" at will. If the militia faltered, it was not due to lack of authority.[19]

The Tejano influence began to appear in the character of the Anglo-American militia in Texas between 1822 and 1832. Much of the subtle change occurred despite the fact that early Anglo colonists failed to take full advantage of either the authority granted to them or the strong Tejano example of an offensive cavalry. For years, the Anglos clung stubbornly to the obsolete ground tactics handed down to them by their forefathers from the experience at Bunker Hill and New Orleans against the British. The battle accounts of early colonists like Gibson Kuykendall, Abner Kuykendall, and Randall Jones reflected a defensive reaction in frontier conflict. The typical campaign in the early colonies, for example, was a retaliatory raid against an Indian camp. The colonists would customarily sneak up on a camp during the night and execute a cross fire on its inhabitants at sunrise.

The Anglo settlements indubitably introduced a new salient into the unconquered *despoblado,* but they were slow in adapting. For example, in 1822, Austin promised to march rifle companies against hostile Indians, but nowhere did his proposal make any mention of cavalry tactics. Even in successful campaigns in 1824 the colonists reportedly "marched" through the woods on foot. For reconnaissance, the expeditions employed "spies" or "rangers," but these were merely scouts sent ahead in the traditional methods of the American Revolution. The Anglo-American settlers had begun to report their "cavalladas" as early as 1823, but rarely did they employ this principle for military advantage. Indeed, the records of the first Anglo militia companies included a fifer and two drummers and no mention whatever of cavalry.[20]

After the 1826 Regulations for Presidios, the Anglo colonists haltingly achieved their mandatory quotas of militia squadrons. But this was only after repeated threats by Governor José María Viesca, who in February, 1829, ordered them to "proceed without delay to the organization of the militia." Only then did the colonists reestablish their militia districts and reelect officers. The new militia organization existed only "on paper," however, and the governor had to remind them of their duty to comply with the law. Even when ordered by the commandant general to ride in retaliation against an Indian attack that year, Austin apologetically declined the order because of the weakness of the horses in the colonies as a result of a feed shortage. Only at the end of the year did the colonists report that they had fielded a party of voluntary "milicianos" to pursue a robber as ordered by the political chief. As late as 1830, the governor admonished the colonies to organize their militia despite their difficulties.[21]

Not until the San Felipe Convention of 1832 did Austin's colonists take the initiative to form a viable, permanent militia. This convention was illegal, so except for one provision, the entire platform was stated in terms of "recommendations" to the government. The one exception was the committee on Indian depredations, which stated that the militia organization "shall" proceed as opposed to suggesting that it "should" proceed, as the other committees had done. Thus, this committee illegitimately issued an order to organize two battalions in the Colorado colonies to rotate in providing forty men for a permanent detachment to serve their frontier. This detachment represented the first Anglo-American commitment to maintaining their own active militia squadron.[22]

In relating the history of the Texas Rangers, General W. H. King indicated that their first, formal organization was in the General Consultation of Texas in 1835. King added, however, "but for a number of years before this the white men of the State, from time to time, by volunteer organizations of temporary character, had been enabled to defend themselves against hostile Indians." In saying they "had been enabled," King was obviously referring to the Tejano authorities who importuned as much as enabled the "white men" to proceed without delay in organizing their squadrons. Indeed, King mentions the specific Texas Rangers who had served in this critical rôle, such as Abner Kuykendall, the captain elected in response to Governor Viesca's threats in 1829. Others were Jack Hays, Henry E. McCulloch, Ben McCulloch, and Tom Green.[23]

At the 1835 Consultation, the Anglo Americans gave ample evidence of having assimilated many of the military principles "rooted in earlier Mexican and colonial practice." On November 13, Consultation President Branch T. Archer submitted as basic provisions for the establishment of the military (1) a regular army of volunteers, (2) a corps of 150 rangers divided into three detachments, and (3) a militia with elected officers and men from each municipality. In familiar terms, Henry Smith added that the ranger leader should be a "bold, energetic commander." Ranging on the *despoblado* would be a primary function of the ranger corps which, as Smith said, "will prove a safeguard to our hitherto unprotected frontier inhabitants, and prevent the depredations of those savage hords that infest our borders." In another recommendation on November 16, Mr. Hanks of the Committee on Military Affairs proposed that an independent cavalry squadron would be "indispensable" to an effective army. Apparently the Anglos were so committed to the concept of an independent flying squadron that they angered the more orthodox militarist, General Sam Houston, who felt that they should establish one large army instead of several small troops.[24] General Houston was later to be converted by the *despoblado*.

As president of the Texas Republic, Sam Houston came to espouse the concept of loose cavalry squadrons to range the *despoblado*. In letters to the frontier outposts, he repeatedly ordered the citizens to avoid large, costly armies, but to employ only small, mobile patrols for spying and defense. In fact, the citizen patrols and the Texas Rangers regularly ranged the region south of Béxar, or San Antonio as the Anglos called it. Their ranging patrols followed the same patterns as the old *cortadas* of the compañía volante of the eighteenth century—from Goliad to San Antonio and from San Antonio across the Nueces River into the Laredo frontier.[25]

Besides the gradual transmission of culture before 1836, the Anglo military learned from Tejanos who actively participated in vital positions in the Texas Republic. These Tejanos played a substantial rôle in the continuing evolutionary process. One of the first commanders of the Texas Cavalry Corps was Jesús Cuellar, a former lieutenant from Tamaulipas who had rendered great assistance to the Anglos in the revolution. In 1836, the General Council commissioned him as a captain in the cavalry. The council had originally offered the position to Juan N. Seguin, who had commanded a Tejano flying squadron, but Seguin declined. Seguin did serve, however, as chairman of the Military Affairs Committee in the Texas Senate in 1839. Other scores of Tejanos served as rangers since the first days of the Republic. Often mislabeled as "Anglo Americans," these Tejanos served as a regular part of Captain John C. Hays's rangers. Described as "very useful and efficient in protecting the western frontier from Mexican and Indian incursions," they rarely have been identified as Tejanos. Indeed, Walter Prescott Webb, a recognized authority on the Texas Rangers, wrote one passage in which he also identified these Tejanos as "the Texans."[26]

The very description of Texas Ranger accouterments recalls the portrait of the Mexican compañía volante. The Texas Rangers were described as neither military nor civilian, but a combination of both. The force was small to afford mobility and limited budgets. A necessary principle was that of the caballada, now called "cavyard," to allow for effective pursuit. Each trooper carried a pistol, a rifle, a knife, a Mexican saddle, a Mexican blanket tied behind the saddle, and a small wallet of parched corn called *pinole* by the Tejanos and "panoln" *(sic)* by the Anglos, and a *reata*.[27]

From Texas, the flying squadron principle gained exposure to the United States Army. This occurred primarily during the Mexican War when the American troops observed the value of ranger squadrons. Among the American troops were such notable future officers of the Civil War era as U.S. Grant, Jefferson Davis, Franklin Pierce, Robert E. Lee, William T. Sherman, George B. Meade, and others. The commanding general, Zachary Taylor, was not favorably impressed with the behavior of the Texas Rangers. He did, however, submit a report on their value in "protection of the frontier." This, of course, was their intended value as a flying squadron. One American colonel noted the influence of the rangers on the troops in horsemanship as well. "They are teaching the United States officers and soldiers how to ride," he said. One of the most impressive feats he related was what the Tejanos had always called the *carrera del gallo*, except that the mounted Anglo rangers grasped dollar bills up from the ground instead grasping a rooster's head. Another significant and extremely ironic step in the continuing spread of the flying squadron concept was a speech in the United States Congress by Senator Sam Houston in 1858. Houston, adamantly opposed to increasing the size of the regular army, instead contended that the army should employ ranger companies which would be more effective against the mobile Indians.[28] So continued the gradual evolution of the old concepts of the Texas *frontera*, the telling effect of which was also apparent in the Civil War.

Undoubtedly the flying squadron had extraordinary effectiveness on the *despoblado* in the nineteenth century. It effectively combined the principles of mobility and incessant pursuit and the advantages of an offensive frontier guard. However, some doubt exists as to its place in a democratic society because of the special privilege inherent in its very nature. Mobility and extended pursuit, for example, presupposed the special privileges of civilian deputization and extraterritorial jurisdiction. Such privileges violated the basic principles of local self-government. The dangers and the remoteness of the *despoblado* inhered in the flying squadron, and was thus by its nature conducive to summary justice—even to include pain of death against citizens without benefit of trial. It created heroic figures who defended their society. But by introducing this personal element, it lent itself to personal prejudice vis-à-vis impartial justice. All of these discrepancies were traced by Paul Vanderwood to the Rurales of Mexico in the 1870s. Considering the characteristics—good and bad—of the rangers in mid-nineteenth-century South Texas, it appears that the Texas Rangers could well have represented something of a connecting link between the Tejano flying squadrons of the 1830s and the Rurales of the 1890s.

VI
Texas Statehood under Coahuila

Texas never enjoyed the independent status of an officially recognized state in the Mexican republic. As a province of New Spain, she had always had her own executive—a governor or political chief—and she maintained certain legislative attributes which tended to draw her away from the central control of Mexico City. But the centripetal forces of the *frontera* leashed Texas to her traditional sister states of the Eastern Interior Provinces. The threat of Anglo-American expansion, the constant burden of Indian wars, and the endemic austerity of life on the northern fringe combined to strengthen a bond with Coahuila which only a revolution could sever.

Texas did exist for at least sixty years as an independent colonial province before 1772. But in that year, New Spain reorganized the northern provinces to secure a better hold of her *frontera*. In the reorganization, Texas joined Coahuila, Nuevo León, and Nuevo Santander in a new entity known as the Eastern Interior Provinces. Each of these provinces had a governor for administrative purposes, but all four were under a commandant general for military purposes. The commandant general in 1776, Teodoro de Croix, actually had quasiviceregal status and was responsible directly to the king in Spain. This binding influence was held over Texas throughout this period in which she struggled to evolve from colonial province to state.

The early years of Mexican independence revealed the major forces which would hamper the course of transition in Texas government. One of these major forces was the political dominance of Miguel Ramos Arizpe. Ramos Arizpe was the delegate of the Eastern Interior Provinces to the parliament or Cortes in Spain. As the Cortes drew up the Constitution of

1812, Ramos Arizpe made major contributions which greatly affected Texas. He introduced the concept of a "provincial deputation" or governing body for each province of Mexico. To reinforce the *frontera* concept, he recommended that the four interior provinces of the east be under the military command of a single commandant. And he employed this same force of logic to recommend an end to the "time-honored tradition" of restricting foreign settlement in Mexico. Swayed by his logic, the Cortes approved his recommendations in 1820. At the same time, Texas Governor Antonio Martínez and the Béxar Ayuntamiento petitioned the provincial deputation of the Eastern Interior Provinces for a colonization program in Texas. The deputation referred the Tejano petition to the Cortes in Spain, where it was incorporated into a new decree. Although it may appear that Ramos Arizpe and the Bexareños were "liberalizing" their attitude toward the United States, they were actually strengthening their position. The new settlement was intended to reinforce the *frontera* as a buffer against United States expansionism.[1]

Another major force acting on Texas in this transitional period was its relationship to the provincial capital in Monterrey. All major governmental functions in Texas were directed to Monterrey, as is illustrated by an election held in Texas in 1820. The ayuntamientos of Béxar and La Bahía conducted the very complicated electoral procedures to select a deputy to the Spanish Cortes from the Eastern Interior Provinces. On August 24, the Béxar Ayuntamiento named twenty-one electors or *compromisarios* to elect two parish electors from Béxar. They elected José Erasmo Seguin and Refugio de la Garza. Seguin and De la Garza joined the La Bahía Parish elector to constitute the Texas Electoral Junta. This junta then elected Juan Manuel Zambrano as the district elector or *elector de partido* to go to Monterrey, where he cast his vote for the two deputies to represent the Eastern Interior Provinces in Spain.[2]

Throughout the independence years, Texas depended on her deputy at the provincial deputation in Monterrey for provincial representation. The first provincial body in these early years was the *junta gubernativa* or governing commission of Nuevo León and Texas, which held its sessions in Monterrey between April 1, 1811, and March 11, 1813. These early juntas have been labeled by Nettie Lee Benson as the "precursors of the deputations" in Mexico. But Tejanos rarely performed active rôles in these early deputations. In 1814, for example, Texas was represented by a delegate from Monterrey for the first officially installed provincial deputation of the East-

ern Interior Provinces. And even in the 1820 deputation, Texas was represented by another delegate from Monterrey. After Mexico achieved her
independence under Agustín de Iturbide in 1821, there was a proposal to
move the provincial capital from Monterrey to Saltillo in 1822, but the
deputation convened in Monterrey after heated arguments. Finally, in 1823,
Texas obtained her own provincial deputation. But even in this transition,
Texas had to struggle to escape from the dying clutches of the Eastern
Interior Provinces.

By late 1822, Emperor Agustín de Iturbide had thoroughly alienated
Mexican republicans by disbanding the national congress in Mexico City.
In response, his own military officers declared a plan which led eventually
to his downfall and the first federal republic of Mexico. General José Antonio Echevarrí issued the Plan de Casa Mata on February 1, 1823. In it, he
called for the people to elect a national congress and for the several provincial deputations to assume control of their respective provinces. The provincial deputations were to authorize the military officers to assume command
of provincial armies. The widespread acceptance of this plan completely
disintegrated Iturbide's imperial hold over Mexico and left in its place a
group of "virtually autonomous provinces." The free hand which the several provincial deputations had over their own affairs made federalism "inevitable" after 1823, according to Nettie Lee Benson. Benson adds that
their experience in self-government "nurtured" federalism and a desire for
state autonomy.[3] Indeed, only after this experience in 1823 did the Texas
Provincial Deputation begin to demand autonomy from the Eastern Interior Provinces.

The first news of the Plan de Casa Mata took Tejanos by surprise. Skepti-
cal at first, the Tejanos were hesitant to commit themselves. On February
24, 1823, the new provincial deputation of Puebla notified the Tejanos of
the plan and of the coming elections for the new national congress. But
Governor José Felix Trespalacios and the Béxar Ayuntamiento declined the
invitation to endorse the plan, and reasserted instead their solemn oath to
the empire. The La Bahía Ayuntamiento also reaffirmed allegiance to Iturbide with a hearty "Viva Agustín I." But as more news filtered up to the
northern frontier about the success of the revolt, Tejanos finally joined
their fellow patriots in welcoming liberalism and federalism.[4] By early
summer, Tejanos had already established their own governing junta in
Béxar which evolved into their first provincial deputation.

In April, 1823, a group of Tejanos met at the home of former Governor

Trespalacios in Béxar to organize the governing junta in accordance with the Plan de Casa Mata. The members included Trespalacios as president, Baron de Bastrop, Erasmo Seguin, Francisco Ruiz, Francisco Roxo, José Antonio Saucedo as secretary, Juan de Castañeda, and Juan Manuel Zambrano. They formally invited the other municipalities to send their deputies to the Provisional Governing Junta of Texas. It would meet in Béxar, and be composed of seven deputies from Béxar and one each from La Bahía, the Colorado colony, the Brazos colony, and Nacogdoches.[5] Trespalacios declared the junta to hold civil, military, and ecclesiastical power over Texas. Without delay, the junta assumed full administrative control over military affairs, the *mesteña* fund, local laws, customs, and commerce in Texas.[6]

Even as the Texas Provisional Governing Junta was adjusting to its new authority, however, another problem was developing at the deliberations in Mexico City. In May, the Supreme Executive in Mexico City appointed General Felipe de la Garza as the new commandant general of the Eastern Interior Provinces, replacing pro-Iturbide General Gaspar López. De la Garza accepted the position, and named General Luciano García as the *ad interim* governor of Texas. Inasmuch as García's appointment included civil and military powers, he immediately dismissed Trespalacios and ordered the Texas Provisional Governing Junta to "cease its functions." As García moved into his new position in Texas, however, the national congress authorized Texas, Nuevo León, and Coahuila to establish permanent provincial deputations. Tamaulipas had already broken away to become an independent state. These developments contributed greatly to the political autonomy of Texas under Mexico.[7]

With their own provincial deputation, Tejanos truly began to develop a sense of autonomy under the new Mexican republic. On September 8, they elected their provincial deputation under Political Chief José Antonio Saucedo. The members, and consequently the men who would become advocates of federalism in Texas, included José María Zambrano, Ramón Músquiz, Juan José Hernández, Miguel Arciniega, Baron de Bastrop, and Mariano Rodriguez. They immediately ordered *ad interim* Governor García to relinquish civil power. And on October 31, the corporation was officially installed as the Texas Provincial Deputation.[8] Texas became, in effect, an independent state at least provisionally as the national congress drew up a new federal constitution.

A necessary factor in the development of the sense of autonomy for Tejanos was to have equal representation in the constituent congress in

Mexico City. For this the Tejano ayuntamientos conducted the same type of electoral procedures that they had practiced for the election of delegates to the Spanish Cortes three years earlier. On September 9, 1823, the electoral junta named Erasmo Seguin as the deputy to Mexico City, and gave him a full slate of instructions in his new duty. He was to insure that the Roman Catholic Church remain supreme in Mexico, and to support a federal, republican form of government. He should work for the establishment of ports at Galveston, Matagorda, and Aransasu (Aransas). One of his major objectives was a colonization program which would allow aliens in the country for a five-year grace period and would establish a system of land grants with preference given to founding families of Texas. Finally, he was to press for the complete reform of the presidial companies and sale of mission lands to pay the retired military in Texas.[9]

José Erasmo Seguin was generally recognized as "the chief" of Tejano statesmen. Born in Béxar in 1782, he became an intellectual and political leader among Tejanos. An avid reader, he collected books and state documents, and even on the most arduous trips as congressman to Mexico City he took along an entire trunkload of his beloved books. He encouraged his son Juan Nepomuceno Seguin to acquire learning, and he had long been an important contributor to education in Béxar. During his lifetime, he had served in several official positions on the ayuntamiento as well as in the national government, including vice-consul and postmaster of Texas. His greatest contribution was in representing Texas during the transitional years of Mexican independence. Although he tended to opt for the conservative view in any political issue, his main concern was for the safety and welfare of his community. He expressed this in a letter to his wife in 1827 when he was representing Texas in Mexico City and his funds had expired. He wrote, "I have no money but I am not hungry and when I am, I shall not request aid from my Province because she exists for us to serve and not to serve us."[10]

One of the most important assignments of Seguin's life was his term in Mexico City in 1824, for the constituent congress that year defined the attributes of the states in the new federation. On January 31, the congress approved Article 7 of the new constitution confirming the existence of the Interior State of the East composed of Coahuila, Nuevo León, and "los Tejas." But the situation was not settled. Nuevo León and Tamaulipas had launched a campaign to become autonomous states, and Ramos Arizpe, the Coahuilan elder statesman, was maneuvering to attach Texas to his own state for a larger combined population. Seguin faced a strong tide in any attempt to resist this union.

In the congress, the deputy of Nuevo León, José Servando Teresa de Mier, successfully maneuvered an act making Nuevo León an autonomous state on May 7. The members of the Texas Provincial Deputation—Saucedo, Arciniega, Bastrop, and Músquiz—issued a statement indicating their own desire for statehood.[11] Their *memoria* stated that Texas was absolutely against union with Coahuila except under certain conditions. This contradictory statement was introduced and effectively exploited by Ramos Arizpe in the congressional debate on the union of Coahuila and Texas. According to Seguin, the contradiction "lost the cause." And he placed the blame squarely on Political Chief Saucedo. Seguin wrote:

> This document and a resolution in the minutes of that corporation [the constituent congress] which contains articles which were placed in the minutes as conditional articles, have lost the cause, which would not have happened had it been clearly represented that union with Coahuila was not desirable, and even though I have worked to make the Congress understand that the will of my province was to remain separated, I have not been able to succeed because of what the minutes indicated, and they insisted upon my presenting a document which expressly stated it: What makes this matter even more painful is that now that the Constitution is concluded and sworn to by the Congress and the Executive Power, no further discussion may be held on this subject, or I should say, this matter may not be considered until the year [18]37 according to the Constitution.[12]

On May 7, 1824, in the same decree that declared Nuevo León an autonomous state, the constituent congress declared Texas to be united with Coahuila as a single state. The decree thus proclaimed the new state as "Coahuila and Tejas, but at such time as the latter should be able to figure as a State by itself, it shall refer this to the general congress for resolution." The state legislature was to meet in Saltillo where Coahuila would have ten deputies and Texas, one. Ramos Arizpe later admitted that he and Erasmo Seguin had arranged the union "with the agreement to promote the distribution of lands in such a manner as to result in a powerful resource equally favorable to both provinces." He added that there were many traditional tenets of nexus between the two sister provinces of the *frontera*. And speaking of Texas, he reasoned that "her inhabitants united by blood, by friendship and by all genre of relations with Coahuila, are so by territory as well, our being, except for the Medina River, close to their capital."[13]

In the summer of 1824, Premier Secretary of State Lucas Alamán officially notified Texas Political Chief Saucedo that Texas had been joined

with Coahuila as a single state. Saucedo and the Texas Provincial Deputation did not accept the decree. In June, they protested the decree to the
constituent congress in Mexico City, and declared it null. Their response
greatly annoyed Alamán, who repeatedly warned them of holding such
"meetings unrecognized by law." He added, "Neither it [such a meeting]
nor anyone has had the faculty to suspend the compliance of the law." He
insisted that Tejanos immediately comply with the law and elect their
deputy to the state legislature.[14]

Even as the national decree of May 7 had shocked the Tejanos, so did the
actions of the state legislature which convened in Saltillo. The deputies
from Coahuila met on August 15 and, in rapid succession, passed laws which
stripped Texas of all political autonomy. In the first week, they drew up
Decree No. 8 abolishing the position of political chief in Texas. They
declared the cessation of duties of the provincial deputation, and ordered it
to transfer the archives to Saltillo. The decree was officially declared on
August 29, before Tejanos even knew that the congress was in session. On
the same day, the congress ordered the election of a new state deputy to the
national congress. And before the end of the year, they ordered the reduc-
tion in size of the ayuntamientos of Béxar and Monclova, as mentioned in a
previous chapter. This was a double blow for Monclova, which had been
the capital of Coahuila until 1823.[15] The actions by Saltillo secured for
those deputies an early political advantage, but neither Monclova nor Texas
accepted the events as a final defeat.

Events in Béxar became heated, and approached a denouement by the
end of the summer. National officials attempted to placate the Tejanos in
order to minimize conflict. Ramos Arizpe wrote them a long, conciliatory
letter on September 15 indicating the advantages of union with Coahuila.
The main advantage he cited was that as occupants of an autonomous
territory, Tejanos would not have enjoyed the sole authority over their
public domain. On the other hand, he pointed out that as part of a state,
Tejanos would stand as "free men and owners of the lands which they have
conquered."[16] The Béxar Ayuntamiento and the alcalde, Gaspar Flores,
concurred with Ramos Arizpe, and enjoined the provincial deputation to
concede.

The provincial deputation responded with an adamant proclamation of
their position. They acknowledged having received the state decree abolishing the Texas Provincial Deputation and political chief. They retorted,
however, that "this Provincial Deputation . . . taking into consideration

that this Province was not represented at that assembly because her representative did not attend as he is awaiting the response of the General Constituent Congress in regard to the exposition dated June 10 directed to those corporations, has found it necessary to resolve that the aforesaid Decree shall be complied with in all its particulars upon arrival of the mail in which it expects to receive a decision."

The political chief relayed their statement to Alcalde Flores, reminding him that they had nullified the decree.[17] It became apparent that the Béxar Ayuntamiento and the Texas Provincial Deputation were rapidly approaching a political stand-off. Whether for political principle or personal pride, the members of the opposing assemblies began to show emotional signs.

The expected mail dispatch arrived on September 30, motivating ayuntamiento members to press the offensive against the deputation. That day, two of the ayuntamiento regidores, Don José Sandoval and Don Fernando Rodriguez, reportedly "threatened" Saucedo on the town plaza, and Alcalde Flores issued a strong ultimatum to the deputation. Saucedo contemptuously dismissed the ayuntamiento's ultimatum. But privately, the other members of his deputation wrote a conciliatory reply to the ayuntamiento. In their memorandum, they began to rationalize their position.[18] Saucedo stood firm. But behind him, his team members blinked.

That night, the entire affair reached a dangerous level of excitement. Saucedo said he feared his personal rights would be "violated," and ordered a citizen to issue the call to arms in the barrio of Valero. He also asked the military commander of Valero, Juan de Castañeda, to lend his troops to the defense of the provincial deputation. Castañeda refused, but by that time a crowd of citizens had responded to the call. They began to gather at the Alamo. Hearing all the commotion, Alcalde Flores issued an urgent plea for Castañeda to prevent an "overthrow" of the ayuntamiento. Castañeda spent the rest of the night trying to disperse the bewildered *vecinos* and calm the anxious adversaries.[19]

The next day, the members of the provincial deputation met and agreed to acquiesce. They apologized to their leader, Saucedo, and explained that they were only conceding to "conserve the peace and public tranquility." They admitted that there was no official procedure for surrendering their power to anyone, and that they were still reluctant to do so at such a critical time. But their foremost aim, they said, was to avert the violent consequences which the ayuntamiento had threatened. The deputation members agreed to surrender their archives to Saltillo. The ordeal was over. On

October 3, Baron de Bastrop left for Saltillo as Texas' first deputy to the state legislature. With him, he took the archives—the literary remains of the short-lived Texas Provincial Deputation. Ramos Arizpe later concluded that "in this manner the ancient provinces of Coahuila and Texas were united in one same State, as they had already been for long periods in the colonial era."[20]

The union of Coahuila and Texas as a single state was a traumatic marriage, "ancient" engagement notwithstanding. It would be easy to castigate the Tejano leadership in the provincial deputation for being "slow" in their conduct of this affair. A more objective analysis of these events—and particularly the events of the following years—reveals the critical rôle played by external factors. There is evidence enough that the Texas Provincial Deputation early made their views known to their deputy in Mexico City. The problem involved not so much the speed of the provincial deputation, but the political views and aims of Seguin and other important Tejanos whose move toward autonomy was intentionally "slow."

Beside the open admission by Ramos Arizpe that he and Seguin had actually prearranged the union, other evidence indicates that Seguin worked less than strenuously to obtain Texas' autonomy. He had reported that he could not accomplish much because of Ramos Arizpe's influence, but he rarely stated his own personal views regarding autonomy. In his own words Seguin once said, "I have been in favor of the union of those two provinces." And in a private letter, he gave his opinion of those Tejanos who argued for autonomy. Seguin described them as men "of little enlightenment." Those men were not so wise as the Navarros and the Ruises, he said. Indeed, his own circle of friends were the same men who led the Béxar Ayuntamiento against the deputation. These included Gaspar Flores, José Antonio de la Garza, Pedro de la Garza, and Manuel Yturri Castillo.

Even more than any political cliques, however, Seguin's actions were dictated by his view of the reality of Texas' position in the new federation. Privately, he shared this view with Baron de Bastrop. Texas would have had the unacceptable option of being reduced to a territory (and thus forfeiting ownership of her public domain), and would have had to face as a territory the taxing burden of Indian wars, the lack of sufficient revenues, the traditional need for a state judicial system, and problems of having minimal population on the northern frontier.[21] Without considering this reality, a modern historian could conclude that the Tejanos were in fact "slow" or that they had, as Henderson Yoakum said, no concept of state rights and "but a dim idea of their civil rights."[22] Actually, Tejanos were quite aware of states' rights and republicanism. Their most significant loss was the bitter disappointment of not achieving state government after the provincial deputation. Disappointment notwithstanding, Tejanos apparently felt that the state government of Coahuila y Texas offered a similar measure of local control as the former provincial structure. They indicated this in a government report in 1826: "This State being composed of the former provinces named Coahuila and Texas, the territory which consists of the latter of these was named Department of Tejas by a decree of the honorable congress of the State, creating for her government and internal administration a political authority with nearly the same attributes held by the former political chiefs during the constitutional system of Spain. Coahuila is administered by the respective ayuntamientos, under the immediate inspection of the government."

The state government of Coahuila y Texas, then, was not substantially unlike the provincial structure. The state hierarchy was still headed by the governor, who was generally responsible for security, administration, and order in his state. The state was divided into departments, each having its own department chief or *jefe de departamento*. Texas being one department, the Texas *jefe* had a large responsibility. He, of course, was responsible to the governor for the security, administration, and order in his respective department. The *jefe de departamento* also supervised the activities of the ayuntamientos, and insured that they would each receive copies of the latest state decrees. He was responsible for education, taxes, censuses, and elections in his department. The department was further divided into *partidos* or districts, each containing one or more municipalities. The *jefe de partido*, or district chief, was the direct-line subordinate of the *jefe de departamento*. Municipalities were governed by the ayuntamiento structure described earlier herein.[23]

The first step in the formalization of Texas as a department was accomplished with the official installation of the Texas deputy in the state constituent congress at Saltillo. Baron de Bastrop arrived there on October 26, 1824.

Baron de Bastrop was not a real baron. He had been born Philip Hendrik Nering Bögel in 1793 in the Netherlands, and had fled to the United States to escape prosecution for embezzlement. Among Tejanos, however, he was known as Señor Felipe Nerí or El Barón. After going bankrupt in Louisiana where he obtained his Spanish citizenship, he had moved to Texas. In 1805, he gained the confidence of Tejanos by giving them a full report on the military and civilian concentrations of the "land hungry" Americans near Natchitoches. Through the years, he had established himself in Béxar as a merchant and "man of the world." By the 1820s, he was serving as regidor and finally in provincial and state deputations. Throughout his long years among Tejanos, Bastrop never escaped an occasional charge or rumor of involvement in nefarious schemes. He was once accused by a Spanish minister of conspiring with Aaron Burr, and in 1827, he was again accused of plotting against the Mexican government. For all his baronial claims and services on provincial assemblies, Bastrop was never elected or appointed to a single executive position in Mexican Texas. This was true also of his tenure in the state legislature, even though he served effectively and was reelected to a second term.[24]

The new election procedures of the state government of Coahuila y Texas were but an extension of the local procedures under former provincial deputations. The elections for state deputy were held on the first Sunday and Monday in August. The assembly followed the same rules at the municipality level. At the municipality level, however, the elections were for the electors who were to go on to the district junta. At the district junta the electors were required to vote "by means of slips which each elector shall deposit in an urn placed upon a table at the foot of a crucifix." At a later election, the electors would elect the governor, vice-governor, and the executive council. By law, a new deputy had to request instructions from his constituents for a legislative agenda. The ayuntamientos customarily prepared the lists of desired legislation, but the deputies often had to remind their constituents to submit their platforms.[25] Tejano deputies to the state legislature established a record of abiding by the instructions of their constituency.

The new legislature of Coahuila y Texas quickly moved to formalize its sessions. It was actually a state constitutional congress while it drew up the Coahuila y Texas constitution, but it served concurrently as a legislature, issuing decrees to conduct state business. In late 1824, the legislature issued its internal *Reglamento* manual titled "Regulations for the Internal Governance of the Council of the Free Independent State of Coahuila y Texas." The regulations set the ordinary legislative sessions from 10:00 A.M. to 1:00 P.M. on Mondays, Wednesdays, and Fridays unless called into secret or extraordinary sessions by the governor. The ordinary business of the day began with the reading and approving of the previous day's minutes. Next the official correspondence was read aloud and referred to the governor for replies or to a specific committee for action if required. If the committee accepted a *dictamen*, recommended legislation, the committee was responsible for preparing the *dictamen* as a bill to present before the legislature. A bill was to be read three times. The first two readings allowed for major amendments, for general discussions, and for rewriting if necessary. On the third reading, the legislature voted on the bill in detail. If approved, it was issued the following day as an official decree. Members of the legislature elected the president, vice-president, and secretary of the legislature every month. For the interim between sessions, they elected a "permanent deputation." The monthly elections were modeled after those of the Spanish Cortes in order to provide actual experience for all deputies through regular rotation. The president of the legislature also served as the vice-governor of the state. Every new session, this individual appointed the members of the several committees.[26] Bastrop served on important committees and as secretary and vice-president of the legislature, but as mentioned above, he never held the position of president.

Bastrop's first legislative objective in the Coahuila y Texas state congress was to secure the reestablishment of a political chieftaincy in the Department of Texas. He initiated his efforts with a long speech before the legislature on January 11, 1825. He indicated the special *frontera* situation of Texas—the distance from Saltillo, the illegitimate presence of many foreigners, and the need for local authority. He argued that the department chief should have the same attributes as the former political chief. The legislature responded favorably, appointing Bastrop to the special committee along with José María Viesca and Ramón Valdés to prepare the *dictamen* as a bill.

The bill passed as Decree No. 13, creating the new position of political chief of the Department of Texas. He was to be responsible for the government of his department. He would reside in Béxar, the department capital, and he should preside *ex officio* over that ayuntamiento. He held judicial powers similar to an ordinary alcalde and was to represent the state in matters of taxes and the administration of justice. The governor appointed José Antonio Saucedo as the first political chief of Texas with a salary of twelve hundred pesos.[27]

Saucedo used his appointment as department chief to establish a full administrative structure for Texas. He submitted a resolution for creation of a *subalterno* or subalternate in the Anglo-American colonies. He then created the position of secretary to the department political chief. After the new positions were approved, Saucedo appointed Ramón Músquiz as secretary and Stephen F. Austin as the subalternate for the colonies. The appointments gave both of these men valuable administrative experience in Mexican government. In addition to the appointments, Texas obtained better representation in the legislature as her population increased. In 1827, the legislative apportionment was restructured for the entire state, giving Texas two deputies. Texas still lagged behind other departments, however, and her representation was later adjusted to three deputies.[28]

Besides the number of deputies, Tejanos sought adjustments to the department structure. Originally, of course, Texas was one department in itself. Its southern boundary, as cited by Ramos Arizpe, was the Medina River. The boundary followed that river to its confluence with the San Antonio River, where the boundary turned southward to the Nueces River, and then followed the Nueces to the Gulf Coast. South of the Nueces was the neighboring state of Tamaulipas. The northern boundary of Texas was defined by the Red River, with the Sabine on the east. The western boundary was undetermined.

The first change in the district boundaries of Texas occurred when the legislature created the new Nacogdoches Partido in 1831. The Béxar and Nacogdoches partidos were divided roughly by the watershed between the Brazos and Trinity Rivers. Decree No. 164 established the exact boundaries of this new district with its political chief at Nacogdoches. The final district division of the Texas Department created the new district of Brazos, with its capital at San Felipe. The Brazos district had as its eastern boundary the Nacogdoches district boundary. The western boundary of the Brazos district was a generally north-south line from the coast to the Red River just east of the Béxar and Goliad settlements.[29] Thus the Department of Texas did attain somewhat equitable representation for each of its three districts by the early 1830s (see map 4).

With the the position of the Department of Texas secured in the state administrative structure, Tejanos directed their attention to their position in the political structure. Bastrop played an important rôle in establishing the Tejano legislative agenda. His most significant contribution was in the state colonization act. Indeed, his experience with colonization in Texas had made him an expert on the subject by the time he arrived as a deputy in Saltillo. As the first land commissioner for Austin's colony in 1823, Bastrop had established San Felipe and other early Anglo settlements in Texas. His

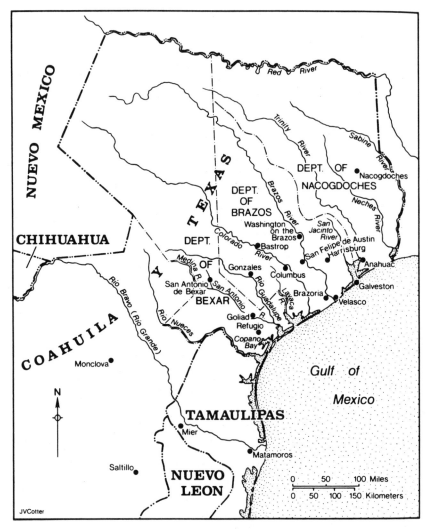

Map 4. Department of Texas in 1834. *From Andreas Reichstein*. Rise of the Lone
Star: The Making of Texas *(College Station: Texas A&M University Press, 1989)*

particular expertise lay in coordinating and often in reconciling the needs
of the colonists and the objectives of the government. He once had reassured Austin of Tejano support, saying, "Be assured that on the deputation
you have two friends Saucedo and me and I believe the others do not think
badly of you." Shortly after his arrival in Saltillo in 1824, Bastrop was

appointed to the Colonization Committee with José María Viesca, Santiago de Valle, and Juan Vicente Campos, state legislators who also proved to be sympathetic to the Texas colonization program.[30] Although Bastrop was effective as a deputy, he had actually been involved in the colonization program since its inception in Texas.

Years earlier, when approving colonization by foreigners, the Spanish Cortes had initiated a long series of legislation on colonization in Texas. Iturbide contributed to this series with his law of January 4, 1823, just before his empire was overthrown. The next major step, and perhaps the most effective, was the National Colonization Law of 1824, Decree No. 416 of the Mexican Congress. This law prevailed during most of the colonization period of Mexican Texas. Under this law, the national government gave the states considerable control of the public domain and immigration programs, with only a few restrictions. States were instructed to remain within the limits of the national constitution, to avoid grants within twenty leagues of international borders or ten leagues of the coast, and to limit grants to eleven leagues per person. Grants were not to be made to religious corporations or to nonresidents, nor were they to be held in mortmain. The national government reserved the right to erect forts and arsenals and to exclude immigration from any specified country. Above all, the government invited foreigners to colonize Mexican lands, promising them security in person and property.[31] Beyond these restrictions, however, the state government was free to develop the legislative provisions for the disposition of public lands.

In Saltillo, Bastrop was instrumental in preparing and securing the state colonization law to implement the national provisions. As a member of the crucial Colonization Committee, he insured that the colonists—particularly Anglo-American colonists—received special advantages. He arranged for the requirement on religion of colonists to be worded so as to specify only "Christianity" instead of the more restrictive label "Catholicism." He included a provision for colonists to be automatically naturalized upon fulfillment of their colonization contracts. He also assured that the article on slavery (Article 46) be worded vaguely enough that it would not immediately prohibit importation of slaves, which Anglo Americans considered a major condition. The law offered one league and one labor to each family for a small fee. Single men were offered one-third of a league, but they could qualify for one-fourth more if they married Mexican women. An empresario would receive five leagues and five labors for completion of his contract to settle one hundred families. Colonists had six years to cultivate their respective lands, and the empresarios had the same period to fulfill their contracts. All colonists were exempt from taxes for ten years.

Bastrop introduced the colonization bill in February of 1825. He obtained a resolution that all discussion on the colonization bill should take priority over any other ordinary bills. He began the final reading—article by article—on February 28. The forty-eighth and final article was approved on March 24 when the bill was issued as Decree No. 16, the Coahuila y Texas Colonization Law of 1825.[32] The state colonization law brought the Anglo-American and Mexican frontiers together for the first time under the legitimate sanction of the laws of Coahuila y Texas. With this foundation for a new society, Tejanos advanced the other parts of their legislative platform.

In working for the Tejano platform, Bastrop was generally following the instructions given him at his election to the office. After the colonization plan and the political chieftaincy, he directed his efforts to ports, the economy, and Indian problems. Another of his successful campaigns was improving the mail service in Texas. The mail had run quite regularly between Coahuila and Béxar and from Béxar to Goliad, but the run to Nacogdoches was irregular. As the population increased in East Texas, effective communication became essential. In July of 1825, Bastrop cited statistical reports and other evidence that any customs agency at Galveston in the future would probably need postal service improvements. In April, 1826, biweekly mail service for Nacogdoches was finally inaugurated, due largely to Bastrop's work.[33]

Bastrop's legislative efforts laid the framework for Texas ports, although the ports were not developed under the Mexican government of Texas. Tejanos maintained that Texas needed at least one port. Through Bastrop and their senators in Mexico City, Tejanos pressed for a port at Galveston. Bastrop reminded the state deputies of the importance of commerce to Coahuila y Texas, and asked them to support a petition which he had submitted to the national congress. Although Galveston was finally declared a legal port, the national government did not appoint a customs collector or develop the port; and it never promoted an official settlement at Galveston. Instead, the port and the coast remained unimproved except for illicit use by Anglo-American colonists. Stephen F. Austin had reportedly conducted a secret survey of the coastal areas shortly after his arrival, and Anglo-American capitalists made much more use of coastal trade than

Tejanos. But, despite Tejano efforts, Galveston waited to be developed by a subsequent government of Texas.[34]

Other major legislative endeavors of Texas in her early years as a department of Coahuila y Texas lay in appealing to the national government for assistance for defense against the Indians in promoting agriculture. Texas managed to obtain tax-exempt status for cotton growers and stock raisers, but she failed to secure a government concession for her tobacco cultivators. Tobacco cultivation and sale was controlled by the national government in Mexico, which had granted a monopoly to Veracruz. Many Anglo colonists had experienced tobacco cultivation in the southern United States, and hoped to develop the industry in Texas. Despite Bastrop's best efforts, however, Texas never obtained the monopoly. Tejanos were even more frustrated in their requests for federal help in the surge of Indian depredations in 1825. One official, the minister of war in Mexico City, suggested that Tejanos attempt to "win the Indians over" with gifts and friendship. Tejanos wryly accused the national government of being "cold and indifferent." The situation continued until Tejanos addressed the problem themselves, as previously mentioned.

The national government eventually became involved in the Indian problem indirectly, however, when the Haden Edwards Rebellion forced their hand in 1827. Edwards had been moving toward a clash with government officials for months before he finally declared his independent Fredonian Republic. The Cherokee Indians of East Texas were his allies in this rebellion under their chief, Richard Fields. Although Austin and Tejanos had attempted to warn the national government of the growing dissent in that region for months, the government failed to take action to preclude the uprising. After national and state troops subdued the rebels, José Antonio Sepúlveda of Nacogdoches criticized the national government for "blindness and imbecility" in not having moved sooner.[35] This undoubtedly encouraged Sepúlveda and other Tejanos to organize their own militia squadrons in Texas after 1826.

Slavery remained one of the most important legislative concerns for Tejanos. As the constituent congress slowly hammered out the several articles of the state constitution, slavery began to emerge as a critical issue. Mexicans had begun to resolve their attitudes toward slavery even before Father Miguel Hidalgo had declared emancipation as part of his independence decrees in 1810. The mestizo population of Mexico moved steadily toward acceptance of black people as equals in society, but the situation in

Texas was unlike that of the remainder of Mexico. The immigration of Anglo Americans introduced the question under different circumstances.

Austin's colonization contract of 1823 had not forbidden slavery, but the national congress began to discuss emancipation in 1824. Austin personally asked Erasmo Seguin in Mexico City to work for the acceptance of slavery in Texas. Seguin agreed to speak favorably for slavery whenever he could, but he promised nothing. In July, the congress issued Decree No. 412 prohibiting forever the commerce and traffic in slaves in Mexico "under any pretense whatever." It further declared all slaves free by virtue of merely setting foot on Mexican soil.[36]

The national emancipation law threatened seriously to limit Anglo-American immigration. Stephen F. Austin wrote a strong letter to the state legislature protesting the national law. He criticized that decree as "an open and positive contravention of the law and the most solemn guarantees," and added, "it will be considered by all as an act of bad faith by the Gov't." He wrote a similar letter to Seguin in Mexico City. Seguin agreed that slavery would help Texas achieve prosperity but added, "but my friend, in my congress they did not even want to hear solicitations of that nature, to the contrary, at the mention of slavery the entire congress became electrified at the consideration of the state of unhappiness of that part of humanity."[37] Seguin had nothing more to offer than a suggestion that Austin seek favorable legislation at the state level.

The Tejano leaders joined Austin in a drive for state legislation that would allow Anglo Americans to bring their slaves. In August of 1825, Austin submitted a proposal for the regulation of slavery to the governor. He proposed that colonists be allowed to introduce slaves until 1840 and that no slave trade be permitted except among the colonists for their own use. The grandchildren of slaves thus introduced were to become free at the ages of twenty-five for males and fifteen for females. But by 1826 the state legislature began to consider an article to the constitution which threatened absolute emancipation in Texas. As proposed, Article 13 read: "The state prohibits slavery absolutely and forever in all its territory, and slaves now in it shall be free from the day the constitution is published in this capital." To this proposal, José Antonio Saucedo sarcastically remarked, "So we begin to see the advantages which the union with Coahuila gives us." The Béxar Ayuntamiento also submitted a protest to the legislature, which Bastrop referred along with Austin's to the Committee on the Constitution.[38]

As the debates in the legislature reached a critical point in the fall of 1826, Tejanos reelected Bastrop, hoping for continuity in their representation. One advantage Texas had lay in the membership of the Committee on the Constitution. Two of the members were José María Viesca and Juan Vicente Campos, who had proven to be sympathetic to Tejano needs. But the opposition in the legislature also held a position of power. Deputy Juan Carrillo, who strongly opposed slavery, was on that key committee. Carrillo was one of the members who were "inimical to the interests of Texas," according to J. E. B. Austin, who was lobbying in the legislature at the time. Compounding the difficulties for Texas, Bastrop became ill on September 22. His absence that day and on many thereafter was the result of an illness from which he never recovered. Adding to this was an atmosphere of rebellion in Coahuila that month. The rebellion was directed at the legislature for taking so long to draw up the constitution. Only the national army saved the legislature from a revolt by several towns in Coahuila.[39] The threatened revolts made legislative expediency something of a premium at a time that Tejanos sought compromise.

Despite all, Tejanos obtained a compromise. It came in November with a long presentation by Dionisio Elizondo. Elizondo used the Béxar *memoria*, and Austin's proposal in favor of slavery. He cited Jeremy Bentham, and readily acknowledged the evil of slavery. But he asked the legislature to consider the position of the Anglo-American colonists who had paid for the slaves as property. Immediate manumission, he argued, would be confiscation and would violate the "public faith." With Elizondo's suggestion, the bill was referred to the committee, where Juan Vicente Campos finally presented a compromise article in January. The wording said merely, "In the State, no one is born a slave." It further set a termination date for the introduction of slaves as six months after publication of the constitution.[40]

The congress finally promulgated the Coahuila y Texas Constitution on March 11, 1827. The people of the state swore allegiance to their new constitution in public ceremonies throughout the state. Even Stephen F. Austin praised the "abundant manifestations of liberal and enlightened principles." The rights of the people were protected as were the different branches of government. It included provisions for education and for a jury system which Tejanos accepted as serious responsibilities.[41]

With the constitution, Coahuila y Texas completed the process of establishing herself as a political entity in the republic. And, most important,

Tejanos were learning the importance of politics in the state legislature. Bastrop had not obtained his few successes in Saltillo by himself; he had to rely on political maneuvering outside the sessions as well. As he said in a letter to Austin in early 1825, "There is a great opposition in the congress against Texas, and in order for me to obtain anything beneficial for Texas and the new colonies I have to win the votes before the congress opens." But Bastrop had gained important legislative successes by finding political allies in the legislature.

As Bastrop said, Texas had opposition in the legislature. He told Austin, "I could not succeed for the rivalry which exists between Cohaguila [*sic*] (or I should say Saltillo) and Texas." He survived, however, by allying himself politically with the deputies from Parras and Monclova, who also opposed the dominance of Saltillo in the legislature. These deputies included José María Viesca, Juan Vicente Campos, Santiago de Valle, and Francisco Gutiérrez. Indeed, Bastrop acknowledged that these were the deputies who, as he said, "have helped me the most" with the colonization bill and the political chieftaincy for Texas. Bastrop had quickly learned to cultivate their friendship, for it was his only hope in Saltillo. More than once the legislative sessions had become ideological confrontations between the Saltillo deputies and the Parras group.[42]

Bastrop had learned to operate within the political system that was forming in the legislature in those early years, but he never wrote of it as a system. He spoke only in terms of political imperatives. In fact, the group of deputies from Parras represented a political faction in Coahuila. Their leaders were José María Viesca in the state legislature and his brother, Agustín, the state senator in Mexico City. The Viesca family was a powerful family of Parras who controlled much of the political power in the *frontera* states. They wanted a modern form of government which would foster the growth of business and prosperity for the Coahuila area. They came to be called federalists and liberals in Mexico. In the 1820s, particularly when Bastrop met them, they were just gathering their political power resources. The records of the legislature, for example, reveal that their allies were steadily gaining in control of the important offices in the state.[43] The group that Bastrop relied on for his support was a nascent political faction, and the politics he witnessed as he maneuvered for votes outside the sessions represented the emergence of a republican political system in Coahuila y Texas.

VII
The Emergence of Tejano Politics

Tejanos attempted to define their own rôle in Coahuila y Texas through politics, and in doing so committed themselves to an unfavorable status in later nineteenth-century Texas. As Coahuiltejanos, they saw their prosperity in the success of Anglo-American colonization. In support of this colonization, they formed a legislative policy which was at the vanguard of liberal thought in Mexico of the 1830s. Indeed, they established in this effort some of the most beneficial legal institutions of their cultural legacy for Texas and the United States. But their protective attitude toward Anglo Americans led Tejanos into direct conflict with the more conservative centralists of Mexico and eventually alienated them from the growing centralist government in Mexico City.

Even as Tejanos loosened the links that bound them to Mother Mexico, they began to conflict with their new Anglo neighbors as well. For years Tejanos alone had resisted the intrusions of Anglo-American adventurers. Their supportive attitude toward colonization struggled against a strong cultural bias which made them perceive many Anglos as crude and asocial. Tejanos thus increasingly defined themselves as an entity different from Mexico and separate from the Anglo. Although Santa Anna and the Anglo Americans in the Texas Revolution have held center stage in the story of Texas, Tejano politics was as much a factor as Mexican centralism or Anglo rebellion in determining the course of Tejanos and Texas.

By the time their constitution was promulgated in 1827, the Tejanos and other liberal Coahuiltejanos had committed themselves to achieving economic prosperity through their state colonization program. The leaders of this liberal group of thinkers were the statesmen from Parras and Monclova. As mentioned earlier, José María Viesca and his brother Agustín, led the group in political ideology and power. Both served in national as well as state positions. They owned two libraries of the latest political and scientific thought, and their family was known in Mexico as very liberal. They supported the growth of capitalism in Coahuila in many ways. One Anglo-American capitalist named Robert Andrews who stayed with the Viescas in Parras described their family as "rich, large, respectable, learned, sensible, and honorable."[1]

Certainly the Viesca political faction did not work in a vacuum in Mexico. They represented a strong liberal party, often referred to as *yorkinos* because of their Masonic affiliation with the York rite, who were struggling to maintain control in Mexican politics in the mid-1820s. Their leaders were revolutionary veterans like Guadalupe Victoria, Lorenzo de Zavala, and Vicente Guerrero. Their antagonists were the centralists who were usually conservatives trying to secure the traditional power of the established military and the Catholic Church in Mexico. From this latter group emerged the generals who fought the Anglo Americans in Texas in 1836—Santa Anna, Filisola, Cos, and Urrea.[2]

In general the Viesca faction supported economic enterprise in a variety of ways. Through legislation, they obtained exemptions from taxes on cotton, foreign imports, and domestic items for colonists and Tejano residents. They granted citizenship and special concessions to many capitalists, including Anglo Americans. James Bowie, for example, acquired a textile mill concession, and Leon R. Almy received a seven-year concession on "a machine to extract water from the depths." Other concessions included cotton gins, ferries, and steamboats.[3] On a visit to Monclova in 1831, Stephen F. Austin stayed at the home of Don Victor Blanco. He acknowledged that Blanco, José Antonio Tijerina, and other deputies of Monclova supported Anglo-American immigration, and later stated that the success of the colonies "stands very high" in the state government.[4]

One of the strongest motives Coahuiltejanos had in supporting economic enterprise, self-interest, is most evident in their efforts to sponsor the cotton industry and to attract U.S. cotton planters to Texas. Knowing that cotton cultivation was labor intensive, Francisco Madero of the Viesca faction suggested and secured a law to import convict labor into Texas. Even more revealing of their motives was their willingness to countenance slave labor. A case in point was that of nascent capitalist Victor Blanco, a long-time politico who aspired to developing a cotton kingdom in Coahuila y Texas. In fact, he held the exclusive cotton ginning concession in the state. A slave owner as recently as 1820, Blanco obviously found it easy to support pro-slavery legislation for a cotton industry based on slavery. The fact that his last legal purchase of a slave was certified by the Béxar Ayuntamiento offers some commentary on that assembly as well. The members of that body in 1820 were such notable Tejanos as Erasmo Seguin, José Flores, Juan Martín Veramendi, Vicente Zambrano, and José María Zambrano.[5]

If the Coahuiltejano capitalists were feathering their nests in cotton, Stephen F. Austin was their nest egg. Austin had a plan for Texas by which he proposed to reconcile the interests of Mexicans and Anglo Americans. He dedicated months to promoting his scheme for prosperity. First, Mexicans would have to accept agriculture—cotton—as the primary enterprise. Discussions leading to the 1828 tariff in the United States had alienated the South as well as the British market. Disaffected by their country's policy, southern cotton planters began to look toward the inviting situation in Mexican Texas. They knew the cotton industry and could teach Coahuiltejanos the means to prosperity. The only thing needed for all this to transpire was for Coahuila y Texas to revoke Article 13 of the constitution prohibiting slavery. Slavery was the factor *sine qua non* in Austin's offer of prosperity. Although Austin did not personally like what he called the "demoralizing influence of slavery," it had already allowed his colony to surpass proportionally the labor supply of any other town in Coahuila y Texas.[6] In slavery, Austin believed he offered Coahuila y Texas its economic future.

The Coahuiltejano effort to establish slavery on a legal basis began in the first Coahuila y Texas Congress in 1827. The two Tejano deputies elected to this congress were Miguel Arciniega and José Antonio Navarro. Arciniega was born in the Alamo in 1807, the son of Gregorio Arciniega of the compañía volante of San Carlos de Parras. He lived in the barrio of Valero all of his life. He was well educated, spoke French and English, and served in numerous public offices including regidor and deputy. He had served as the land commissioner in the colonies and was favorable to Anglo-American immigration. Having owned slaves only a few years before his election, he also spoke in favor of slavery in the congress. Navarro, one of the best known Tejanos, needs little biographical description except to say that he came from a long line of Spaniards—a characteristic which set him somewhat apart from anti-Spanish liberals of Coahuila y Texas. Although neither of them served as president of the state congress, they were politically astute and effective from the time of their arrival in Saltillo.[7]

As Arciniega and Navarro entered the state congress in the summer of 1827, the obstacles were mounting against the Texas cotton hopes. Many Mexican statesmen—liberal and conservative—actively opposed the slavery interests. They acknowledged the benefits which Caucasians would reap from slavery, but one slavery opponent responded, "God forbid the payment of such a price for prosperity."[8] Just as the Tejanos arrived in the Saltillo congress, Coahuilan conservatives were launching a campaign against the entire liberal federalist platform including slavery. They began by introducing a bill to halt all traffic in slaves. This bill, which passed as Decree No. 18 on September 15, 1827, made slaveowners responsible for enumerating and educating their slaves. It also set rigorous penalties for the introduction of slaves six months after publication of the constitution.[9] The next spring, the conservatives introduced a bill for Decree No. 50 which would suspend the offices of the governor's cabinet members, treasurer, vice-governor, and all district and department chiefs except those of Texas. The highly controversial bill proposed that ayuntamientos be placed directly under the control of the governor. Tejano deputies, meanwhile, inconspicuously prepared their own bill for slavery in Texas.

While the legislative battle raged over Decree No. 50, José Antonio Navarro introduced his bill for indentured servitude in Texas. In April, Governor José María Viesca opened the liberal offensive against Decree No. 50 as an attack on the constitution. During the heated debate, Navarro maneuvered his own bill through the committee. Coahuiltejanos were quite familiar with such servant contracts for peons; therefore, even the centralists saw no new threat in Navarro's bill. His bill was passed as Decree No. 56 on May 5, 1828. It validated contracts of servitude made in foreign countries by immigrants to Coahuila y Texas as long as they did not conflict with state laws. Navarro obtained legal sanction for Anglo-American colonists to bring slaves as permanently indentured servants into the state. The bill was a legal subterfuge, but as a political maneuver, it succeeded. Arciniega later admitted that the bill would never have passed had it not been for the heated discussion over Decree No. 50. Meanwhile, Decree No. 50 finally passed, and led to constant bickering between centralists and federalists in the state for years to come.[10]

Another incident in 1829 revealed the pro-slavery commitment of the liberal Coahuiltejanos who wanted a cotton industry. On September 15, President Guerrero chose to commemorate Father Hidalgo's 1810 emancipation decree by declaring anew the abolition of slavery in Mexico. Presi-

Fig. 3. Agustin Viesca, the last Mexican governor of Texas under the Mexican flag. *Courtesy Agustín Viesca Cardenas, México, D.F.*

dent Guerrero's declaration naturally upset the Anglo-American colonists, but the followers of Viesca immediately set their political machine to work. José María Viesca protested the declaration in letters to the new Texas political chief, Ramón Músquiz, to his own brother Agustín Viesca, and to the president. Músquiz automatically suspended action on the decree and told the colonists to calm themselves until something could be done to repeal the decree. Agustín Viesca, who was then serving as the national secretary of relations in Mexico City, personally explained to the president how destructive the decree would be to the Texas economy. In a similar protest to the president, José María Viesca added that "the advancement of Coahuila was so dependent upon that of Texas." In response to such pressure, President Guerrero exempted Texas from the decree, and once again the Anglo-American nest egg lay secure in the hands of the Viesca faction.[11]

Just as Coahuiltejanos sponsored pro-slavery measures to induce Anglo-American immigration, they similarly established a program of land laws as a foundation for settlement and prosperity. Some, such as the homestead protection, were developed explicitly to attract southern U.S. debtors. Many of their laws were based upon ancient Hispanic tradition; others were imaginative answers to frontier imperative. Almost all of them were continued under different titles by Anglo Americans in Texas and the United States after 1836.

The best known of the Coahuiltejano land laws was the system of empresario contracts which was generally successful from the time it was initiated. It continued in the Republic of Texas as the third class headright and served as the basis for the Mercer, Peters, Fisher and Miller, and Castro colonies.[12] Another system used in Texas under Spain allowed settlers to claim land even before it was opened for public sale. This method constituted, of course, the preemption type of grant. The early Spanish law was described by an investigative commission under James R. Miller and W. H. Bourland for the state of Texas in 1854. The Miller and Bourland report description stated as follows:

"The mode of acquiring this kind of title was in the first place by application or denouncement [*denuncio*] whereupon the land was ordered to be and was inspected as to quality, surveyed, appraised, passed through the appropriate departments of the colony, and also of the Intendency of San Luís Potosí, and declared in due form. The Intendent of that province would issue a title to the applicant, and also a commission to some person in authority to put him in judicial possession of the same. The act of possession made the title perfect, except as to subsequent conditions."

The writing of this law presupposed that, despite the "public auction," the applicant would receive the title. Miller and Bourland went on to cite examples of grants in early Texas, such as that of Don Vicente López de Herrera, who applied in 1798 and received his title in 1806.[13]

The congress of Coahuila y Texas enacted this system of grants in a law scarcely appreciated by historians, Decree No. 272 of March 26, 1834. The decree stated that the lands were to be sold at public auction whenever the executive opened them for survey and sale "or on notice from any person interested in purchasing any land, which he may point out, and of which he may request a survey." The sale was to be advertised for three months and auctioned to the highest bidder for at least the minimum price of ten dollars for a million square varas or yards, approximately. An appointed land commissioner would then "issue to purchasers in the name of the state the titles to the land sold in accordance with the certificates they present him from the subordinate commissioners, describing the lands and surveys thereof."[14]

The above system was almost identical to one being proposed in the United States by Senator Thomas Hart Benton in 1824 as his "graduation" bill. Benton's "log cabin" bill was not passed until 1841 as the Pre-Emption Act by another senator. In contrast, the Tejanos had been claiming their lands under their *denuncio* system since the eighteenth century.[15]

Another Coahuiltejano land program from Hispanic tradition was the grant of one league and one labor as a bounty for military service or for serving as a settler on the defensive frontier. These *frontera* settlement programs were employed when the colonial government of Mexico had tried to settle Palafox, Trinidad, and the other Texas settlements of the early nineteenth century. They were later used by the Republic of Texas as first class headrights.[16]

Through the implementation and development of ancient Hispanic land policies, Coahuiltejanos provided a major impetus in drawing the Anglo-American tide southward to Texas. After years of actively seeking solutions to peopling the *frontera*, Coahuiltejanos had developed their land programs far in advance of the Anglo-American systems. Even Stephen F. Austin admitted that Coahuila y Texas had "the most liberal and munificent government on earth to emigrants." He added that he opposed annexation of Texas by the United States because the American land system would totally ruin "thousands" of settlers. One of Austin's settlers, Jonas Harrison, voiced a similar complaint of the "illiberal" land policies of the United States. He added that if the United States had "radically changed" its policies before the 1820s, "we had most of us never seen Texas." But the Coahuiltejano land laws provided a tremendous attraction. In effect, the land laws played a vital role in making Texas from its very beginning. Land historians have generally agreed with the statement of former Texas land commissioner Bascom Giles that "Texas history is largely based upon the history of its lands."[17] And its land laws were solidly based in the Hispanic land policies forged by Tejanos to attract Anglo-American colonization.

Coahuila y Texas land laws included many principles rarely acknowledged in history, but which also contributed to the "munificence" of Texas.

One of the most important of these is the basic premise of Mexican federalism that the state—not the federal government—should administer its own public domain. Indeed, Miguel Ramos Arizpe justified the union of Coahuila and Texas on the basis that Texas would own her own public domain. And this principle was implicit in many of the other programs such as the education laws which Anglo Americans retained after 1836, and which were likewise called "munificent" by an education historian of the state. According to Hispanic tradition, the state also gained possession of any intestate property or any subsurface minerals not expressly granted as part of the land grant.[18] Another Coahuiltejano law issued as Decree No. 95 on July 3, 1829, granted the state the right to establish its own territorial limits. This law became particularly important to Texas when oil was discovered in the Gulf of Mexico near the Texas coast. In a major court case, *United States vs. the State of Texas* (1950), prominent Texans Allan Shivers, Price Daniels, and Bascom Giles testified to the fact that Texas boundaries were set by the Mexican state laws in Mexican terms of three *leguas*—not three miles. The Texas tidelands, therefore, extended ten and one-half miles into the Gulf while those in other American states extended only three miles. The tidelands combined with the state ownership of the public domain and mineral rights to reap millions of dollars for Texas schools and public facilities. These advantages were not serendipitous or incidental, but well-prepared programs intentionally designed to attract and hold settlers for the *frontera*.[19]

The best example of Coahuiltejano land policy development is seen perhaps in the homestead law of Coahuila y Texas. The principle of homestead protection had its origin in fifteenth-century Spain when Ferdinand and Isabella ruled that a man's oxen, work animals, and tools were not to be seized for payment of debt. In time, this protection was extended to cover all tools, all work animals, and a person's land as well. The principle was transmitted to the New World by the *Recopilación*, where it offered an excellent solution for Coahuiltejanos who needed to attract and hold Anglo-American immigrants.

The congress of Coahuila y Texas was well aware of the fact that Austin's colonists were constantly threatened with ruin by creditors from the United States. In response to their pleas, the congress passed Decree No. 70 on January 13, 1829. The decree offered the citizens protection from seizure of their land, tools, and work animals or from any debt which would "affect their attention to their families." This law was also retained by the Lamar Administration under the Republic of Texas and, according to Eugene C.

Barker, "has been regarded as the foundation of the successive homestead exemption laws that have ruled in Texas since that day and as the prototype of a goodly progeny in other states."[20]

A significant feature in all of these property laws was the equal right of women to own, trade, and sue for property. A high proportion of the women in Texas were widows in the first half of the nineteenth century. And though excluded from prominent office, these women served a vital rôle in Tejano society by virtue of their estate inheritance and management. Many of them were involved in law suits, particularly those suing for military survivor's benefits. Others were involved in land sales. These economic activities enabled many women to achieve financial superiority over their male contemporaries. Women were landowners; they were employers; and they were some of the most generous contributors to pious funds and school-fund drives. As a concession to this economic reality, Coahuilte-janos passed laws allowing for community property of husband and wife. The laws recognized the wife's personal ownership of property which she owned before marriage and thus after the possible death of her spouse. They were among the laws retained in Texas government after 1836.[21]

One principle that Coahuiltejanos were slow to exclude from their land programs was religious intolerance. They modified the interpretations of pertinent laws, because they realized that intolerance hindered immigration of Protestant Anglo Americans, but even this concession was difficult to obtain. This is not to say that all Coahuiltejanos were staunch Catholics, although many accepted Catholicism as the state religion. For example, Senator Erasmo Seguin had been given official instructions in 1823 to see that the Roman Catholic Church reign supreme at the constitutional convention in Mexico City. There are indications, however, that many Tejanos strongly opposed the Church. As early as 1805, for example, a citizen of Nacogdoches was arrested for his campaign to criticize the Church publicly by posting "indecorous" broadsides on trees. In the 1820s Bexareños were reported to have protested the presence of clergy, shouting, "Out with the friars, out with the good-for-nothings."[22] These attacks were related to the Tejanos' adamant position that the mission lands justly belonged to the people and not to the Church. Opposition to the Church was therefore not new to Tejanos when they wanted liberal land policies.

Ever since the mission lands had been secularized in 1792, Tejanos had fought to gain title to those lands. On numerous occasions Tejanos petitioned the national and state government for distribution of these lands, but most requests went unanswered. Tejanos were able to acquire the mission lands in the mid-1820s, only after years of petitioning. Then they began to demand that the missions themselves be sold for back payment of military and public officials.[23] After years of opposition to the Church's claim to property in Texas, Tejanos came to challenge the Church's spiritual influence on the colonization program as well.

For years, the only way Tejanos could minimize the effects of intolerance on the colonization program was to obtain loose interpretation of the laws. The Coahuila y Texas Constitution expressly prohibited any religion except the Roman Catholic. The state Colonization Law stated that original settlers should be Catholics in accordance with the constitution, but it allowed new colonists to qualify by being merely "Christian." In practice the Anglo colonists were not persecuted or harassed, but neither were they allowed to practice openly their Protestant religions. In fact, they were given their own priest in 1831. Father Miguel Muldoon, an Irish Mexican, served as the vicar-general of the colonies until 1833. And religious instruction was encouraged in Tejano education law. One such decree allowed for reading, writing, arithmetic, and "catechism of the Christian religion." Finally the liberal Coahuiltejanos in the state congress succeeded in including religious toleration as a provision in the new law of 1834. Article 10 of Decree No. 272 explicitly stated: "No person shall be molested for political or religious opinions, provided, he shall not disturb the public order." This provision is particularly instructive in demonstrating the definite relationship between liberal land policy and Coahuiltejano efforts for religious toleration.[24]

Even as the Tejanos were striving to promote Anglo-American colonization, however, they began to manifest a crosscurrent of antagonism with those colonists. In the mid-1820s a pattern of conflict began to emerge between the Tejanos and Anglo Americans around Goliad and Victoria. The conflict began when state authorities in Saltillo granted Green DeWitt an empresario contract in 1825. The Tejanos in Victoria and Goliad were shocked to learn only after the fact that their towns and ranches were included in DeWitt's grant. They protested repeatedly to the authorities, but obtained no response. Then, as if to exacerbate the situation purposely, the congress granted to James Power and James Hewetson a tract which not only was located within the ten-league coastal reserve but which also overlapped a Tejano ranch community (later named San Patricio). These conflicting grants created an atmosphere of distrust, conflict, and rivalry which prevailed from the day DeWitt claimed his lands.

The tense situation between DeWitt's colony and the Tejanos erupted into open conflict within a year of DeWitt's arrival. In March, 1826, the Tejano leader and empresario, Martín de León, sued an Anglo colonist in a dispute over livestock. Although the political chief contained the ire of De León, within a few months a worse incident rekindled the flames of conflict. In October, the political chief ordered De León to confiscate some contraband goods which Anglo colonists had hidden in DeWitt's colony. The political chief also ordered the commander of La Bahía Presidio, Rafael Antonio Manchola, to escort De León with an armed troop. When the colonists heard that the Tejanos were coming and that De Leon had sworn to return with DeWitt's head, the Anglo Americans armed themselves for resistance. An armed conflict was averted only by the timely intervention of Stephen F. Austin, whom the Tejanos respected as a singularly honorable Anglo.[25] These incidents were only the beginning of a long series of conflicts between the Anglos and Tejanos in that region. For years, these Tejanos repeatedly arrested Anglos with illegally acquired property, either contraband goods or rustled livestock. Indeed, the point of contact between Tejano and Anglo-American settlements was nowhere closer than between Victoria and Gonzales; and nowhere did it seem so strongly to portend such eternal conflict between the two ethnic communities. Tejanos and their descendants would become embittered at Anglo encroachments—legal and illegal—onto these Tejano lands.[26] The events gave Tejanos an unfavorable opinion of Anglo-American character.

In the disputes of 1826, the Anglo Americans alienated a significant person, Rafael Antonio Manchola. Manchola was the son-in-law of Martín de León, a rich and powerful man. After his tour as presidial commander between 1826 and 1828, Manchola became a state deputy until 1830, and then the primary alcalde of Goliad in 1831. As military commander, he had personally observed many illegal activities of the Anglo colonists. He had also participated as troop commander in the government campaign against the Haden Edwards rebellion.[27] By alienating Manchola, the colonists not only forfeited the favor of a powerful statesman—this was the man who was actively writing the munificent provisions of the colonization program for them in the Saltillo legislature—but they incurred a strong resentment which contributed to the restrictive Law of April 6, 1830.

Manchola's attitude toward the Anglos was best demonstrated in a letter to Mateo Ahumada, the commandant of Texas. In his own words, Manchola "violently" reported the events of the October, 1826, confrontation with DeWitt. Heavily underlining the phrases for emphasis, Manchola wrote:

"I have been told verbally that Gren DeWitt [*sic*] has said that *if I had arrived by day instead of by night as I did he would not have let me come near*; and I consider him . . . to be very capable of it because of his total lack of respect for our authority, which is completely scoffed at by him as well as by his colonists and those of the Brazos and the Colorado, all of whom need to be forced to live an orderly life and to stop the libertine way they live now."

Manchola went on to recommend that military detachments be stationed in the Anglo colonies to guard the rivers and bays for contraband activities. His recommendations continued:

> . . . no faith can be placed in the Anglo-American colonists because they are continually demonstrating that they absolutely refuse to be subordinate, unless they find it convenient to what they want anyway, all of which I believe will be very detrimental to us for them to be our neighbors if we do not in time, clip the wings of their audacity by stationing a strong detachment in each new settlement which will enforce the laws and jurisdiction of a Mexican Alcalde which should be placed in each of them, since under their own colonists as judges, they do nothing more than practice their own laws which they have practiced since they were born, forgetting the ones they have sworn to obey, these being the laws of our Supreme Government . . .

Almost as if in response to Manchola's recommendations, Colonel José de las Piedras arrived in East Texas with a detachment of two hundred men the following summer with orders to enforce the colonization laws among the Anglo-American colonies.[28]

The Tejanos of Manchola's sentiment began to report that Anglo Americans were generally undesirable in society. One Mexican diarist in 1828 wrote that they were a "lazy people of vicious character." When he encountered a kind or courteous Anglo, he said these qualities were "a very rare thing among individuals of his [Anglo-American] nationality." The Goliad Tejanos were particularly upset at DeWitt, whom they contemptuously described as being "drunk in the streets constantly." They felt that this Anglo American was an "adventurer" and that his activities were "fraudulent." In one report to a state authority, they said, "Let us be honest with ourselves, Sir, the foreign empresarios are nothing more than money-changing speculators caring only for their own well-being and hesitating not in their unbecoming methods."[29] Though relatively liberal in the Mexican political spectrum of the 1830s, Tejanos were nevertheless quite nationalistic in regard to the Anglos.

Tejanos were very much aware of the widening cultural gap between them and the rest of Mexico as well. In correspondence, they explicitly indicated that their life on the *frontera* marked their distinction. In a special report to the Béxar Ayuntamiento in 1829 a special committee cochaired by Juan Nepomuceno Seguin and Luciano Navarro identified these burdensome effects of the *frontera* on Tejanos. The report listed several grievances directed to the state congress; moreover, it revealed graphically that cultural distinction was manifesting itself in economic—and ultimately in political—differences.

The Béxar special report of 1829 listed many demands similar to those of the Laredo Ayuntamiento mentioned in a previous chapter. The Bexareños demanded an additional alcalde, reaffirmed their claim to extra land grants as defenders of the *frontera*, and requested a seven-year extension of tax and *mercader* exemption. They complained that Texas had to cry like a baby for its busy mother to give it any attention. Specifically, the Bexareños protested their subordinate status to remote capitals in Coahuila and Mexico City. The report mentioned "men who are ignorant of the political state of the Department of Texas, men who know neither her topographical situation nor her class of inhabitants neither in her hinterland nor on her borders." And in the first formal indication of dissatisfaction with their union with Coahuila, the Tejanos added the sarcastic remark that "the government cannot be convinced that the Department of Tejas is not just a newborn population which lacks the strength to govern itself." The report was forwarded by the ayuntamiento to the congress.[30]

At approximately the same time that the Béxar Ayuntamiento submitted its *memoria*, events in national politics in Mexico City turned against Texas. One of these events was a tour of inspection by General Manuel Mier y Terán through Texas. Mier y Terán was sent to investigate the possible Anglo-American threat in Texas. Anglo colonists believed Mier y Terán was sent "for the purpose of determining the dividing line between the two Governments," and most Tejanos undoubtedly thought likewise. Another national event involved a power shift from the liberal federalists to the conservatives. This shift was initiated by a conservative declaration and coup called the Plan de Jalapa of 1829. The plan declared that "any functionaries denounced by public opinion should be expelled." President Guerrero was "denounced" by the centralists, and a new centralist administration under Anastacio Bustamante ascended in December.[31]

The power shift in national politics stirred matters in Coahuila y Texas proportionally. To begin with, the two Tejano deputies, Rafael Antonio Manchola and José María Balmaceda, vere strongly committed to the liberal Viesca machine in the congress. They were therefore automatically out of favor with the new national administration. In describing them, Stephen F. Austin said, "The people of this place are unanimously hostile to the present administration [Bustamante], and they are more friendly to the North American emigration than they ever were." They were indeed hostile to centralism and in favor of colonization, but they paid a price for their stance against the new power block in Mexico City. In the state congress, Manchola and Balmaceda, particularly the latter, came under bitter attack for their liberal stance. Conservative representatives in Saltillo succeeded in having Balmaceda publicly denounced by citizens in Saltillo. By virtue of Article 4 of the Plan de Jalapa, Balmaceda and Parras Deputy Ignacio Sendejas were reprimanded and expelled from the congress by Decree No. 149 on September 18, 1830.[32]

José María Balmaceda was a military officer who had just retired in 1827 in Béxar. He had become a leading merchant and "principal citizen" of Béxar and served as regidor on the ayuntamiento. Between 1828 and 1830, he was a state deputy. In the congress, he and Manchola took advantage of their alliance with the Viesca group to secure important offices and committee positions. For example, Balmaceda and Manchola presided over the congress for all except two months of the entire one-year period between January, 1829, and February, 1830. Unfortunately, this prominence in liberal politics attracted the scorn of conservatives. The Plan de Jalapa was designed as an opposition party maneuver, and succeeded in Saltillo as well as in Mexico City.[33]

In response to Decree No. 149, Balmaceda and Manchola immediately issued a call for public support. Although, as they stated, the Saltillo "anarchists" had charged that the Tejanos did not merit the public's confidence, the Tejano deputies requested that the ayuntamientos of Texas write to affirm their support. The ayuntamientos of Béxar, Goliad, and San Felipe responded immediately, proclaiming that only the appropriate constituents would determine the merit of a deputy.[34] The congressional session ended before this particular dispute became any more critical. But this was one of the major events at the state level in the commitment of Tejanos to the liberal federalist standard.

The events surrounding Decree No. 149 almost automatically committed the incoming Texas deputies, Stephen F. Austin and Manuel Músquiz, a priest. In a letter to his confidant, Samuel M. Williams, Austin indicated the animosity between the liberal Coahuiltejanos and the centralist powers of Mexico City. These latter individuals included President Bustamante, his centralist ideologue, Lucas Alamán, and General Mier y Terán. Austin warned that in case of an outright break, he "must go with the Viescas."[35] This clearly revealed that by taking their liberal stance, the Coahuiltejanos committed Texas and its Anglo colonists to an adverse position under an increasingly hostile centralist administration as early as 1829. The next year began under foreboding political circumstances for Texas.

After his trip to Texas, General Mier y Terán submitted his report to the chief executive who, at that time, was Bustamante. Bustamante's minister of relations, Lucas Alamán, used Mier y Terán's recommendations to frame the Law of April 6, 1830. This law represented but another effort of the conservative Mexicans to control Anglo-American immigration. Indeed, the most important provision of the law prohibited further immigration from the United States. It provided for military installations in the heart of the Anglo colonies in Central and East Texas. It welcomed European colonists, but it absolutely forbade further importation of slaves. It also terminated any empresario contracts which were incomplete at the time the law was published.

The similarity of these legal provisions with the earlier recommendations of Rafael Antonio Manchola was, of course, not a complete coincidence. As mentioned, Manchola was a much respected Tejano with access not only to Saltillo, but to Mexico City as well. This is not to say that Tejanos were suddenly opposed to Anglo-American colonization, for they were not. In fact, Tejanos were the only Mexicans to intervene in favor of the colonists, and who eventually repealed the provisions of the Law of April 6, 1830. But Manchola's recommendations did not fall on deaf ears in Saltillo; and his report was submitted just as the conservative element was growing in that city. Manchola's report was not a break in Anglo-Tejano relations in Texas, but it was a turning point for the worse.

In the Coahuila y Texas Congress, matters deteriorated as the conservatives expanded the policy of the Law of April 6, 1830, at the state level. They began their campaign in late 1830 with a bill to prohibit foreigners from practicing retail trade. The debates over this bill, aimed directly at the Anglo capitalists, caused a sharp polarization between the vying political factions. On April 11, 1831, Manuel Músquiz of Béxar made a strong appeal against the bill. Voting in support of Músquiz were Stephen F.

Austin and all of the deputies from Parras and Monclova except two. In favor of the bill were the Saltillo deputies and the two dissenting Parras deputies. The voting continued as a stalemate until a compromise was reached in February, 1832. Decree No. 183 forbade the practice of retail trade to all foreigners except to those in the Texas Department.[36] After the debate on this decree, the sectional lines were drawn in the congress.

The liberals concentrated their efforts on the reform of the colonization program. Músquiz and a Monclova deputy, Pedro Fuentes, passed a new colonization law welcoming Mexicans and foreigners not included in the Law of April 6, 1830. The Coahuila y Texas Colonization Law of 1825 was amended, however, in accordance with the Law of April 6, 1830. And the congress allowed the extension of two major Anglo-American colonization contracts which General Mier y Terán had recommended. The contract applicants were John Cameron, and the contract group of Lorenzo de Zavala, Joseph Vehlein, and David G. Burnet. These empresarios promised to settle foreigners other than Anglo Americans. Ironically, their contract extensions irritated the Tejano deputies, who considered these particular empresarios to be fraudulent.[37]

While Tejanos were struggling to overcome the detrimental effects of the Law of April 6, 1830, another wave of national disturbances promised even more partisan conflict. General Santa Anna, perceiving the growth of liberal power, endorsed a liberal proclamation against the Bustamante Administration. By joining the liberal revolt, Santa Anna only added to the nation's instability. As the summer progressed, other generals and other states declared in favor of the liberal plan, the Plan de Veracruz.

In Coahuila y Texas the liberals were sympathetic with national liberals, but the Coahuiltejanos withheld their endorsement of any faction. They proclaimed that Coahuila y Texas would not support any government other than a liberal federalist system of sovereign states. Their position, according to Stephen F. Austin, was "decidedly in favor of the colonists" and in favor of Santa Anna only as he offered to overthrow centralist power. Otherwise, they opposed Santa Anna as well.[38] Austin and the colonists were not so cautious.

In early 1832, the Anglo colonists began to venture into politics on their own. To begin with, they engaged in a politically hazardous confrontation with Colonel John Davis Bradburn, an Anglo-American adventurer who had joined the centralist cause in Mexico. Bradburn was one of the commanders stationed in Texas to enforce the provisions of the Law of April 6,

1830. He had dealt rather tactlessly with the colonists in a dispute which almost ignited a major rebellion. Austin has been credited with calming the colonists with his perennial advice to them, that "if the whole of the settlers will accept my motto 'Fidelity to Mexico,' and act and talk in conformity, they will flourish beyond their own expectations."[39]

In July, Colonel José Antonio Mexía marched to Anáhuac to preclude any revolutionary activities there. Mexía was a liberal who was supporting the Plan de Veracruz when he decided to investigate the situation among the colonies. The colonists convinced him that their actions were directed only at Bradburn and not against the Mexican government. They affirmed their support of the latter, especially Mexía's liberal party. While Mexía was in Texas, Colonel José de las Piedras declared in favor of the Plan de Veracruz and joined Mexía. Mexía and De las Piedras left Texas later that summer, taking their combined armies to join the struggle against centralism in Mexico. With them they took all of the national army troops which had been sent to enforce the Law of April 6, 1830.

Mexía's visit sparked a wave of liberal enthusiasm among the colonists, who were greatly encouraged to declare also for Santa Anna. But when they attempted to induce Tejanos to do likewise, the Tejanos declined. The colonists proceeded unilaterally to declare for Santa Anna in July. In August, when Tejanos declared themselves in favor of the Plan de Veracruz, the colonists went one step further and called a convention for October in San Felipe. They felt it appropriate under the circumstances to draft a list of demands from the government which they supposed, by now, to welcome liberal pronouncements.

The convention was called by Horatio Chriesman and John Austin. Settlers from all of the Anglo colonies met on October 1, 1832, and drew up their list of demands. They petitioned the government for repeal of the exclusion article in the Law of April 6, 1830. As mentioned earlier, they petitioned the government for school land grants, and they provided for a permanent troop to guard their frontier against Indians. They also requested land grants and customs privileges in the colonies. Just as the convention adjourned, Rafael Antonio Manchola arrived as the one Tejano delegate to the convention. In a last-minute appeal for Tejano support, the colonists appointed Manchola as commissioner along with William H. Wharton to transmit the *memoria* to the government authorities. Manchola agreed to do it, but the government's reaction precluded any need for Manchola's commission.[40]

The impact of the Anglos' unilateral convention shocked and upset authorities in Béxar. In particular, Political Chief Ramón Músquiz complained that although he concurred with the intent of the petitions, the Anglo community had acted "beyond its faculties." Regardless of their grievances, he added, such meetings simply were not legal. Austin apologized for his colonists and denied having organized the convention. In an effort to assuage the political chief, he said, "With regard to the meeting, it did not originate with me, but I believe some good will result from its action; the public is satisfied, and we have enjoyed more quiet than heretofore." Actually, Austin was being less than forthright with the authorities, and his first deceptive response led to another convention, which also lacked the official sanction of Tejanos. Austin thus inadvertently added to the growing distrust between colonists and Tejanos.

Austin later admitted in a private letter that he had been involved in the call for the convention. He had planned the convention, but he had expected to convene it personally at a later date. In a letter to Samuel M. Williams in 1834, he revealed how his plan had gone awry in his efforts to win the Bexareños over to the Anglo movement. He wrote that "although I had agreed to the calling of a convention before I went to Béxar, I did not expect it would have been done in my absence." Austin's biographer asserts that "the language of the call is probably his," but adds that it is difficult to prove that Austin actually arranged the convention because many of his letters are missing for the time in question. Nevertheless, much can be inferred from letters written by colonists in reply to Austin's missing letters. One letter from John A. Williams, for example, implied strongly that Austin had arranged the convention in deliberate contravention of directive and law. In biting satire, Williams quoted Austin's letter as saying, "Let the organization go on by the election of [militia] officers as ordered by the convention." Williams accusingly warned Austin that "short-sighted, aspiring ambitious politicians" would be responsible for any deaths or "civil war" resulting from the convention. Chiding Austin, he added, "Remember your excellent *Moto* [*sic*], *fidelity* to Mexico."[41]

In his impatience for action Austin had in effect preempted the Tejano authorities in approving the convention. Tejanos had declared for the Plan de Veracruz, but they withheld formal action until national liberals had actually overthrown Bustamante on December 9, 1832. Austin's action was even more revealing of his nerve in lobbying among Tejano communities while simultaneously planning a second convention for 1833 in the colonies. Here also his biographer asserts that "of the actual calling of the second convention we know very little." But another colonist's letter to Austin offers some compensation for the other missing letters. On December 8, Jonas Harrison replied to a letter from Austin regarding "another convention." Harrison closed with, "Your early notice to us, of this subject, is another evidence of the good feelings and kindness you hold."[42] Thus a convention had been held and a second one planned while Austin denied one and concealed the other.

Tejanos resolved to hold their own convention ten days after Santa Anna had actually deposed Bustamante—not before. In effect the Tejanos and the Anglos both committed themselves formally to declaring their rights. But in their commitment the people of Texas stood in separate camps. Although their object was common, their paths had begun to diverge.

On December 19, 1832, the leading citizens of Béxar met in a convention to draw up their *memoria* to the state congress. Present were forty Bexareños, including many younger men like Juan Nepomuceno Seguin, Ambrosio Rodriguez, and Balmaceda. One of the major grievances listed in the Béxar *memoria* was the constant intervention of the national government in the state colonization program. Specifically the Law of April 6, 1830, threatened to exclude useful "capitalists" from moving into Texas. It also threatened the promising trade with Santa Fe which was growing, thanks to the *"norte-americanos capitalistas."* Bexareños argued that "the complete sanction" of power in the colonization program should rest with the *vecinos* and ayuntamientos of Texas as the water laws allowed. Tejanos had a close "topographical" knowledge of their department. The national government had granted contracts in Decrees No. 184, 185, and 192 (Powers, Cameron, Vehlein, Burnet, and Zavala) which were detrimental to Tejano settlements.

Other grievances listed in the Béxar *memoria* included Decree No. 50, which they said "dissolved the social compact," and the expulsion of a Texas deputy from the state congress in accordance with the Plan de Jalapa. This insult alone, they said, "gave them another most justifiable cause to secede." The list included demands for bilingual administrators, more judges, militia salaries, and tax exemptions.[43]

Nacogdoches and Goliad also drew up *memorias* in January, 1833. Both of these approved of the Béxar positions, but the Goliad *memoria* is perhaps the most revealing of Tejano sentiments at the time. It began with a declaration of the social contract and ended with a threat of secession by the same sanction.

If the people who are ruled by despots are permitted the natural right of revolutionary measures against their oppression then those people, who by their own consent live under the divine republican system, have also had conceded to them by the political compact the right to petition as a primary measure which they may use toward remedying the evils which afflict them, whether those evils originate from the inertia of the laws, by the ignorance of the Legislators, or by the ineptitude of their governing officials.

In a classic Mexican phrase of protest, the Goliad leaders exhorted, *"Basta ya."* [Enough]

We have had enough of these legislators who insult through their very capriciousness the sacred charter such as those who passed the unconstitutional Decrees Numbers 50, 149, and 183; We want no more of legislators such as the one who disregarded the sacred rights of this community for no other reason than to protect the false pretensions of two colonization empresarios. Bring to an end this administration of justice so defective and so backward as this semi-Gothic one which we are practicing. In a word, let the laws be complied with, let's be republicans, let's be men, let's defend our rights, or let's not exist at all.

The *memoria* added statements supporting all of the arguments of the Béxar *memoria*. It protested the conflict with the Powers and DeWitt grants, citing the illegal aspects and activities of these colonies. It spoke of Don Esteban Austin as the only "true empresario." Citing the many times Goliad had submitted pleas for rectification of these evils, the *memoria* described the Tejano attitude toward the colonization program.

Ah, Sir! If this outrage had been committed against any other people, they would have seceded in an instant from such an unjust and impolitic government, but such has not been the conduct of Goliad, for she will always be obedient, but never again will she allow such odium on her social rights. And let it not be said that because of this, colonization is not desired, far from such an absurd idea, only an effort to correct the defects in the laws [is desired].

And in the peculiar admixture of sublime courtesy with deadly advertence which the Mexican demeanor seemed to possess, the Goliad leaders stated their position most respectfully.

Finally, Sir, these inhabitants confide in the goodness of Thy Honor, having heard the representation of the Illustrious Ayuntamiento . . . that the constitutional laws and the remedies which our grievances decry shall be dignified with a response; for their inattention will force Tejanos to the hard but necessary task of demanding of the Honorable Assembled Chambers of the union the compliance of the Second Article of Decree No 35 of the General Constituent Congress of the year 1824.[44]

The political chief, Ramón Músquiz, was even more upset to receive the Tejano *memorias* on the heels of the Anglo conventions. He referred the *memorias* to the governor, apologizing for his boisterous brethren. He attempted to cushion the effect of the strong threats by explaining that the Tejanos wrote them only to propitiate the revolutionary fervor among the colonists. But it was difficult to portray as anxious supplicants the steadfast men who invoked the social contract. And even as Músquiz offered his apology, a confident Juan N. Seguin stepped in as the new political chief of Texas, a harbinger of a new generation of Tejanos.

There were new leaders among the Anglo Texans as well. The membership of the second convention in 1833 revealed names like Sam Houston, William H. Wharton, and David G. Burnet, all in important positions. These are the men of whom Austin spoke when he said, "I wished the [second] convention to meet in Béxar, but at that time it was death to any man's popularity to speak in favor of the Mexicans." Austin also used descriptions of some of these men whom he called "demagogues, pettyfoggers, visionary speculators and schemers," or people who were constantly "damning those who are in office merely because they are in office."[45]

The identity of Austin's targets in the above epithets was not always obvious, but certain individuals did emerge as opponents to what Austin considered to be a reasonable course of action. Two of these men who led a school of thought among colonists were the Wharton brothers, William and John. William had felt very strongly that the Anglo Americans should have maintained a more adamant stance in the first convention of 1832. Both brothers published a newspaper in 1833 which, according to Eugene C. Barker, opposed "Austin's policy of forbearance and conciliation with Mexico."

Many other such new faces were arriving daily in the colonies after 1832. Few others, however, reveal so clearly the impact of the newer immigrants on politics as Sam Houston. Houston had first become intimately interested in Texas in 1822 when he invested in the Texas Association of Tennessee, which held an empresario contract later transferred to Sterling C. Robertson in a highly controversial incident. By 1832, Houston felt that "a change must soon take place in Texas" and in order to take advantage of that change, he said, "So I will pass that way and see my old friends."

Contemporary Mexican officials as well as later Mexican historians have felt that Houston represented "the aims of [Andrew] Jackson." Indeed, Barker affirms Houston's almost familial relationship with Jackson. Whether Houston was an agent of Anglo-American designs on Texas, he was an extremely influential individual. He had significant political access in Washington, D.C. and represented an important element of change in the Anglo attitude toward Tejanos and Texas.[46]

Meanwhile affairs in Mexico offered liberal Coahuiltejanos a brief respite from conservative pressures. In January, 1833, Santa Anna had succeeded in ushering Manuel Gómez Pedraza into the Mexican presidency, which Gómez Pedraza was to have held in the first place, having been elected in 1828. In April, Santa Anna became president with arch-liberal Valentín Gómez Farías as his vice-president. Santa Anna immediately handed the executive reigns to Gómez Farías in a move for which contemporaries and historians have offered only speculation of the president's motives. Santa Anna's motives notwithstanding, the Mexican executive under Gómez Farías unleashed a liberal tide in Mexico City which sent waves of political repercussions all the way to Coahuila y Texas.

When the Coahuila y Texas Congress met in February, 1833, the deputies from Monclova and Parras united as a majority bloc. From Parras were José María Viesca, Agustín Viesca, and Juan de Dios Delgado. From Monclova were Marcial Borrego, Dionisio Elizondo, and José María Uranga. These deputies secured control of the congress, and in response to *memorias* from Béxar, Parras, and Goliad, voted to move the state capital to Monclova.[47] The Monclova legislature then proceeded to enact a full slate of liberal reforms. In their efforts to compensate for lost time, however, the Viescas lost the confidence of their Texas allies.

The Monclova Congress began with a strong appeal to the Texas constituency. In March, they legalized popular petitions, and on April 2, they provided for preferential treatment to any discussion in the state congress concerning Texas. The Viesca brothers immediately arranged for the congress to petition the national government for the repeal of the Law of April 6, 1830, and in the same month, introduced a bill to allow foreigners in the retail trade. Both efforts passed by the end of the year.[48]

In January, 1834, Stephen F. Austin was arrested and imprisoned in Mexico City for imprudent remarks about the separation of Texas from Coahuila. The state and the national governments retained their salutary attitude toward colonization, however. Austin reported from Mexico that Santa Anna, who returned intermittently to the presidency, was "friendly to Texas and to me." In fact, Santa Anna recommended a few basic reforms in Coahuila y Texas—reforms which the Coahuila y Texas Congress added to their own efforts. On February 6, 1834, Marcial Borrego, president of the state congress, appointed a "committee of analysis" to draw up a "project of legislation" incorporating all of the desired reforms.[49]

The liberal legislation spree continued in Monclova. The liberal land law of March 26, 1834, which incorporated the aforementioned religious provision, was secured as part of the analysis. This law attracted the attention of all Mexico. An Anglo American, John Durst, was elected as the additional deputy from Texas (joining José Antonio Vásquez and Oliver Jones), and Thomas J. Chambers was appointed as *asesor general* for the state. Other liberal acts included the acceptance of English as a legal language of the state, the extension of empresario contracts, and the implementation of the jury system. With these new laws to digest, the congress closed its legislative session of April 30.[50] With its closing ended the normal, if uneasy, life of the state of Coahuila y Texas. Worsening conditions in Mexico City that summer made unlikely the continued existence of such a liberal state as Coahuila y Texas.

Santa Anna returned to reclaim the presidency in May after the liberal congress under Gómez Farías had thoroughly alienated the power of the Church and the established military. After closing the doors to the congress, the reestablished president then endorsed the Plan de Cuernavaca. This plan proclaimed him the "only authority" in the Mexican government, and nullified all of the liberal laws of Gómez Farías.

Santa Anna then held elections for a new congress composed of centralists. The centralist congress set about creating a centralist state of Mexico; reformed itself as a unicameral assembly; dissolved all state legislatures and state officials, making departments of the former states; and finally abrogated the Federal Constitution of 1824, replacing it with the centralist code of the Siete Leyes or Seven Laws of 1836.[51]

In Monclova, the permanent deputation of the state congress reaffirmed its stance against Mexican centralism. After a strong declaration against Santa Anna on June 24, 1834, the permanent deputation came under severe attack from centralist forces. The military and civilian centralists of Saltillo declared for Santa Anna, and against the claim of the Monclova congress as the legitimate government. At this time the Texas deputies, José Antonio Vásquez and Oliver Jones, wrote to Béxar recommending that the municipalities of Texas unilaterally convene in November to determine their own course of action. The convention failed to attract the delegates who by November had been disaffected by further disintegration in the state government.

In March and April, the new governor in Monclova, Agustín Viesca, passed two land laws strictly for political expediency. The laws, in effect, allowed him as governor to sell state lands for public defense. His intention was to defend the liberal congress from increasing threats of violence from the Saltillo forces. While a few Anglo Americans leaped at the opportunity for huge purchases, many more Anglo Americans were completely averse to the speculative aspects of such land sales. Thus, when centralist forces finally overthrew and arrested Governor Viesca, neither Tejanos nor Anglos responded to his call to arms.

Governor Viesca's call to arms in June, 1835, logically should have been the commencement of overt hostilities with the Mexican centralist government forces. Instead, Texas ignored him. In his call, Viesca attempted to alert the citizens to the presence of a real danger: "Citizens of Texas, arise in arms or sleep forever! Thy dearest interests, thy liberty, thy properties, what is more, thy very existence depends on the deceitful capriciousness of thy most malevolent enemies. Thy destruction is already resolved, and only thy firmness and thy special energy can save thee!"[52]

Viesca's efforts to use land laws to support the liberal cause failed in Texas, but such appeals had received lively response in other liberal states. In other parts of Mexico, liberal legislatures had employed similar measures to gain the adherence of capitalists in support of liberal reforms. Vito Alessio Robles, the Coahuilan historian, explains the trend succinctly: "Since that time [1834] there appears a willingness to obtain resources at all costs to sustain the crumbling vice presidency of Gómez Farías and the continued effect of his reform laws, even to the point of going beyond the law itself."[53]

By the end of the year, legislative conflict grew into open warfare against Santa Anna's conservative forces. In Zacatecas a citizens' army had answered their governor's call to arms, only to be crushed mercilessly by Santa Anna's army in May, 1835.[54] The Zacatecas defeat discouraged other liberal revolts. Texas finally arose in arms, but as in 1832, the people of Texas stood in separate camps. By October, the Anglo colonists began to resist militarily also. With the fall of the Alamo and Goliad to Santa Anna in 1836, they realized the deadly earnestness of Viesca's unheeded warning.

VIII
The Tejanos between Two Frontiers

If life had been difficult for Tejanos before the coming of the Anglo Americans, it was even more so after 1836. For years, Tejanos had defended their *frontera* against threats from the French, Anglos, and Indians. In 1836, Tejanos discovered that Mexican centralists presented just as much of a threat to Tejano security as did foreign enemies. They realized that the Texas *frontera* was not simply a frontier boundary or buffer zone, but a separate entity between two frontiers.

The Texas Revolution and the Mexican War brought years of turmoil for Texas and for Tejanos. The Tejanos, who could claim Texas in 1820, had lost that claim by 1836. Anglo-American people poured into Texas after the revolution, making the Tejanos a distinct minority in their native land. Tejanos remained in large enough numbers, however, to provide a degree of continuity of their Mexican culture in Texas. Those who had held their ground during the revolution and those who returned afterward continued the process of cultural transmission to the incoming order.

The most traumatic effects of the revolution were the initial wave of racial conflict and the resulting land exchange between Anglo and Tejano. At first, people fought for political principle, but soon political principle became racial polarization as well. Tejanos quickly were forced to choose sides. Those who did not voluntarily side with Mexico were either forced to do so, or were subjected to harassment. Juan N. Seguin, who had originally joined the Anglo revolutionaries, soon found himself a "foreigner in [his] native land." With a hundred other Bexareños, Seguin hid on his ranch which was robbed by Mexican troops one day and burned by Anglo troops on another. Fernando de León of Victoria, who had contributed generously

to the Texas forces, was arrested by a Mexican general in 1836 and again by
an Anglo commander in 1837—each time for conspiring with the enemy.
All the townspeople of Goliad were stripped of their arms, and their Tejano
leaders were physically abused by a Mexican general in 1835. When the
Texas army arrived there a year later, Anglo troops robbed and plundered
the homes, driving Tejano families out. Similar conditions prevailed at
Nacogdoches where Tejano families were continually robbed of their livestock, grain, and belongings. The military campaigns of the war brought a
"restive Texas Army, a force greatly augmented by volunteers" and too
often perpetrating "a piratical and predatory war."[1]

Many Tejanos such as Carlos de la Garza, Vicente Córdova, and eventually Juan N. Seguin turned against the militant Anglos. Hundreds of Tejano
families, however, scattered onto the ranches and eventually into Coahuila.
Most Nacogdoches Tejanos took their families to Louisiana. But at least
120 of them left their wives and children at home, and launched a short-
lived guerrilla war against the Anglo settlements. Goliad also had some
ranch-based Tejano guerrillas, but most of the families fled to Tamaulipas,
Nuevo León, and Louisiana, reportedly leaving Goliad in a "virtual state of
abandonment."[2] Across the state, Tejano emigrés lost lands to "fictitious
law suits," sheriffs' auctions, and dubious transfers of title. Manuel Sabriego,
for example, who had fled to Monterrey, lost his two-and-a-half-league
ranch to a ninety-six-dollar law suit. By 1845, forty of the forty-nine Goliad
Tejano ranches had gone into Anglo hands for a pittance of their value. And
fortunate were the former owners of these, for many received no recompense at all. In an official report, one Texas Army officer stated that one
particular band of Anglo-American gangsters had boasted of their plan to
"visit Carlos Rancho[,] burn it down[,] kill all the Mexicans belonging to
it[,] and as they said *make a clean turn* of every kind of cattle on the perarie
[*sic*]." As the 1840s progressed, Tejanos were either driven out, or their
movement was restricted in these counties. Anglos flooded in and took the
ranches, the livestock, and indeed the livelihood of the old Tejanos around
Béxar, Goliad, and Nacogdoches.[3]

Throughout the decade following the revolution, many Tejanos were
able to find some semblance of refuge in the southern part of Texas—the
part formerly claimed by Tamaulipas along the Río Grande. As mentioned
in an earlier chapter, the Río Grande frontier was just on the threshold of
an upward thrust in the 1830s from the Río Grande to the Nueces. This
region proved to be more stable for Tejanos because of its strong popula-

tion base and also because few Anglo Americans ventured south of the Nueces until many years after the revolutionary war. These people were not Tejanos until Texas claimed the Río Grande as a border after the war. In effect, many of them became Tejanos initially by annexation. Actually these were people of the same *frontera* culture group as the Bexareños and other Tejanos. Most significantly, however, they became citizens of Texas by virtue of land grants they received from the Republic of Texas.

The Texas land grants, as mentioned above, were very similar to the Coahuila y Texas or Tamaulipas grants on the same land just a few years earlier. The first class headright offered by the Republic of Texas, for example, involved little more than a change in language to the Río Grande ranchero who claimed a land grant under the new republic. He would still receive a league and one labor; he had to have remained in the country during 1836; he could not have aided the Mexican army in the revolution; and he had to defend the land against Indian incursion. As long as he had not previously received land from Spain or Mexico, the ranchero could obtain his land and his Texas citizenship by merely living on his ranch for one year. Thus did 450 ranchero families register in this region by March, 1837. By 1840, another 175 had, in the language of the land grant, "arrived in this republic" to defend the Río Grande frontier under the various other headright inducements of Texas.

Although the Río Grande region experienced a great influx of Mexicans as headright claimants, other areas of the republic attracted them as well (see table 12). The Béxar-Goliad region recorded the highest number, many of these being original Tejanos who qualified for the first class headrights. The important distinction in these two regions is that the Río Grande settlers not only claimed the headrights, but were able to hold and patent them as well. Only twenty-five percent of the Béxar-Goliad claimants patented their headrights while sixty-eight percent of the Río Grande claimants patented theirs.[4] Many of these immigrant Tejanos lost their claims to the Anglo "cowboys" who frequently raided along the San Antonio River and sometimes even south of the Nueces during these years. As one historian stated, "their only excuse was that those whom they robbed were Mexicans." Many Tejanos lost their patents due to ignorance of procedures or lack of documentation. But the substantial difference in patent rates between the regions indicates the more destructive effects of the raids in the northern region.[5] In any case, the rancheros held the frontier against marauding Anglos and Indians alike.

TABLE 12 Tejano Headrights Patented by Region and Year

Headrights	Béxar-Goliad			Nacogdoches			Rio Grande		
	Granted	Ptd.	% Ptd.	Granted	Ptd.	% Ptd.	Granted	Ptd.	% Ptd.
1st Class (to 1836)	556	103	19%	94	11	12%	448	296	66%
2nd Class (to 1837)	163	31	19%	8	3	38%	13	3	23%
3rd Class (to 1840)	302	109	36%	11	6	55%	148	117	79%
Bounty (Revolution)	95	30	32%	5	1	20%	6	4	67%
Donation	112	28	25%	0	0	0	8	1	13%
REGIONAL TOTALS	1,228	301	0	118	21	0	623	421	1

Headrights	Other Texas Counties			Class Totals		
	Granted	Ptd.	% Ptd.	Granted	Patented	Avg. % Ptd.
1st Class (to 1836)	183	29	16%	1,281	439	28%
2nd Class (to 1837)	44	4	9%	228	41	22%
3rd Class (to 1840)	22	0	0%	483	232	42%
Bounty (Revolution)	28	2	7%	134	37	31%
Donation	15	2	13%	135	31	13%
REGIONAL TOTALS	292	37	0	2,261	780	27%

SOURCE: GLO, *Abstract of Original Titles*

The campaigns of the Mexican War actually spurred the population growth of the Río Grande. The most immediate effects of General Taylor's occupation, for example, were to stimulate trade and introduce some semblance of order—albeit military—to the region. Even as the war raged in central Mexico, the modern towns of the Río Grande region were being born. From the old ranches eventually grew the new American towns of Corpus Christi, Eagle Pass, Brownsville, Edinburgh, and Río Grande City. The San Patricio land district of Texas was finally organized into several new counties. An American diocese was created, an official census was taken, and American city governments were organized with new government officials, including some old ranchero patriarchs. By 1848, the number of Tejanos was in an upward swing, led particularly by the robust ranch frontier of the Río Grande.[6]

The United States census of 1850 was the first and most revealing of Tejano demography during the period after the Texas revolution. It revealed, for example, that although only about fifteen hundred of the original Tejanos remained in the old Béxar-Goliad region, more than six hundred Mexican-born heads of household had entered the region since the revolution. Many of the old Adaesaños who had evacuated Nacogdoches during the revolutionary years had also returned by 1850. Although reduced in number to 171, they brought with them the old Adaesaño blood of the Chirino, Procela, Acosta, Chavana, and the Sánchez families to include a few children born in Louisiana during the intervening years. In Victoria, the De León and Benavides families returned from Louisiana by 1850 to join fifty other Tejano families living at "New La Bahía."[7] With the great thrust of the Río Grande ranch frontier, the three groups more than compensated for the numerical losses sustained in the revolution, and provided a racial and cultural holdover of the old Tejano frontier.

There are few enumerative data based exclusively on the Tejanos of the Río Grande region before 1850. But the vast majority of the "Mexican-born" persons tallied in the 1850 census were living in this region, and the enumeration almost necessarily included the Tejano headright families of the republic period. In fact, the Mexican-born heads of household in 1850 are strikingly similar to the Tejano headrights in number as well as in other characteristics. Sixty-six percent of all the Mexican-born heads of household in the 1850 census lived in the same Río Grande region—that is, the ranchero salient extending from the Río Grande to Nueces County. The census provides strong indications of the old ranching frontier. It is this

TABLE 13 Mexican-Born Heads of Household by Occupation by Region
Texas, 1850

Counties	Béxar-Goliad	Río Grande	Nacogdoches	Other
Laborer	248	1,038	1	27
Artisan	181	122	0	5
Professional/				
Mercantile	3	8	0	0
Other	278	497	7	31
TOTALS	710	1,665	8	63

NOTE: All figures include Mexican-born persons in Texas, according to the U.S. Census, 1850 *MS*, who qualified as heads of household.

region, for example, that reflects some of the greatest numbers of sheep, goats, and cattle in Texas. Most of the Mexican-born ranch workers listed as "laborers" were south of the Nueces. Very common in this region were households including a landowner with several such workers. It is possible, therefore, that the census taker may have misunderstood the Tejano term *labrador*, which actually denotes a landowner.

Further analysis reveals other interesting statistics on the Mexican-born in the 1850 census. The mean age, for example, was thirty-one years for males and twenty-seven years for females—considerably higher than those of their old Tejano counterparts. Families averaged about five persons including parents, although many households were much larger including the servants and workers. The occupational breakdown indicates that eighty percent of the heads of household were "laborers," sixteen percent were artisans, and less than five percent were mercantile and professional. Béxar had the highest number of artisans while the Río Grande counties had the most laborers (see table 13). The migration figures computed through the "child-ladder" method indicate substantial numbers of Mexican families flowing into the entire area northward to the San Antonio River throughout the 1840s.[8] Thus by 1850, the old Béxar-Goliad region was becoming unified at last with the Río Grande frontier into a cultural salient which stamped an indelible Mexican character throughout the south of Texas.

A seemingly inescapable conclusion in reading of the difficult experience of Tejanos is that Texas was simply too big for them. As mentioned earlier, the most memorable events in Texas history were caused at the national level—the National Colonization Law of 1823, the Law of April 6, 1830, Santa Anna's centralist plan, and ultimately a war between Mexico and the United States. National events notwithstanding, Tejanos first gave life to Texas. If Texas had countless herds of livestock for the taking, it was because Tejanos purposely propagated them. If Texas legal institutions were "munificent," as historians have said, it was because Tejanos offered generous and family-oriented land grants; because Tejanos devised a system for tapping the public domain for continuous educational finance; because Tejanos maintained a firm hold over their mineral and water rights for the people of the state; and because Tejanos offered inviting franchises to entrepreneurs. Texas to the settler in the 1820s and the 1830s was not simply land; it was land with a homestead protection and tax exemptions. These factors constituted an invitation to prosper on the land.

Austin has been seen by historians as the harbinger of a new race to Mexican Texas. He may also be seen as the usher of capitalism into Texas. Timing was an important factor for capitalism in the meeting of the Anglo-American frontier and the Mexican frontier in Texas. While the Mexicans were barely crawling out from years of oppression under a colonial government, the United States population and enterprise was burgeoning. The Anglo-American capitalists and cotton planters arrived just in time to benefit from the federalist experiment of the Viesca political faction in Coahuila y Texas.

In Texas the emigrants found franchises and land-grant programs not possible in the Unites States at that time. Even Austin once admitted that such concessions would not be fair or practical in a more established country. Yet, he and the Viescas worked hand in hand to erect a governmental system which would support capitalism in Texas. While the federal government in the Unites States continued to grow more secure in strength and dominance in national affairs, Mexican states like Coahuila y Texas were just beginning to solidify their bonds with their federal government. This time lag combined with liberal land policies to give Texas an added brilliance on the horizon for frustrated Anglo Americans. The fervent efforts to attract the Anglo-American capitalists caused an imbalance in the legislative programs of Tejanos and the Viescas. Their laws seemed always to offer property and the protections of property more than the protection of persons and personal freedom. In the slavery issues, for example, Tejano former slave owners were more inclined to see black people as an Anglo capitalist saw them—as property—than as people. Even the religious freedom which Tejanos finally allowed in Decree No. 272 of 1834 was granted only as an added clause to a land law. Perhaps their own strong sense of mission on the *frontera* made it easier for the Tejanos to undervalue the individual. Such attitudes gave the Tejanos a reputation for harshness and cruelty which made them easy targets for unjust criticism and attack after San Jacinto.

The distinctiveness of Tejano culture is in its combination of conflict and heritage. Conflict inhered in Tejano life on the *frontera*. From their first settlement on the Texas *frontera* to the postrevolutionary decades of unrest, Tejanos knew conflict in their daily lives. Defense had become a part of their unique culture. Their heritage was more than simply Mexican. It was a Mexican heritage which retained significant aspects of Indian and Spanish culture and developed under constant conditions of conflict.

The story of the Tejano culture is definitely not one of decline. The Tejano population dwindled in relation to the flood of Anglo Americans arriving in Texas, but the Tejanos and their families remained in the Texas Republic. In fact, the strongest surge that Tejano population experienced was between San Antonio and the Río Grande after 1836. More significantly, the Tejano culture has been adopted and spread by the Anglo Americans themselves. Because Texas was the first Mexican state settled by the Anglo-American tide, Texas probably had a greater influence initially on that westward-moving frontier. The use of words like lasso, corral, and mustang in distant western states like Wyoming and Montana indicate the extent to which the tools, techniques, and animals of the Tejanos have spread across the United States. With those tools and animals, of course, spread the laws for water, land, and resource management. Aspects of Tejano life have colored and benefited American life. The tremendous herds of Tejano cattle provided beef for a steak- and hamburger-eating nation in its dynamic industrialization phase. And Tejano laws laid much of the foundation for a prosperous Texan society. Indeed, the history of Texas can never be complete without the story of her original founders—the Tejanos.

Notes

Abbreviations Used in Notes

AGC   Coahuila. Archivo General del Estado de Coahuila. Saltillo, Coahuila.

AGI   Spain. Archivo General de las Indias (transcripts). Audencia de Guadalajara. Barker Texas History Center. University of Texas at Austin.

AGM   Mexico. Archivo General de la Nación. West Transcripts. Barker Texas History Center. University of Texas at Austin.

AGN   Mexico. Archivo General de la Nación. México, D.F., México.

BA   Texas. Béxar Archives. Barker Texas History Center. University of Texas at Austin.

BLAKE   Blake Transcripts. Barker Texas History Center. University of Texas at Austin.

GLO   Texas. General Land Office. Spanish Archives.

NA   Texas. Nacogdoches Archives. Texas State Library. Austin, Texas.

SFA   San Antonio. San Fernando Archives. San Fernando Cathedral. San Antonio, Texas.

Chapter 1. Tejano Settlements on the Frontera

1. Herbert Eugene Bolton, *Texas in the Middle Eighteenth Century: Studies in Spanish Colonial History and Administration,* pp. 4–8.

2. *AGI,* Guadalajara, Miguel Ramos Arispe to Commandant General, vol. 62, pp. 56, 58.

3. William Kennedy, *Texas: The Rise, Progress, and Prospects of the Republic of Texas,* p. 394.

4. *BA,* Victor Blanco to Juan Antonio Saucedo, Sept. 9, 1826.

5. *AGC,* Census and Statistical Report, Oct. 1, 1831, Legajo 25, Expediente 1051; *BA,* Governor Cordero to Prudencio de León, March 14, 1806; *BA,* Governor Cordero to Felipe R. de la Portilla, Dec. 16, 1807; *BA,* Representación, Dec. 19, 1832.

6. Frederick C. Chabot, *With the Makers of San Antonio: Genealogies of the Early Latin, Anglo-American, and German Families with Occasional Biographies, Each Group Being Prefaced with a Brief Historical Sketch and Illustrations,* pp. 40–42, 91–94, 144. A more recent study of presidial amalgamation is Gerald E. Poyo and Gilberto M. Hinojosa, eds., *Tejano Origins in Eighteenth-Century San Antonio,* pp. 3, 33.

7. *SFA*, Marriage Register, p. 50; D. B. Adams, "The Tlascalan Colonies of Northern Coahuila," p. 269; *BA*, Census of "Pueblo de San Antonio Balero [*sic*]," Dec. 31, 1806.

8. Examples of such unqualified allusions to the Mexican *mestizaje* can be seen in Walter Prescott Webb, *The Texas Rangers: A Century of Frontier Defense*, p. 10, in which he compares the "self-willed and cocksure group of Americans with the vague desires of a conglomerate Latin-Indian population," and Alicia V. Tjarks, "Comparative Demographic Analysis of Texas, 1777–1793," p. 294. More specific descriptions appear in Harold Driver, *Indians of North America*, and W. W. Newcomb, Jr., *The Indians of Texas, from Prehistoric to Modern Times*.

9. *AGI*, Guadalajara, Petition, 1698, vol. 17, p. 205; Alejandro Prieto, *Historia, geografía, y estadística del estado de Tamaulipas*, pp. 141, 179; Bolton, *Texas in the Middle Eighteenth Century*, p. 345; Adams, "Tlascalan Colonies," pp. 100, 140.

10. J. M. Rodriguez, *Rodriguez Memoirs of Early Texas*, p. 38.

11. *GLO, Spanish Archives*, vol. 31, p. 22; *SFA*, Marriage Register, 1798–1823; Richard Santos, "A Preliminary Survey of the San Fernando Archives," p. 155; *BA*, Béxar Presidio Report, Sept. 30, 1805.

12. *NA*, Béxar Census, June 30, 1833; José María Sánchez, "A Trip to Texas in 1828," pp. 257–59; Rodriguez, *Rodriguez Memoirs*, p. 45; *BA*, Béxar Census, Jan. 1, 1820.

13. *AGC*, Census and Statistical Report, June 1, 1828, "Notas."

14. Nuestra Señora del Refugio de la Bahía Mission (Refugio, Texas), "Record Book," vol. 2; A. B. J. Hammett, *The Empresario Don Martín de Leon*, pp. 17, 22; Hobart Huson, *Refugio: A Comprehensive History of Refugio County from Aboriginal Times to 1955*, vol. 1, p. 82; Harbert Davenport, "The Men of Goliad," pp. 11–13. For Rafael Antonio Manchola, see Coahuila y Texas, "Actas del congreso constitucional del estado libre de Coahuila y Texas," 1828–30 (typescript) at University of Texas. Kathryn Stoner O'Connor, *The Presidio La Bahía del Espíritu Santo de Zuñiga, 1721 to 1846*, p. 96; Pat Nixon, *Medical Story of Early Texas, 1528–1853*, p. 130.

15. *BA*, Pudientes of Béxar, Dec. 31, 1808; *BA*, Indian War Casualties, Feb. 1, 1820; *BA*, Béxar Census, Dec. 31, 1820; Mattie Austin Hatcher, "Texas in 1820: Report of the Barbarous Indians of the Province of Texas, by Juan Antonio Padilla, Made December 27, 1819 . . .," p. 61; Henderson K. Yoakum, *History of Texas from Its First Settlement in 1685 to Its Annexation to the United States in 1846*, vol. 1, p. 176; O'Connor, *Presidio La Bahía*, pp. 97, 257; Chabot, *With the Makers of San Antonio*, p. 168. For the best account of ranch population just prior to 1821, see Jack Jackson, *Los Mesteños: Spanish Ranching in Texas, 1721–1821*, appendix.

16. *AGC*, Legajos 20–28, 1828 to 1833; *GLO, Maps of All Texas Counties*; *GLO, Spanish Archives*, vol. 31, p. 22; Sánchez, "Trip to Texas in 1828," p. 260; Kennedy, *Texas: The Rise, Progress, and Prospects*, pp. 395, 396, 404; Huson, *Refugio: A Comprehensive History*, vol. 1, pp. 160, 161.

17. *BA*, Census, Dec. 31, 1790; Isaac Cox, "The Louisiana-Texas Frontier," pp. 27–30; Tjarks, "Demographic Analysis," p. 338; Bolton, *Texas in the Middle Eighteenth Century*, pp. 109–33, 432–46.

18. George P. Garrison, *Texas: A Contest of Civilizations*, pp. 118–24.

19. Lester G. Bugbee, "The Texas Frontier, 1820–1845," pp. 111, 112; Juan N. Almonte, *Nota Estadística Sobre Tejas*, p. 72; Winnie Allen, "History of Nacogdoches, 1691–1830," pp. 48–68.

20. Eugene C. Barker, *The Life of Stephen F. Austin Founder of Texas, 1793–1836*, p. 345; *BA*, Ranches, Mar. 7, 1806; *BA*, Representación, Dec. 19, 1832; *BLAKE*, vol. 19, p. 149, and Census, Apr. 30, 1835; Bolton, *Texas in the Middle Eighteenth Century*, pp. 109–33, 432–46.

21. *BA*, Béxar Census, Jan. 1, 1820; *BLAKE*, vol. 19, pp. 108–66, Nacogdoches Census, June 30,

1834, and vol. 18, p. 260, Nacogdoches Census, Jan. 1, 1806; Tjarks, "Demographic Analysis," p. 326; Yoakum, *History of Texas*, vol. 2, p. 245.

22. Leroy P. Graf, "Colonization Projects in Texas South of the Nueces, 1820–1845," p. 437; J. B. Wilkinson, *Laredo and the Río Grande Frontier*, pp. 99, 109; Kennedy, *Texas: The Rise, Progress, and Prospects*, pp. 391, 410; *AGC*, Leg. 15, Exped. 756; Military Report, 1815, Carlos E. Castañeda Collection, Barker Texas History Center, University of Texas at Austin, vol. 5, p. 96; *GLO, Spanish Archives*, James R. Miller and W. H. Bourland, "Report of James R. Miller and W. H. Bourland, Commissioners to Investigate Land Titles West of the Nueces" (*MS*, 1854). applications of Joaquin Galán (San Pat. 1–554) and Antonio Guerra (Bex. 1–1781).

23. An example of the validity of the ranchero claims is the claim entitled "El Potrero" in *GLO*, Miller and Bourland, "Land Titles West of the Nueces," pp. 47, 48 in which the descendants of the original grantee claimed to have brought "numerous heads of stock, many tenants and servants [and] to occupy and hold absolute possession of said tract never having abandoned it at any time on account of Indian incursions, down to the approach of the U.S. Army in 1846." *AGN*, Decreto No. 47, Nov. 18, 1830, vol. 314, p. 55; Jovita González, "Social Life in Cameron, Starr, and Zapata Counties," p. 38; J. Lee Stambaugh and Lillian J. Stambaugh, *The Lower Rio Grande Valley of Texas*, p. 96; Paul S. Taylor, "Historical Note on Dimmit County, Texas," p. 82; Gilberto Miguel Hinojosa, *A Borderlands Town in Transition: Laredo, 1755–1870;* Florence Johnson Scott, *Historical Heritage of the Lower Rio Grande.*

24. H. P. N. Gammel, comp., *The Laws of Texas, 1822–1897*, vol. 1, p. 100; Yoakum, *History of Texas*, vol. 1, p. 254.

Chapter 2. *Governing the Towns of the* Frontera

1. Real Academia Española, *Diccionario de la Lengua Española* (Madrid: Real Academia Española, 1956), p. 639.
2. C. H. Haring, *The Spanish Empire in America*, p. 159.
3. Wilkinson, *Laredo*, p. 145.
4. Mattie Austin Hatcher, "Municipal Government of San Fernando de Béxar, 1730–1800," p. 299.
5. Hatcher, "Municipal Government of Béxar," p. 299; Colin M. MacLachlan, *Criminal Justice in Eighteenth Century Mexico: A Study of the Tribunal of the Acordada*, p. 3.
6. Haring, *Spanish Empire in America*, p. 162; O. Garfield Jones, "Local Government in the Spanish Colonies as Provided by the Recopilación de Leyes de los Reinos de las Indias," pp. 67–70.
7. Hatcher, "Municipal Government of Béxar," pp. 295, 298; Jones, "Local Government in the Spanish Colonies," p. 65.
8. Adams, "Tlascalan Colonies," pp. 241–96; MacLachlan, *Tribunal of the Acordada*, p. 15.
9. Tamaulipas, "Gobernación: Decreto Número 73," Nov. 13, 1828; Kathleen DeCamara, *Laredo on the Rio Grande*, p. 14; Wilkinson, *Laredo*, pp. 40, 64.
10. *BA*, Election Returns, Dec. 23, 1827; *AGC*, Leg. 15, Exped. 756 (1924), *passim; GLO*, Miller and Bourland, "Land Titles West of the Nueces," Webb County; *BA*, Nicasio Sánchez to Antonio Elozúa, Apr. 23, 1826; Antonio Elozúa to Alcalde, May 31, 1826; John P. Kimball, comp., *Laws and Decrees of the State of Coahuila and Texas*, p. 154.
11. Cox, "Louisiana-Texas Frontier," pp., 32, 33; Barker, *Life of Stephen F. Austin*, pp. 149, 150, 157; *BA*, Nacogdoches Citizens to José Antonio Saucedo, Jan. 16, 1824.
12. Leonard Cardenas, Jr., "The Municipality in Northern Mexico," p. 9; Nettie Lee Benson,

La diputación provincial y el federalismo Mexicano, p. 82. The Béxar Ayuntamiento did not immediately implement the changes of the Spanish Constitution of 1812 as seen in Nettie Lee Benson, ed., *Mexico and the Spanish Cortes, 1810–1822: Eight Essays*, p. 61, but did so later as seen in *BA*, Minutes of the Béxar Ayuntamiento, Aug. 24, 1820; José Ramirez to Antonio Martinez, Aug. 30, 1820; and La Bahía Ayuntamiento to Béxar Junta Gubernativa, Apr. 23, 1823.

13. *BA*, Luciano García to Béxar Ayuntamiento, Sept. 25, 1823; Kimball, *Laws of Coahuila and Texas*, p. 154; Coahuila y Texas, "Actas del congreso," Dec. 14, 1824.

14. *BA*, Béxar Ayuntamiento Special Committee, Report, Nov. 18, 1829; Kimball, *Laws of Coahuila and Texas*, Article 156, p. 444, Decree No. 33, pp. 166–68, and Decree No. 262, pp. 347–49.

15. *BA*, Nacogdoches Ayuntamiento, Minutes, June 24, 1827; Nacogdoches Ayuntamiento, Announcement of Installation, June 29, 1827; Coahuila y Texas, "Actas del congreso," Jan. 29, 1829; Cosme Garza García, *Prontuario de leyes y decretos del estado de Coahuila de Zaragoza*, p. 37.

16. Coahuila y Texas, Reglamento para el gobierno ecónomico político del estado libre de Coahuila y Texas, Article 150; *BA*, Regulations (Guidelines) for Ayuntamientos, Dec. 20, 1827.

17. *BA*, L. Duboys to Ramón Músquiz, Jan. 8, 1828; José María Viesca to Ramón Músquiz, May 21, 1828; José María Viesca to Ramón Músquiz, Aug. 6, 1828; Ramón Músquiz to Nacogdoches Ayuntamiento, May 6, 1831.

18. For the best overall description of municipality establishment, see Gilbert R. Cruz, *Let There Be Towns: Spanish Municipal Origins in the American Southwest, 1610–1810*, pp. 6, 68. Coahuila y Texas, Ordnanzas [sic] municipales para el gobierno y manejo interior del ayuntamiento de la ciudad de San Antonio de Béjar; Coahuila y Texas, Ordenanzas municipales para el gobierno y manejo interior del ayuntamiento de la villa de Goliad; Ethel Zivley Rather, "DeWitt's Colony," p. 121; Wilkinson, *Laredo*, p. 38.

19. Kimball, *Laws of Coahuila and Texas*, p. 21; John Sayles and Henry Sayles, *Early Laws of Texas*, vol. 1, p. 73; Rupert Norval Richardson, Ernest Wallace, and Adrian N. Anderson, *Texas: The Lone Star State*, p. 61.

20. San Felipe de Austin, Miscellaneous Papers, Barker Texas History Center, University of Texas.

21. Earl S. Pomeroy, *The Territories and the United States, 1861–1890: Studies in Colonial Administration*, p. 94; Gordon M. Bakken, "The English Common Law in the Rocky Mountain West," p. 110.

22. Kimball, *Laws of Coahuila and Texas*, Constitution of Coahuila y Texas, Section II, "Municipal Electoral Assemblies," Articles 48, 49, and 50, and Section VII, Article 164; Constitution of Coahuila y Texas, Article 47; Coahuila y Texas Constituent Congress, Decree No. 31, Article 17, and Decree No. 24, Article 5.

23. Kimball, *Laws of Coahuila and Texas*, Constitution of Coahuila y Texas, Articles 51–61, 160–62, and 167; Hatcher, "Municipal Government of Béxar," p. 323; *BA*, La Bahía Ayuntamiento, Election Report, 1826.

24. *BA*, Béxar Ayuntamiento to provincial deputation, Oct. 20, 1823; Béxar Municipal Regulations, Mar. 20, 1825; Coahuila y Texas, *Ordenanzas municipales de Goliad*.

25. Regular reports include *BA*, Gaspar Flores to Ramón Músquiz, Aug. 3, 1829; José Guadalupe de los Santos to Ramón Músquiz, Aug. 1, 1828; La Bahía Ayuntamiento, Report, June 30, 1830; special reports include *BA*, Béxar Municipal Ordinance, June 14, 1829, and Anastacio Bustamante to Antonio Elozúa, Nov. 4, 1827.

26. *Nueva Recopilación de las leyes de España*, Tomo II, Libro 8; Coahuila y Texas, *Reglamento*,

Articles 109–23; *BA, Sumaria, Francisco Balboa,* Apr. 12, 1827; Juan Martín de Veramendi, Jail Inspection Report, June 30, 1828; Juan Martín de Veramendi, List of Vagabonds, 1828; José Guadalupe de los Santos to Ramón Músquiz, List of Vagabonds, July 4, 1828.

27. *BA,* José Guadalupe de los Santos to Juan Martín de Veramendi, Sept. 11, 1828; Francisco Ruiz to Gaspar Flores, Oct. 18, 1824; Coahuila y Texas, "Actas del congreso," Feb. 21, 1831.

28. Coahuila y Texas, *Reglamento, 1827,* Articles 115 and 145; Coahuila y Texas, *Ordnanzas Municipales de Béjar,* "Salubridad Publica," and "Seguridad Publica."

29. Eugene C. Barker, "The Government of Austin's Colony 1821–1831," p. 246.

30. For the comisario and syndico, see Coahuila y Texas, *Reglamento, 1827,* chapter 7; Coahuila y Texas, *Ordnanzas Municipales de Béjar,* Article 34; Coahuila y Texas, *Ordenanzas municipales de Goliad,* Article 36. For the syndico procurador, see *BA,* Béxar Municipal Regulations, Mar. 20, 1825, Articles 2 and 11.

31. Wilkinson, *Laredo,* pp. 109, 117, 126; Haring, *Spanish Empire in America,* p. 168; *BA, Sumaria, Juan Bordes,* Oct. 30, 1824; José Nicolás Páez y Colomo to Béxar Alcalde, May 8, 1826.

32. Coahuila y Texas, *Reglamento, 1827,* Article 146; Coahuila y Texas Decree No. 39, Section I, see C. R. Wharton, "The Jurisdiction of the Alcalde Courts in Texas prior to the Revolution"; *Novísima Recopilación de las leyes de España,* Tomo V, Libro 11, Título XX, Ley viii; *BA,* Libro de juicios conciliarios, 1825–1828; Wharton, "Alcalde Courts in Texas," p. 31; *BLAKE,* vol. II, Judgment by Arbitration, Aug. 30, 1826.

33. Coahuila y Texas, *Arancel de los derechos que deben percibir los escribanos públicos, alcaldes constitucionales, secretario del tribunal de justicia, receptor, abogados, asesores, procurador, apoderados, alcaides, y alguaciles, del estado de Coahuila y Texas; BA, Sumaria, Juan Bordes,* Oct. 30, 1824.

34. Kimball, *Laws of Coahuila and Texas,* Decree No. 262, pp. 347–49; Constitution of Coahuila y Texas, Article 192; *NA,* Goliad Ayuntamiento to Coahuila y Texas Congress, Jan. 15, 1833; *BA, Sumaria, Agustín Valdés,* Jan. 8, 1827.

35. *BA,* José Salvador Díaz, Memorial, Sept. 18, 1825.

36. William Chambers, *Old Bullion Benton, Senator from the New West: Thomas Hart Benton, 1782–1858,* p. 28; Barker, "Government of Austin's Colony," p. 252.

37. Barker, "Government of Austin's Colony," p. 229; Barker, *Life of Stephen F. Austin,* p. 189; Dudley G. Wooten, ed., *A Comprehensive History of Texas, 1685 to 1897,* vol. 1, pp. 483, 486; Vito Alessio Robles, *Coahuila y Texas desde la consumación de la independencia hasta el Tratado de Paz de Guadalupe Hidalgo,* vol. 1, p. 170; Wharton, "Alcalde Courts in Texas," p. 3; Wooten, *Comprehensive History of Texas,* vol. 1, p. 486; Coahuila y Texas, "Actas del Congreso," Feb. 3, 1834.

38. Coahuila y Texas, "Actas del congreso," Mar. 24, 1834; Barker, *Life of Stephen F. Austin,* p. 396; Cardenas, "Municipality in Northern Mexico," p. 10; Seymour V. Connor, "The Evolution of County Government in the Republic of Texas," p. 163.

39. Connor, "Evolution of County Government," pp. 163, 169, 180; Gerald Ashford, "Jacksonian Liberalism and Spanish Law in Early Texas," p. 25. For an explanation of how these lands were later "liberated" from Tejano hands, see David Montejano, *Anglos and Mexicans in the Making of Texas, 1836–1986,* p. 21.

40. Wharton, "Alcalde Courts in Texas," pp. 17–19.

41. Hinojosa, *Borderlands Town in Transition,* p. 58; Wilkinson, *Laredo,* pp. 210, 218.

Chapter 3. The Tejano Community

1. None of the Texas missions had a total population of over one hundred by the close of the eighteenth century, according to the figures in *BA,* Texas Mission Census, Dec. 31, 1804.

Although few Spaniards lived in the missions, they often outnumbered the Indian neophyte population, as seen in Missions Espada and San Juan above. For the fusion of *calpulli* and barrio, see MacLachlan, *Tribunal of the Acordada*, p. 15.

2. *BA*, Béxar Municipal Regulations, Mar. 20, 1825; Coahuila y Texas, *Ordenanzas municipales de Goliad*, Article 39.

3. Wooten, *Comprehensive History of Texas*, p. 597; Barker, *Life of Stephen F. Austin*, p. 89.

4. San Felipe de Austin, Misc. Papers, U.T.; Bette E. Dobkins, *The Spanish Element in Texas Water Law*, p. 97.

5. *BA*, Gaspar Flores, "Address to the People of the Province of Texas," Dec. 5, 1824; Francisco Javier Bustillo, Receipts, Dec., 13, 1824; Gaspar Flores, Receipt, Dec. 22, 1824; List of National Holidays, June 16, 1824; Eugenio Flores to Junta Patriotica, June 24, 1828; Junta Patriotica, Proceedings, Sept. 12, 1829; José Antonio Saucedo to Juan Martín Veramendi, Sept. 24, 1825; Kennedy, *Texas: The Rise, Progress, and Prospects*, p. 397.

6. Nixon, *Medical Story of Early Texas*, p. 132; *BA*, Junta Patriotica, Proceedings, Sept. 12, 1829; José Antonio Saucedo to Juan Martín de Veramendi, Sept. 24, 1825; Citizens Meeting on Smallpox, Jan. 22, 1831; Ramón Músquiz, Instructions, Jan. 23, 1831.

7. *BA*, Ramón Músquiz to Syndico of Goliad, July 2, 1824; Wilkinson, *Laredo*, p. 125; J. Villasaña Haggard, "Epidemic Cholera in Texas, 1833—1834," p. 230; Charles Ramsdell, Jr., "Spanish Goliad," *MSS*, Barker Texas History Center Archives, University of Texas; Nixon, *Medical Story of Early Texas*, pp. 138–39.

8. Dobkins, *Spanish Element in Texas Water Law*, p. 122; Rafael Aguáyo Spencer, comp., *Obras de D. Lucas Alamán: Documentos Diversos*, vol. 4, p. 197.

9. *BA*, Béxar Tabla Estadística, Aug. 19, 1826; Dobkins, *Spanish Element in Texas Water Law*, pp. 86, 129; *GLO, Maps of All Texas Counties*.

10. *Nueva Recopilación*, 1772, Tomo II, Libro V, Título III, Ley xix; Wells A. Hutchins, "The Community Acequia: Its Origins and Development," p. 265.

11. Edwin P. Arneson, "Early Irrigation in Texas," pp. 121, 127, 129; *BA*, Juan Nepomuceno Seguin to Erasmo Seguin, Sept. 6, 1824.

12. Gammel, *Laws of Texas*, vol. 1, p. 299.

13. *BA*, Béxar Ayuntamiento to José Antonio Saucedo, Jan. 20, 1826; Béxar Municipal Regulations, Mar. 20, 1825; Coahuila y Texas, *Ordenanzas municipales de Béjar*, Articles 21, 34, 38–40, and 52; Coahuila y Texas, *Reglamento*, 1827, Articles 137–39; Arneson, "Early Irrigation in Texas," pp. 128–29.

14. *GLO, Abstract of All Original Texas Land Titles Comprising Grants and Locations to August 31, 1942*, vol. 4, Béxar County, *passim*; Roger N. Conger, "The Tomas de la Vega Eleven League Grant on the Brazos," pp. 370–82; Dobkins, *Spanish Element in Texas Water Law*, p. 128; Arneson, "Early Irrigation in Texas," pp. 128–29.

15. Wells A. Hutchins, *The Texas Law of Water Rights*, pp. 50–51; Gammel, *Laws of Texas*, vol. 3, pp. 958–59; Dobkins, *Spanish Element in Texas Water Law*, pp. 137–39. See also San Antonio, "Minutes of the City Council of the City of San Antonio [Béxar], 1815–1835" (transcript), pp. 502, 504–508.

16. Hutchins, *Texas Laws of Water Rights*, pp. 108–109, 130, 376; Dobkins, *Spanish Element in Texas Water Law*, pp. 28, 28n, 29.

17. Dobkins, *Spanish Element in Texas Water Law*, pp. 18, 22; Hutchins, *Texas Laws of Water Rights*, p. 107; Hutchins, "Community Acequia," p. 263.

18. Gammel, *Laws of Texas*, vol. 1, p. 451; I. J. Cox, "Education Effort in San Fernando de Bexar," p. 54; Coahuila y Texas, *Ordnanzas municipales de Béjar; Ordenanzas municipales de Goliad; Reglamento, 1827.*

19. Coahuila y Texas, *Reglamento, 1827*, Article 131; *BA*, Béxar Ayuntamiento to José Antonio

Saucedo, Apr. 14, 11825; Alejandro Treviño to Juan Martín de Veramendi, Dec. 31, 1828; Coahuila y Texas, 1826, *Nota estadística remitida por el gobierno supremo del Estado de Coahuila y Tejas a la cámara de senadores del soberano congreso general con arreglo al artículo 161 número 8° de la Constitución Federal de los Estados Unidos Mexicanos,* p. 7.

20. BA, List of Contributors, Jan. 12, 1828; Junta Piadosa, Minutes, Jan. 16, 1831; List of Contributors, Aug. 1, 1831; Cox, "Education in San Fernando," p. 42; Max Berger, "Education in Texas during the Spanish and Mexican Periods," p. 43.

21. BA, Refugio de la Garza, Report, July 28, 1831; Béxar Ayuntamiento Account Book, Jan. 2, 1826; Cox, "Education in San Fernando," pp. 45–49.

22. For Goliad, see BA, Nemesio Salcedo to Governor of Texas, Feb. 11, 1805, and Berger, "Education in Texas during the Spanish and Mexican Periods," p. 43. For Nacogdoches, see BA, José María Mora to Ramón Músquiz, July 21, 1828 and Ramón Músquiz to Goliad Ayuntamiento, June 13, 1831. For Laredo, see Wilkinson, *Laredo,* pp. 114–15. For enrollment statistics, see Almonte, *Nota estadística sobre Texas,* p. 40; William R. Hogan, *The Texas Republic: A Social and Economic History,* p. 137.

23. Cox, "Education in San Fernando," p. 54; BA, Refugio de la Garza, Report, July 28, 1831; Béxar Ayuntamiento to Ramón Músquiz, Aug. 29, 1838; AGN, Secretría de Gobernación, Legajo 37, Expediente 1; Coahuila y Texas, "Actas del congreso," Apr. 6, 1832 [Nacogdoches bill], Apr. 15, 1826, May 20, 1826, and June 6, 1826.

24. For the proceedings of the San Felipe Convention on October 5, 1832, see Gammel, *Laws of Texas,* vol. 1, p. 493. Max Berger claims in his article "Education in Texas during the Spanish and Mexican Periods" that the Anglo Americans in Texas were the first to demand state land grants for education at the San Felipe Convention of 1832. He says, "Shortly thereafter the Mexican residents of Béxar added their protests to those of the American settlers," and refers to a Bexareño memorial dated December, 1832.

25. AGN, Secretría de Gobernación, Legajo 37, Expediente 13; Kimball, *Laws of Coahuila and Texas,* pp. 333, 336; Cox, "Education in San Fernando," p. 54; Gammel, *Laws of Texas,* vol. 1, p. 325.

26. Frederick Eby, comp., *Education in Texas: Source Materials,* pp. 88–92; Wooten, *Comprehensive History of Texas,* vol. 1, p. 809.

27. William H. Wharton was intimately involved with the statement on education of the San Felipe Convention in 1832, as see in Barker, *Life of Stephen F. Austin,* p. 350. His brother, John A. Wharton, was on the Committee on Education which drew up the bill in 1839, according to Herbert Pickens Gambrell, *Mirabeau Buonaparte Lamar: Troubadour and Crusader,* p. 231.

28. Berger, "Education in Texas during the Spanish and Mexican Periods," p. 49; Hogan, *Texas Republic,* p. 136; Eby, *Education in Texas,* pp. 88–92.

29. Jovita González, "Social Life in Cameron, Starr, and Zapata Counties," p. 76; Cox, "Education in San Fernando," pp. 45–49; Berger, "Education in Texas during the Spanish and Mexican Periods," p. 31. For later development of private Hispanic schools, see Guadalupe San Miguel, Jr., *"Let All of them Take Heed": Mexican Americans and the Campaign for Educational Equality in Texas, 1910–1981,* pp. 9, 10.

30. Eby, *Education in Texas,* p. 84.

Chapter 4. Tejano Justice on the Frontera

1. William H. Dusenberry, *The Mexican Mesta: The Administration of Ranching in Colonial Mexico,* p. 38; Wilkinson, *Laredo,* p. 17; Ramsdell, "Spanish Goliad"; Robert H. Thonhoff, "The First Ranch in Texas," p. 1; Odie B. Faulk, "Ranching in Spanish Texas," p. 257.

2. *BA*, Béxar Statistical Report, Aug. 19, 1826; Charles Gibson, *Spain in America*, p. 193; Haring, *Spanish Empire in America*, p. 159.
3. Sandra L. Myers, *The Ranch in Spanish Texas, 1691–1800*, p. 21; Dobkins, *Spanish Element in Texas Water Law*, p. 114.
4. Juan Agustín Morfi, *Viaje de Indios y diario del Nuevo México con una introducción bibliográfica y anotaciones por Vito Alessio Robles*, p. 211; Kennedy, *Texas: The Rise, Progress, and Prospects*, p. 172.
5. Francisco J. Santamaría, *Diccionario de Mejicanismos*, p. 719; Dusenberry, *The Mexican Mesta*, p. 59; Myers, *The Ranch in Spanish Texas*, p. 26.
6. *AGI*, Guadalajara, Miguel Ramos Arizpe to Commandant General, vol. 62, p. 27; Guadalajara, Report of Bishop of Nuevo Leon, vol. 61, p. 154; Almonte, *Nota estadística sobre Tejas*, p. 31.
7. *AGM*, Mexico, Archivo General de la Nación (West Transcripts), vol. 315, p. 126. The papers of Stephen F. Austin were published in three volumes, edited by Eugene C. Barker, and are hereinafter referred to as Barker, *The Austin Papers* (although the three volumes have different publishers—see bibliography). For the citation on the word "mestango," see Barker, *The Austin Papers*, vol. 2, p. 902.
8. *BA*, José Antonio Saucedo to Béxar Ayuntamiento, Dec. 6, 1825; Faulk, "Ranching in Spanish Texas," pp. 263–65; Kennedy, *Texas: The Rise, Progress, and Prospects*, pp. 120–21.
9. For *arbitrios*, see *BA*, Béxar Ayuntamiento, 1824, *passim*. For taxes, see *Nueva Recopilación*, Tomo 2, Libro 6, Título 13, Ley 2; Wilkinson, *Laredo*, p. 76; Myers, *The Ranch in Spanish Texas*, pp. 37–38.
10. *BA*, Béxar Ayuntamiento to Provincial Deputation, Oct. 20, 1823; Coahuila y Texas, "Actas del congreso," Aug. 8, 1827; Kimball, *Laws of Coahuila and Texas*, pp. 178–79.
11. *BA*, *Sumaria vs. Juan Bordes*, Oct. 30, 1824; Ramón Músquiz to Béxar Ayuntamiento, July 22, 1828; Virginia H. Taylor, ed. and trans., *The Letters of Antonio Martínez: Last Spanish Governor of Texas, 1817–1822*, p. 274.
12. William H. Dusenberry, "The Regulation of Meat Supply in Sixteenth-Century Mexico City," pp. 38, 41–42; Myers, *The Ranch in Spanish Texas*, pp. 34, 36; Wilkinson, *Laredo*, p. 67. For *mercader*, see Kimball, *Laws of Coahuila and Texas*, pp. 178–79, 291, 334; San Antonio, "Minutes of the City Council, 1815–1835," p. 524; *BA*, Juan Martín de Veramendi to Antonio Elozúa, Apr. 24, 1828; Béxar Ayuntamiento Special Committee Report, Nov. 18, 1829; Francisco Flores to Ramón Músquiz, Oct. 30, 1830.
13. *BA*, *Sumaria vs. Juan Bordes*, Oct. 30, 1824; see livestock censuses for Béxar, Nacogdoches, and Goliad in *NA*, 1833, *passim*.
14. *Nueva Recopilación*, Tomo 2, Libro 6, Título 17, Ley 1; *Novisima Recopilación*, Tomo 3, Libro 6, Título 15, Ley 1; Wooten, *Comprehensive History of Texas*, vol. 1, p. 598; Lewis Birdsall Harris, "Journey of Lewis Birdsall Harris, 1836–1842," p. 141.
15. Abbe Emmanuel Henri Dieudonné Domenech, *Missionary Adventures in Texas and Mexico*, p. 255; Wilkinson, *Laredo*, pp. 70, 180, 215; Kennedy, *Texas: The Rise, Progress, and Prospects*, pp. 120–21; Ramsdell, "Spanish Goliad"; Myers, *The Ranch in Spanish Texas*, p. 30.
16. Walter P. Webb, *The Great Plains*, p. 210; Terry G. Jordan, "The Origin of Anglo-American Cattle Ranching in Texas; A Documentation of Diffusion from the Lower South," p. 81; C. C. Cox and D. Harris, "Reminiscences of C. C. Cox," p. 208.
17. William A. McClintock, "Journal of a Trip through Texas and Northern Mexico in 1846–1847," p. 241; Wooten, *Comprehensive History of Texas*, vol. 1, p. 595.
18. U.S. Bureau of the Census, *The Seventh Census of the United States: 1850*, p. 513; in the original documents, U.S. Census, 1850 *MS*, see occupations listed as "cartman" in Béxar County, *passim.*; Lewis Birdsall Harris, "Journal," p. 186; Jordan, "Anglo-American Cattle Ranching," pp. 82–83; Myers, *The Ranch in Spanish Texas*, pp. 178–79.

19. Barker, "Government of Austin's Colony," p. 299; *BLAKE*, vol. 1, p. 155; San Antonio, "Minutes of the City Council, 1815–1835," p. 524; Kimball, *Laws of Coahuila and Texas*, pp. 178–79; Wilkinson, *Laredo*, p. 67.

20. Coahuila y Texas, *Reglamento, 1827*, Article 69; Sánchez, "Trip to Texas in 1828," pp. 251–56; Almonte, *Nota estadística sobre Tejas*, p. 46; John W. Audubon, *Audubon's Western Journal: 1849–1850*, p. 54.

21. *BA*, José Guadiana to Manuel Salcedo, Nov. 15, 1810; Ranch Census, Oct. 1, 1811; Béxar Municipal Regulations, Mar. 20, 1825. Also see Kimball, *Laws of Coahuila and Texas*, pp. 191–92, 446; Myers, *The Ranch in Spanish Texas*, pp. 36, 55.

22. *Novísima Recopilación*, Libro 12, Título 35, Ley 2–3; *Nueva Recopilación*, 1774, Tomo 2, Libro 5, Título 4; Hatcher, "Municipal Government of Béxar," pp. 323–25; MacLachlan, *Tribunal of the Acordada*, pp. 10, 27.

23. MacLachlan, *Tribunal of the Acordada*, p. 33.

24. Gibson, *Spain in America*, p. 119; Myers, *The Ranch in Spanish Texas*, p. 55; *Nueva Recopilación*, Tomo 3, Libro 5, Título 5, Ley 1; Dusenberry, *The Mexican Mesta*, pp. 51, 88, 157.

25. MacLachlan, *Tribunal of the Acordada*, pp. 106–107; Paul Vanderwood, "Genesis of the Rurales: Mexico's Early Struggle for Public Security," p. 323.

26. Hatcher, "Municipal Government of Bexar," appendix 7, p. 350.

27. Coahuila y Texas, *Ordnanzas* [sic] *municipales de Béjar*, Articles 31 and 32, p. 21; Coahuila y Texas, *Ordenanzas municipales de Goliad*, Articles 30–34; Dusenberry, *The Mexican Mesta*, pp. 195–203; Myers, *The Ranch in Spanish Texas*, p. 35.

Chapter 5. Military Reorganization in Texas

1. Adams, "Tlascalan Colonies," pp. 162, 163, 224, 225; J. McAlister, "The Reorganization of the Army of New Spain, 1763–1767," p. 3.

2. *SFA*, Marriage Records, p. 50; Adams, "Tlascalan Colonies," p. 230. For patrol procedures and journals, see *BA*, Order, Apr. 12, 1828, and Diary of Expedition, *passim.*, Dec. 1, 1803, Oct. 7, 1805, Apr. 20, 1828, and Jan. 7, 1830.

3. *BA*, Felipe de la Garza to Luciano Garza, Jan. 15, 1824; Juan de Castañeda to José Antonio Saucedo, July 3, 1824; Max L. Moorhead, *The Apache Frontier: Jacobo Ugarte and Spanish-Indian Relations in Northern New Spain, 1769–1791*, pp. 88–93.

4. *BA*, Military Order, Mar. 24, 1808; Wilkinson, *Laredo*, pp. 56, 65.

5. *BA*, Antonio Elozúa to Felipe de la Garza, June 19, 1829; Jerry Don Thompson, *Sabers on the Rio Grande*, pp. 45–46.

6. *BA*, List, Feb. 1, 1820, and Felipe de la Garza to Béxar Ayuntamiento, Sept. 27, 1823; Coahuila y Texas, *Nota Estadística*, 1826, pp. 3,4; Wilkinson, *Laredo*, p. 98.

7. *BA*, Rafael González to José Antonio Saucedo, Mar. 20, 1824; José Antonio Saucedo to La Bahía Ayuntamiento, Sept. 19, 1825, *passim.*

8. *BA*, José Antonio Saucedo to Béxar Alcalde, June 26, 1872. For militia exemption, see Kimball, *Laws of Coahuila and Texas*, pp. 152–53.

9. *BA*, Rafael González to Mateo Ahumada, May 17, 1825; Coahuila y Texas, "Actas del congreso," May 2, 1829; Wilkinson, *Laredo*, pp. 64, 72.

10. *BA*, Juan José Zambrano to José Antonio Saucedo, Aug. 5, 1826; Wilkinson, *Laredo*, pp. 118–20.

11. *BA*, "Guarnición de la Provincia de Texas," Dec. 1, 1819. For the Béxar company, see Coahuila y Texas, *Nota Estadística, 1826*, p. 4. For other units, see *BA*, La Bahía Civil Militia Roster, Oct. 10, 1825; Samuel Norris to José Antonio Sepulveda, Aug 8, 1826; José Guadalupe de los Santos to Ramón Músquiz, Nov. 19, 1828.

12. Coahuila y Texas, *Nota estadística, 1826*, p. 9; *BA*, Río Grande Ayuntamiento to Bustamante, Oct. 18, 1826, and Antonio Elozúa to commandant of San Bartolo, Mar. 18, 1827; see also in *BA* correspondence of alcaldes of Laredo, Mier, Revilla, and Río Grande for 1826–27, *passim.*

13. Thompson, *Sabers on the Rio Grande*, p. 50. *BA*, Antonio Elozúa to Company Commanders, June 30, 1829; Gaspar Flores to Ramón Músquiz, Sept. 19, 1830; Ramón Músquiz to Goliad Alcalde, Feb. 15, 1831; Mariano Cosío to Antonio Elozúa, Feb. 22, 1831; Béxar Alcalde to Ramón Músquiz, Nov. 27, 1831.

14. Emilio del Castillo Negrete, *México en el siglo XIX*, p. 432; Barker, *The Austin Papers*, vol. 2, p. 520; Barker, *Life of Stephen F. Austin*, p. 345; *BA*, Ramón Músquiz to Mier y Terán, May 28, 1830; Edna Rowe, "The Disturbances at Anahuac in 1832," pp. 270, 280.

15. Rodriguez, *Rodriguez Memoirs*, pp. 40, 53; Davenport, "Men of Goliad," p. 12; Paul Schuster Taylor, *An American-Mexican Frontier, Nueces County, Texas*, p. 12; Wilkinson, *Laredo*, pp. 169, 170, 180; Barker, *Life of Stephen F. Austin*, p. 421.

16. For typical Anglo-American perspective on this subject, see Joseph Milton Nance, *After San Jacinto: The Texas-Mexican Frontier, 1836–1841*, p. 409, and Yoakum, *History of Texas*, vol. 2, p. 365. For an excellent example of investigative historical research, see Harbert Davenport, "Captain Jesús Cuellar, Texas Cavalry, Otherwise 'Comanche,'" p. 56 in which Davenport pieces together the rôle of Jesús Cuellar in the Republic of Texas Cavalry. Davenport states that "although the services rendered to revolutionary Texas by Jesús Cuellar were by no means inconsiderable, and are in part well known, his name appears but once in the archives of Texas, and not at all in any English account of the Texas Revolution."

17. For De la Garza, see Davenport, "Men of Goliad," p. 12, and O'Connor, *Presidio La Bahía*, p. 251. For Córdova, see Carlos E. Castañeda, *Our Catholic Heritage in Texas, 1519–1936*, vol. 7, p. 21, and Yoakum, *History of Texas*, vol. 2, pp. 245, 258–59.

18. Barker, *The Austin Papers*, vol. 1, pt. 1, pp. 420, 475, 557; vol. 2, pp. 1,027–33.

19. Compare Austin's phrase "strike and pursue" to the Tejano phrase *"vatir y perseguir."* Barker, *The Austin Papers*, vol. 1, pt. 1, pp. 594, 677, 715; Barker, *Life of Stephen F. Austin*, p. 96.

20. J. H. Kuykendall, ed., "Reminiscences of Capt. Gibson Kuykendall," p. 29, passim; J. H. Kuykendall, ed., "Reminiscences of Barzillai Kuykendall," p. 314; Yoakum, *History of Texas*, vol. 1, pp. 223–26; Barker, *The Austin Papers*, vol. 1, pt. 1, pp. 510, 678, 831, 839, 885; Barker, *Life of Stephen F. Austin*, p. 92.

21. Eugene C. Barker, ed., "Minutes of the Ayuntamiento of San Felipe de Austin, 1828–1832," pp. 397, 408; *BA*, José María Viesca to Ramón Músquiz, June 13, 1829, and June 4, 1830; Estevan F. Austin to Antonio Elozúa, June 30, 1829; Thomas Daves to Ramón Músquiz, June 4, 1830.

22. Barker, *Life of Stephen F. Austin*, p. 349; Gammel, *Laws of Texas*, vol. 1, pp. 497–500.

23. Wooten, *Comprehensive History of Texas*, vol. 2, p. 336; Barker, *The Austin Papers*, vol. 1, pt. 1, p. 420.

24. Gammel, *Laws of Texas*, vol. 1, pp. 543, 558, 671; Connor, "County Government in the Republic," p. 168; Llerena B. Friend, *Sam Houston: The Great Designer*, p. 64.

25. Nance, *After San Jacinto*, p. 489; Amelia W. Williams and Eugene C. Barker, eds., *The Writings of Sam Houston, 1813–1836*, vol. 4, p. 89.

26. Texas, Republic, *Journals of the Fourth Congress of the Republic of Texas, 1839–1840 to Which Are Added the Relief Laws*, vol. 1, p. 207; Davenport, "Jesús Cuellar, Texas Cavalry," p. 58; Nance, *After San Jacinto*, pp. 411, 142; Yoakum, *History of Texas*, vol. 2, pp. 320–21; Webb, *The Texas Rangers*, p. 70.

27. For the best description of the Texas Rangers, see Webb, *The Texas Rangers*, pp. 79–82.
28. Joseph Dorst Patch, *The Concentration of General Zachary Taylor's Army at Corpus Christi, Texas*, p. 25; U.S., Congress, U.S. House Executive Document 60, p. 107; Holman Hamilton, *Zachary Taylor*, vol. 1, p. 165; Friend, *Sam Houston*, p. 257.

Chapter 6. Texas Statehood under Coahuila

1. Castañeda, *Our Catholic Heritage*, vol. 6, pp. 186, 187. For the basic study of Ramos Arizpe and the origin of the provincial deputation in the Spanish Cortes, see Benson, *Diputación provincial*, p. 14; see also *AGI*, Guadalajara, vol. 62, pp. 53–56. For Texas colonization request, see Alessio Robles, *Coahuila y Texas*, vol. 1, p. 105.
2. *BA*, Béxar Ayuntamiento, Minutes, Aug. 24 and 27, 1820; José Ramirez to Antonio Martínez, Aug. 31, 1820; [Antonio Martínez] to José Encarnación Vásquez.
3. Benson, *Diputación provincial*, pp. 28, 30, 77–78, 90; Nettie Lee Benson, "The Plan of Casa Mata," pp. 51, 55; Barker, "Government of Austin's Colony," pp. 223–25.
4. *BA*, Puebla Provincial Deputation to Texas Provincial Deputation, Feb. 24, 1823; Béxar Ayuntamiento to Monclova Junta Provisional Gubernativa, Mar. 22, 1823; La Bahía Ayuntamiento, Proclamation, Mar. 24, 1823; San Carlos, Tamaulipas Ayuntamiento to Béxar Ayuntamiento, July 5, 1823; Monclova Junta Gubernativa to Béxar Ayuntamiento, Aug. 2, 1823.
5. *BA*, Béxar Junta Gubernativa to Béxar Ayuntamiento, April 15, 1823; José Felix Trespalacios to La Bahía Ayuntamiento and Commandant, April 17, 1823; La Bahía Ayuntamiento to Béxar Junta Gubernativa, April 23, 1823; Charles A. Bacarisse, "The Baron de Bastrop: The Life and Times of Philip Hendrick Nering Bögel, 1759–1827," p. 277.
6. *BA*, José Felix Trespalacios to Béxar Junta Provisional Gubernativa, April 17, 18, and 24, 1823; Béxar Junta Provisional Gubernativa to Béxar Ayuntamiento, April 28, 1823; Béxar Ayuntamiento to Béxar Junta Provisional Gubernativa, April 29, 1823.
7. *BA*, Felipe de la Garza to Texas Junta Provisional Gubernativa, June 16, 1823, and Béxar Junta Provisional Gubernativa to Béxar Ayuntamiento, June 17, 1823; Alessio Robles, *Coahuila y Texas*, vol. 1, pp. 150, 153; Benson, *Diputación provincial*, p. 82.
8. *BA*, Lucas Alamán to Luciano García, Sept. 17, 1823, Luciano García to Béxar Ayuntamiento, Sept. 24, and 25, 1823, and Lucas Alamán to José Antonio Saucedo, Nov. 15, 1823; Benson, *Diputación provincial*, p. 82; Bacarisse, "Baron de Bastrop," p. 297.
9. *BA*, José Miguel Aldrete to Governor, Aug. 17, 1823; Béxar Sala Capitular, Election Results, Aug. 17, 1823; La Bahía Ayuntamiento to Luciano García, Sept. 14, 1823; Luciano García to Béxar Ayuntamiento, Sept. 9, 1823.
10. *BA*, Erasmo Seguin to María Josefa Becerra [Seguin], Jan. 7, 1824, and Alcabala Permit: Erasmo Seguin, Feb. 21, 1825; Chabot, *With the Makers of San Antonio*, pp. 118–29; Barker, *The Austin Papers*, vol. 2, p. 897; Bacarisse, "Baron de Bastrop," p. 200; Charles A. Bacarisse, "The Union of Coahuila and Texas," p. 740.
11. Manuel Dublán and José María Lozano, *Legislación Mexicana o colección completa de las disposiciones legislativas expedidas desde la independencia de la república ordenada por los licenciados Manuel Dublán and José María Lozano*, pp. 693, 697; Bacarisse, "Union of Coahuila and Texas," pp. 342, 740; *BA*, Béxar Provincial Deputation to Béxar Ayuntamiento, Jan. 12, 1824.
12. *BA*, Erasmo Seguin to Texas Provincial Deputation, Oct. 5, 1824.
13. Dublán and Lozano, *Legislación Mexicana*, p. 706; Alessio Robles, *Coahuila y Texas*, vol. 1, p. 175.

14. *BA*, Primera Secretaría de Estado to José Antonio Saucedo, May 8 and July 8, 1824; Béxar Provincial Deputation to José Antonio Saucedo, Sept. 22, 1824.

15. Coahuila y Texas, "Actas del congreso," Aug. 10 and 27, and Dec. 14, 1824; Garza García, *Leyes de Coahuila*, pp. 35, 72; Bacarisse, "Union of Coahuila and Texas," p. 347; Bacarisse, "Baron de Bastrop," p. 321; Alessio Robles, *Coahuila y Texas*, vol. 1, p. 75.

16. *BA*, Miguel Ramos de Arizpe to Béxar Ayuntamiento, Sept. 15, 1824.

17. *BA*, Béxar Provincial Deputation to José Antonio Saucedo, Sept. 22, 1824; José Antonio Saucedo to Gaspar Flores, Sept. 23, 1824.

18. *BA*, Béxar Provincial Deputation, Minutes, Sept. 30, 1824; José Antonio Saucedo to Ayuntamiento, Sept. 30, 1824; Béxar Ayuntamiento to Gefe Político [José Antonio Saucedo], Sept. 30, 1824.

19. *BA*, Juan de Castañeda to Gaspar Flores, Sept. 30, 1824; Gaspar Flores to Juan de Castañeda, Sept. 30, 1824; Juan de Castañeda to Rafael González, Oct. 1, 1824; Alessio Robles, *Coahuila y Texas*, vol. 1, p. 233.

20. *BA*, Béxar Provincial Deputation to José Antonio Saucedo, Oct. 1, 1824, and Juan de Castañeda to Rafael González, Oct. 3, 1824; Alessio Robles, *Coahuila y Texas*, vol. 1, p. 168.

21. Bacarisse, "Union of Coahuila and Texas," pp. 346, 740; *BA*, Erasmo Seguin to Texas Provincial Deputation, Oct. 5, 1824, and Erasmo Seguin to María Josefa Seguin, Oct. 20, 1824; Barker, *The Austin Papers*, vol. 2, pt. 1, pp. 775–77.

22. Yoakum, *History of Texas*, vol. 1, pp. 230–31.

23. Coahuila y Texas, *Nota estadística, 1826*, p. 3; Coahuila y Texas, *Reglamento, 1827, passim*.

24. *BA*, José María Zambrano to Gaspar Flores, May 10, 1824; Coahuila y Texas, "Actas del congreso," Oct. 28, 1824; Bacarisse, "Baron de Bastrop," pp. 18, 94, 118, 147, 318; Barker, *The Austin Papers*, vol. 1, pt. 2, pp. 1,723–26.

25. Kimball, *Laws of Coahuila and Texas*, see Coahuila y Texas Constitution, Section II, Paragraph I, Municipal Electoral Assemblies, and Paragraph II, District Electoral Assemblies; *BA*, Juan Vicente Campos to Béxar Ayuntamiento, Nov. 29, 1828; Barker, *The Austin Papers*, vol. 1, pt. 2, p. 1,486; Barker, "Government of Austin's Colony," p. 251.

26. *BA*, Reglamento p.ª el Gobierno interior del Consejo de Gobierno del Estado Libre Independent de Coahuila y Tejas, 1824.

27. *BA*, Coahuila y Texas Congress, Minutes, Feb. 8, 1825; Coahuila y Texas, "Actas del congreso," Jan. and Feb., *passim.*, and May 31, 1825; Garza García, *Leyes de Coahuila*, p. 29.

28. *BA*, Rafael González to José Antonio Saucedo, May 18, 1825, and José Antonio Saucedo to Béxar Ayuntamiento, July 28, 1825; Coahuila y Texas, "Actas del congreso," Mar. 22 and 23, 1827, and Mar. 7, 1834.

29. Compare Alessio Robles, *Coahuila y Texas*, vol. 1, pp. 2–6 and map opposite p. 8 to GLO, "J. de Cordova's Map of the State of Texas, 1849" (K-4-11); Garza García, *Leyes de Coahuila*, pp. 47, 48; Coahuila y Texas, "Actas del congreso," Jan. 25, 1831, and Mar. 5, 1834.

30. Barker, *The Austin Papers*, vol. 1, pt. 1, p. 752; Coahuila y Texas, "Actas del congreso," Dec. 2, 1824; Bacarisse, "Baron de Bastrop," p. 336.

31. Dublán and Lozano, *Legislación Mexicana*, p. 712.

32. Coahuila y Texas, "Actas del congreso," Feb. 10 and Mar. 24, 1825; Bacarisse, "Baron de Bastrop," pp. 335, 336.

33. *BA*, José Antonio Saucedo to Alcaldes of Texas, Apr. 13, 1825; Coahuila y Texas, *Nota estadística, 1826*, p. 5; Bacarisse, "Baron de Bastrop," p. 343.

34. Barker, *The Austin Papers*, vol. 2, p. 110; Marilyn McAdams Sibley, *The Port of Houston: A History*, p. 20; Bacarisse, "Baron de Bastrop," pp. 337–48; Abel G. Rubio, *Stolen Heritage: A Mexican-American's Rediscovery of His Family's Lost Land Grant*, p. 94.

35. Coahuila y Texas, "Actas del congreso," Nov. 16, 1824, Sept. 20, 1825, Feb. 11, 1826, and

May 30, 1826; Alessio Robles, *Coahuila y Texas*, vol. 1, p. 222; Allen, "History of Nacog-doches," p. 67.

36. Dublán and Lozano, *Legislación Mexicana*, pp. 339, 710; Barker, *The Austin Papers*, vol. 1, pt. 1, p. 723.

37. Barker, *The Austin Papers*, vol. 1, pt. 1, p. 1406 and pt. 2, p. 1,157.

38. *BA*, Juan José Zambrano to José Antonio Saucedo, Aug. 24, 1826; Coahuila y Texas, "Actas del congreso," Sept. 2, 1826; Barker, *The Austin Papers*, vol. 1, pt. 2, pp. 1,170, 1,371.

39. Coahuila y Texas, "Actas del congreso," May 7, 1825, and Sept. 22, 1826; Barker, *The Austin Papers*, vol. 1, pt. 2, p. 1462; Bacarisse, "Baron de Bastrop," pp. 366.

40. Coahuila y Texas, "Actas del congreso," Nov. 30, 1826, and Jan. 18, 1827; Garza García, *Leyes de Coahuila*, p. 82.

41. Coahuila y Texas, "Actas del congreso," Feb. 5, 1828; Kimball, *Laws of Coahuila and Texas*, p. 154; Barker, *The Austin Papers*, vol. 1, pt. 2, p. 1,648.

42. Barker, *The Austin Papers*, vol. 1, pt. 2, pp. 1,147, 1,057–60; Coahuila y Texas, "Actas del congreso," Sept. 4, 1826.

43. Coahuila y Texas, "Actas del congreso," 1824–26, *passim*.

Chapter 7. The Emergence of Tejano Politics

1. Ildefonso Villarello Vélez, *Historia de Coahuila*, appendix; Barker, *The Austin Papers*, vol. 1, pt. 1, p. 694.

2. This period of the Mexican Republic is surveyed in Michael P. Costeloe, *La Primera República Federal de México (1824–1835): Un estudio de los partidos políticos en el México independiente.*

3. *AGN*, Secretaría de *Gobernación*, Legajo 37, Exped. 13; Coahuila y Texas, "Actas del congreso," Oct. 16, p. 86; Barker, *The Austin Papers*, vol. 2, p. 767.

4. Barker, *The Austin Papers*, vol. 2, p. 582.

5. *BA*, Béxar Ayuntamiento, Bill of Sale, May 5, 1820; *BA*, Béxar Ayuntamiento, Minutes, Aug. 24, 1828; Coahuila y Texas, "Actas del congreso," June 4, and Nov. 28, 1827, and Mar. 26, 1831.

6. Barker, *The Austin Papers*, vol. 2, pp. 122, 793–96; Alessio Robles, *Coahuila y Tejas*, vol. 1, pp. 329–34; Montejano, *Anglos and Mexicans*, p. 16.

7. *BA*, Béxar Ayuntamiento, Bill of Sale, July 15, 1820; *BA*, *Sumaria, Juan Bordes*, Oct. 30, 1824; Barker, *The Life of Stephen F. Austin*, p. 138; Chabot, *With the Makers of San Antonio*, p. 234; *BA*, Census of Valerio, July 7, 1830; Coahuila y Texas, "Actas del congreso."

8. Barker, *Life of Stephen F. Austin*, p. 262.

9. Coahuila y Texas, "Actas del congreso," July 7, 1827; Garza García, *Leyes de Coahuila*, p. 82.

10. *BA*, Protest of Decree No. 50, Apr. 24, 1828; Garza García, *Leyes de Coahuila*, p. 81; Kimball, *Laws of Coahuila and Texas*, p. 101; Barker, *The Austin Papers*, vol. 2, p. 41.

11. Barker, *Life of Stephen F. Austin*, p. 215; Barker, *The Austin Papers*, vol. 2, pp. 273, 286, 303; *BA*, José de las Piedras to Antonio Elozúa, Dec. 8, 1829.

12. Bascom Giles, *History and Disposition of Texas Public Domain*, p. 7.

13. *GLO*, *Spanish Archives*, Miller and Bourland, "Land Titles West of the Nueces."

14. Kimball, *Laws of Coahuila and Texas*, pp. 248–49; Thomas Lloyd Miller, *The Public Lands of Texas, 1519–1970*, p. 35.

15. Chambers, *Old Bullion Benton: Senator from the New West*, p. 114.

16. *BA*, Antonio Cordero to Nemesio Salcedo, May 1, 1806; Coahuila y Texas, "Actas del congreso," Jan. 20, 1829.

17. Barker, *Life of Stephen F. Austin*, p. 272; Barker, *The Austin Papers*, vol. 2, p. 900; Giles, *Texas Public Domain*, p. 3.
18. Gammel, *Laws of Texas*, vol. 1, p. 424; James P. Hart, "Oil, The Courts, and the Railroad Commission," p. 303.
19. *BA*, José Antonio Vásquez to Ramón Músquiz, July 3, 1829; Ernest R. Bartley, *The Tidelands Oil Controversy: A Legal and Historical Analysis*, pp. 82, 89; Miller, *Public Lands of Texas*, p. 12.
20. Coahuila y Texas, "Actas del congreso," Jan. 13, 1829; Barker, *Life of Stephen F. Austin*, pp. 198, 199.
21. *BA*, José Bonifacio Galán to Mateo Ahumada, Jan. 31, 1826; Hogan, *Texas Republic*, p. 246; Cox, "Education in San Fernando," p. 42; Wilkinson, *Laredo*, p. 68, says, "There were usually more women than men in the Spanish towns of the Rio Grande frontier and more widows in the middle years than widowers."
22. *BA*, Dionisio Valle to Juan Bautista Elguezabal, May 23, 1805; Sánchez, "Trip to Texas in 1828," p. 259.
23. *BA*, La Bahía Ayuntamiento to Luciano García, Sept. 14, 1823; Coahuila y Texas, "Actas del congreso," July 16, 1825; *NA*, "Estadística" Note No. 4, June 30, 1833; *BCA*, "Mission Records," 1823, *passim*.
24. Coahuila y Texas, "Actas del congreso," Jan. 2 and Aug. 10, 1827, and Jan. 7, 1833; Barker, *Life of Stephen F. Austin*, p. 121; Joseph Martin Dawson, *Jose Antonio Navarro: Co-Creator of Texas*, p. 45; Kimball, *Laws of Coahuila and Texas*, p. 248.
25. *BA*, Representación, Dec. 19, 1832, and Mateo Ahumada, Military Order, Oct. 29, 1826; Rather, "DeWitt's Colony," pp. 108–13; Miller, *Public Lands of Texas*, p. 18; Barker, *Life of Stephen F. Austin*, p. 112.
26. *BA*, Green DeWitt to Ramón Músquiz, July 28, 1830, and Francisco Flores to Ramón Músquiz, Oct. 30, 1830; Rubio, *Stolen Heritage*, p. 85.
27. *BA*, Cavalry Report, Sept. 15, 1826, and Mateo Ahumada to Francisco Rojo, Dec. 10, 1826; *NA*, Goliad Census, Dec. 31, 1831.
28. *BA*, Rafael Antonio Manchola to Mateo Ahumada, Oct. 29, 1826; Castañeda, *Our Catholic Heritage*, vol. 6, p. 235.
29. Sánchez, "Trip to Texas in 1828," *passim.; NA*, Goliad Ayuntamiento to State Congress, Jan. 15, 1833.
30. *BA*, Béxar Ayuntamiento Special Committee, Report, Nov. 18, 1829.
31. J. C. Clopper, "J. C. Clopper's Journal and Book of Memoranda for 1828," p. 60; Costeloe, *Primera República*, pp. 243, 247.
32. Barker, *The Austin Papers*, vol. 2, p. 568; Kimball, *Laws of Coahuila and Texas*, p. 160.
33. Coahuila y Texas, "Actas del congreso," 1829–30 *passim.*; Barker, *The Austin Papers*, vol. 2, pp. 105, 897; *BA*, Lucas de Palacio to Erasmo Seguin, Oct. 25, 1827; Alessio Robles, *Coahuila y Texas*, vol. 1, p. 536.
34. *BA*, Leona Vicario [Saltillo] Permanent Deputation to Béxar Ayuntamiento, Sept. 4, 1830; Barker, *The Austin Papers*, vol. 2, pp. 500, 501.
35. Coahuila y Texas, "Actas del congreso," Jan. 11, 1831; Barker, *The Austin Papers*, vol. 2, p. 568.
36. *AGN*, Secretría de Gobernación, Legajo 37, Exped. 14; Ernest Wallace, *Documents of Texas History*, p. 66; Coahuila y Texas, "Actas del congreso," Feb. 25 and Apr. 11, 1831; Feb. 8, 1832.
37. Coahuila y Texas, "Actas del congreso," Apr., 1832; *passim*.
38. Coahuila y Texas, "Actas del congreso" Mar. 25 and Dec. 28, 1832; Barker, *The Austin Papers*, vol. 2, p. 762; Costeloe, *Primera República*, p. 337.

39. Barker, *Life of Stephen F. Austin*, pp. 332–33.
40. Barker, *Life of Stephen F. Austin*, pp. 344–51 *passim*.
41. Barker, *Life of Stephen F. Austin*, p. 356; Barker, *The Austin Papers*, vol. 2, pp. 903–906. Although Barker stated that he could find no specific evidence of Austin's complicity among Austin's letters, another historian, Herbert Eugene Bolton, claimed in *Guide to Materials for the History of the United States in the Principal Archives of Mexico* to have found such evidence at the Archivo General de la Nación of Mexico. Bolton cites the section on Secretaría de Fomento, Colonización, e Industria, Archivo General, Legajo 2 (1833), for a "Stephen F. Austin circular to the States, transmitting a copy of a communication by Stephen F. Austin in which he invites the ayuntamientos of Texas to separate from Coahuila even though the national authorities should refuse their consent." This document is hardly traceable in the radical reorganization which the Mexican archives have undergone since Bolton's survey in 1913.
42. Barker, *The Austin Papers*, vol. 2, pp. 897, 899–901; Barker, *Life of Stephen F. Austin*, p. 359; Costeloe, *Primera República*, p. 346.
43. *BA*, Representación, Dec. 19, 1832.
44. *NA*, Nacogdoches Ayuntamiento to State Congress, Jan. 30, 1833, and Goliad Ayuntamiento to State Congress, Jan. 15, 1833.
45. For Tejanos, see *BA*, Juan Nepomuceno Seguin to Béxar Ayuntamiento, Jan. 2, 1833, and Barker, *Life of Stephen F. Austin*, p. 356. For Anglo Americans, see Barker, *The Austin Papers*, vol. 2, pp. 1,024–26, and Barker, *Life of Stephen F. Austin*, pp. 219, 360.
46. Barker, *Life of Stephen F. Austin*, pp. 335, 390; Friend, *Sam Houston*, pp. 34, 35, 41, 54; Alessio Robles, *Coahuila y Texas*, vol. 1, p. 314.
47. Costeloe, *Primera República*, p. 396; Coahuila y Texas, "Actas del congreso," Feb., 1833–Apr., 1833 *passim*.
48. Coahuila y Texas, "Actas del congreso," Apr. 2 and Apr. 26, 1833; Garza García, *Leyes de Coahuila*, p. 96; Barker, *The Austin Papers*, vol. 2, p. 1,016.
49. Barker, *The Austin Papers*, vol. 2, p. 1,077; Coahuila y Texas, "Actas del congreso," Feb. 6, 1834; Hubert Howe Bancroft, *History of the North Mexican States and Texas*, vol. 16, p. 137.
50. Coahuila y Texas, "Actas del congreso," Jan.–Apr., 1834 *passim*.; Alessio Robles, *Coahuila y Texas*, vol. 2, p. 13; Costeloe, *Primera República*, p. 381.
51. Bancroft, *North Mexican States and Texas*, vol. 16, p. 143; Costeloe, *Primera República*, pp. 428, 435.
52. Barker, *Life of Stephen F. Austin*, p. 401; Alessio Robles, *Coahuila y Texas*, vol. 1, p. 449; vol. 2, p. 22.
53. Alessio Robles, *Coahuila y Texas*, vol. 1, p. 495.
54. Yoakum, *History of Texas*, vol. 1, p. 449.

Chapter 8. The Tejanos between Two Frontiers

1. Williams, *Writings of Sam Houston*, vol. 4, pp. 63, 64; Nance, *After San Jacinto*, pp. 30, 53, 54; Friend, *Sam Houston*, pp. 66, 73; O'Connor, *Presidio La Bahía*, pp. 100, 126, 253; Hammet, *Empresario Martín de Leon*, p. 75.
2. Gerald S. Pierce, *Texas under Arms: The Camps, Posts, and Military Towns of the Republic of Texas, 1836–1846*, p. 144; Yoakum, *History of Texas*, vol. 2, pp. 245, 265; Chabot, *With the Makers of San Antonio*, p. 35; Hammet, *Empresario Martín de Leon*, pp. 83, 84; O'Connor, *Presidio La Bahía*, p. 259.
3. James Ernest Crisp, "Anglo-Texan Attitudes Toward the Mexican, 1821–1845," p. 342; Deed Records, County Clerk's Office, Refugio County; Deed Records, County Clerk's Office,

Goliad County; Webb, *Great Plains*, p. 210; Rodriguez, *Rodriguez Memoirs*, p. 53; Williams, *Writings of Sam Houston*, vol. 2, p. 77 and vol. 4, pp. 65, 101; Arnoldo De León, *They Called Them Greasers: Anglo Attitudes Toward Mexicans in Texas, 1821–1900*, p. 77.

4. Gammel, *Laws of Texas*, vol. 1, pp. 19, 20, 925, 1,408, 1,414, and vol. 2, p. 35; Miller, *Public Lands of Texas*, p. 49; Texas headright data were compiled from *GLO* files and *GLO, Abstract of Original Titles.*

5. Nance, *After San Jacinto*, p. 547; Miller, *Public Lands of Texas*, p. 56; Williams, *Writings of Sam Houston*, vol. 4, pp. 115; Pierce, *Texas Under Arms*, p. 120.

6. Castañeda, *Our Catholic Heritage*, vol. 7, pp. 112–14; Seb S. Wilcox, "Laredo during the Texas Republic," pp. 104, 105; Frank Cushman Pierce, *Texas' Last Frontier: A Brief History of the Lower Rio Grande Valley*, p. 138; Stambaugh, *Lower Rio Grande Valley*, pp. 88–92; González, "Cameron, Starr, and Zapata Counties," p. 26; Pierce, *Texas under Arms*, pp. 151, 152.

7. U.S. Census, 1850 *MS;* Nance, *After San Jacinto*, p. 286; O'Connor, *Presidio La Bahía*, p. 259; Hammet, *Empresario Martín de Leon*, p. 75.

8. The "child-ladder" method indicates migration patterns in census records by determining date and place of births of the offsprings in a family. It is fully explained in Barnes F. Lathrop, *Migration into East Texas, 1835–1860: A Study from the United States Census.* For the definition of *labrador,* see Poyo and Hinojasa, *Tejano Origins in Eighteenth-Century San Antonio*, p. 87.

Bibliography

All bibliographic entries are included in a single alphabetical listing in order to facilitate reference. Numerous primary sources—such as minutes, deeds, laws, record books, and other unpublished documents—are listed under the name of the states, towns, or jurisdictions which produced them as in the case of Refugio County, Deed Records. Other primary sources such as memoirs that have been published in books or journal articles are listed under the name of the compiler or diarist. The bibliography entry is listed under the same name that is used for the endnote, although a few archive names are abbreviated as indicated in the notes.

Adams, David Bergen. "The Tlascalan Colonies of Northern Coahuila." Ph.D. diss., University of Texas at Austin, 1971.

Alessio Robles, Vito. *Coahuila y Texas desde la consumación de la independencia hasta el Tratado de Paz de Guadalupe Hidalgo.* 2 vols.; México: n.p., 1945.

Allen, Winnie. "History of Nacogdoches, 1691–1830." M.A. thesis, University of Texas, 1925.

Almonte, Juan N. *Nota estadística sobre Tejas por Juan N. Almonte.* México: Ignacio Cumplido, 1835.

Arneson, Edwin P. "Early Irrigation in Texas." *Southwestern Historical Quarterly* 25 (Oct., 1921): 121–30.

Audubon, John W. *Audubon's Western Journal: 1849–1850 Being the MS record of a trip from New York to Texas, and an overland journey through Mexico and Arizona to the gold-fields of California.* Cleveland: Arthur H. Clark Company, 1906.

Bacarisse, Charles. "The Baron de Bastrop: The Life and Times of Philip Hendrick Nering Bögel, 1759–1827." Ph.D. diss., University of Texas at Austin, 1955.

———. "The Union of Coahuila and Texas." *Southwestern Historical Quarterly* 61 (Jan., 1958): 341–49.

Bakken, Gordon M. "The English Common Law in the Rocky Mountain West." *Arizona and the West* 2 (Summer, 1969): 109–28.

Bancroft, Hubert Howe. *The Works of Hubert Howe Bancroft.* Vols. 15 and 16, *History of the North Mexican States and Texas*. 2 vols. San Francisco: The History Company, Publishers, 1886–89.

Barker, Eugene C. *The Austin Papers*, vol. 1. *Annual Report of the American Historical Association for the Year 1919, vol. 2*. 2 pts. Washington, D.C.: Government Printing Office, 1924.

————. *The Austin Papers*, vol. 2. *Annual Report of the American Historical Association for the Year 1922, vol. 2*. 2 vols. Washington, D.C.: Government Printing Office, 1928.

————. *The Austin Papers, Volume III*. Austin: University of Texas Press, 1927.

————. "The Government of Austin's Colony, 1821–1831." *Southwestern Historical Quarterly* 21 (January, 1918): 223–52.

————. *The Life of Stephen F. Austin, Founder of Texas, 1793–1836: A Chapter in the Westward Movement of the Anglo-American People*. Austin: University of Texas Press, 1969.

————, ed. "Minutes of the Ayuntamiento of San Felipe de Austin, 1828–1832," *Southwestern Historical Quarterly* 21 (January, 1918): 299–326 and (April, 1918): 395–423.

Bartley, Ernest R. *The Tidelands Oil Controversy: A Legal and Historical Analysis*. Austin: University of Texas Press, 1953.

Benson, Nettie Lee. *La diputación provincial y el federalismo Mexicano*. México: Colegio de México, 1955.

————. "The Plan of Casa Mata." *Hispanic American Historical Review* 25 (Feb., 1945): 45–56.

————, ed. *Mexico and the Spanish Cortes, 1810–1822: Eight Essays*. Austin: University of Texas Press, 1966.

Berger, Max. "Education in Texas during the Spanish and Mexican Periods." *Southwestern Historical Quarterly* 51 (July, 1947): 41–53.

"Blake Transcripts." Barker Texas History Center. University of Texas at Austin.

Bolton, Herbert Eugene. *Guide to Materials for the History of the United States in the Principal Archives of Mexico*. Washington, D.C.: Carnegie Institute of Washington, 1913.

————. *Texas in the Middle Eighteenth Century: Studies in Spanish Colonial History and Administration*. Austin: University of Texas Press, 1970.

Bugbee, Lester G. "The Texas Frontier, 1820–1845." *Publications of Southern History Association* 4 (March, 1900): 102–21.

Cardenas, Leonard, Jr., "The Municipality in Northern Mexico." *Southwestern Studies* 1 (Spring, 1963): no. 1.

Castañeda, Carlos E. Collection. Barker Texas History Center. University of Texas at Austin.

————. *Our Catholic Heritage in Texas, 1519–1936*. Vol. 2, *The Mission Era: The Winning of Texas 1693–1731*. Austin: Von Boeckmann-Jones Co., 1936.

Chabot, Frederick C. *With the Makers of San Antonio: Genealogies of the Early Latin, Anglo-American, and German Families with Occasional Biographies, Each Group Being Prefaced with a Brief Historical Sketch and Illustrations*. San Antonio: Privately published by Artes Gráficas, 1937.

Chambers, William. *Old Bullion Benton, Senator from the New West: Thomas Hart Benton, 1782–1858.* 1st ed. Boston: Little, Brown, 1956.

Clopper, J. C. "J. C. Clopper's Journal and Book of Memoranda for 1828," *Quarterly of the Texas State Historical Association* 13 (July, 1909–April, 1910): 44–80.

Coahuila. Archivo General del Estado de Coahuila. Saltillo, Coahuila.

Coahuila y Texas. "Actas del congreso constitucional del estado libre de Coahuila y Texas" (typescript). Barker Texas History Center. University of Texas at Austin.

————. *Arancel de los derechos que deben percibir los escribanos públicos, alcaldes constitucionales, secretario del tribunal de justicia, receptor, abogados, asesores, procurador, apoderados, alcaides, y alguaciles, del estado de Coahuila y Texas.* Leona Vicario, Coahuila: Imprenta del Govierno, 1828.

————. *Nota estadística remitida por el gobierno supremo del Estado de Coahuila y Tejas a la cámara de senadores del soberano congreso general con arreglo al artículo 161 número 8° de la Constitución Federal de los Estados Unidos Mexicanos.* México: La Imprenta del Aguila, 1826.

————. *Nota estadística remitida por el gobierno supremo del Estado de Coahuila y Tejas a la cámara de senadores del soberano congreso general con arreglo al artículo 161 número 8° de la Constitución Federal de los Estados Unidos Mexicanos el año de 1827.* México: Imprenta del Supremo Gobierno, 1827.

————. *Ordenanzas municipales para el gobierno y manejo interior del ayuntamiento de la villa de Goliad.* Leona Vicario, Coahuila: Imprenta del Gobierno, 1829.

————. *Ordnanzas* [sic] *municipales para el gobierno y manejo interior del ayuntamiento de la ciudad de San Antonio de Béjar.* Leona Vicario, Coahuila: Imprenta del Govierno, 1829.

————. *Reglamento para el gobierno ecónomico político del estado libre de Coahuila y Tejas.* Monterrey, México: Imprenta del Gobierno, 1827.

Conger, Roger N. "The Tomas de la Vega Eleven League Grant on the Brazos." *Southwestern Historical Quarterly* 61 (Jan., 1958): 370–82.

Connor, Seymour V. "The Evolution of County Government in the Republic of Texas." *Southwestern Historical Quarterly* 55 (Oct., 1951): 163–200.

Costeloe, Michael P. *La primera república federal de México (1824–1835): Un estudio de los partidos políticos en el México independiente.* México: Fondo de Cultura Económica, 1975.

Cox, C. C., and D. Harris. "Reminiscences of C. C. Cox," *Quarterly of the Texas State Historical Association* 6 (1902–1903): 128–38, 204–35.

Cox, Isaac Joslin. "Education Effort in San Fernando de Bexar." *Quarterly of the Texas State Historical Association* 6 (July, 1902): 27–63.

————. "The Louisiana-Texas Frontier." *Quarterly of the Texas State Historical Association* 10 (July, 1906): 27–30.

Crisp, James Ernest. "Anglo-Texan Attitudes Toward the Mexican, 1821–1845." Ph.D. diss., Yale University, 1976.

Cruz, Gilbert R. *Let There Be Towns: Spanish Municipal Origins in the American Southwest, 1610–1810.* College Station: Texas A&M University Press, 1988.

Davenport, Harbert. "Captain Jesús Cuellar, Texas Cavalry, Otherwise 'Comanche.'" *Southwestern Historical Quarterly* 30 (July, 1926): 56–62.

———. "The Men of Goliad." *Southwestern Historical Quarterly* 48 (July, 1939): 1–27.

Dawson, Joseph Martin. *José Antonio Navarro: Co-Creator of Texas.* Waco, Texas: Baylor University Press, 1969.

DeCamara, Kathleen. *Laredo on the Rio Grande.* San Antonio: Naylor, 1949.

Del Castillo Negrete, Emilio. *México en el siglo XIX, Tomo XVIII.* 1st ed. México: Imprenta del Editor, 1889.

De León, Arnoldo. *They Called Them Greasers: Anglo Attitudes Toward Mexicans in Texas, 1821–1900.* Austin: University of Texas Press, 1983.

Dobkins, Bette E. *The Spanish Element in Texas Water Law.* Austin: University of Texas Press, 1959.

Domenech, Abbe Emmanuel Henri Dieudonné. *Missionary Adventures in Texas and Mexico.* London: Longman, Brown Green, Longmans, and Roberts, 1858.

Driver, Harold. *Indians of North America.* 2nd ed., revised; Chicago: University of Chicago Press, 1969.

Dublán, Manuel, and José María Lozano. *Legislación Mexicana o colección completa de las disposiciones legislativas expedidas desde la independencia de la república ordenada por los licenciados Manuel Dublán and José María Lozano.* México: Imprenta del Comercio, 1876.

Dusenberry, William H. *The Mexican Mesta: The Administration of Ranching in Colonial Mexico.* Urbana: University of Illinois Press, 1963.

———. "The Regulation of Meat Supply in Sixteenth-Century Mexico City." *Hispanic American Historical Review* 28 (Feb., 1948): 38–52.

Eby, Frederick, comp. *Education in Texas: Source Materials.* University of Texas Bulletin No. 1824 (Apr., 1918).

Faulk, Odie B. "Ranching in Spanish Texas." *Hispanic American Historical Review* 44 (May, 1965): 257–66.

Friend, Llerena B. *Sam Houston: The Great Designer.* Austin: University of Texas Press, 1969.

Gambrell, Herbert Pickens. *Mirabeau Buonaparte Lamar: Troubadour and Crusader.* Dallas: Southwest Press, 1934.

Gammel, H. P. N., comp. *The Laws of Texas, 1822–1897.* 10 vols. Austin: Gammel Book Company, 1898.

Garrison, George P. *Texas: A Contest of Civilizations.* Boston: Houghton, Mifflin and Company, 1903.

Garza García, Cosme. *Prontuario de leyes y decretos del estado de Coahuila de Zaragoza.* Saltillo: Oficina Tipográfica del Gobierno, 1902.

Gibson, Charles. *Spain in America.* New York: Harper and Row, 1966.

Giles, Bascom. *History and Disposition of Texas Public Domain.* Austin: General Land Office, 1942.

Goliad County. Deed Records. County Clerk's Office. Goliad, Texas.

González, Jovita. "Social Life in Cameron, Starr, and Zapata Counties." M.A. thesis, University of Texas at Austin, 1930.

Graf, Leroy P. "Colonization Projects in Texas South of the Nueces, 1820–1845." *Southwestern Historical Quarterly* 50 (Apr., 1947): 431–48.

Bibliography

Haggard, J. Villasaña. "Epidemic Cholera in Texas, 1833–1834." *Southwestern Historical Quarterly* 40 (Jan., 1837): 216–30.

Hamilton, Holman. *Zachary Taylor.* Vol. 1 *Soldier of the Republic.* 2 vols. New York: Bobbs-Merrill Company, 1941.

Hammett, A. B. J. *The Empresario Don Martín de Leon.* Kerrville, Texas: Braswell Printing Co., 1971.

Haring, C. H. *The Spanish Empire in America.* New York: Oxford University Press, 1947.

Harris, Lewis Birdsall. "Journey of Lewis Birdsall Harris, 1836–1842," *Southwestern Historical Quarterly* 25 (October, 1921): 63–71, 131–46, 185–97.

Hart, James P. "Oil, the Courts, and the Railroad Commission." *Southwestern Historical Quarterly* 44 (Jan., 1941): 303–20.

Hatcher, Mattie Austin. "Municipal Government of San Fernando de Béxar, 1730–1800." *Southwestern Historical Quarterly* 8 (Apr., 1905): 277–352.

———. "Texas in 1820: Report of the Barbarous Indians of the Province of Texas, by Juan Antonio Padilla, Made December 27, 1819 . . ." *Southwestern Historical Quarterly* 23 (1919–20): 47–48.

Hinojosa, Gilberto Miguel. *A Borderlands Town in Transition: Laredo, 1755–1870.* College Station: Texas A&M University Press, 1983.

Hogan, William R. *The Texas Republic: A Social and Economic History.* Austin: University of Texas Press, 1969.

Huson, Hobart. *Refugio: A Comprehensive History of Refugio County from Aboriginal Times to 1955.* 2 vols. Woodsboro, Texas: Rooke Foundation, 1955.

Hutchins, Wells A. "The Community Acequia: Its Origins and Development." *Southwestern Historical Quarterly* 31 (Jan., 1928): 261–84.

———. *The Texas Law of Water Rights.* Austin: Texas Board of Water Engineers, 1961.

Jackson, Jack. *Los Mesteños: Spanish Ranching in Texas, 1721–1821.* College Station: Texas A&M University Press, 1986.

Jones, O. Garfield. "Local Government in the Spanish Colonies as Provided by the Recopilación de Leyes de los Reinos de las Indias." *Southwestern Historical Quarterly* 19 (July, 1915): 65–90.

Jordan, Terry G. "The Origin of Anglo-American Cattle Ranching in Texas: A Documentation of Diffusion from the Lower South." *Economic Geography* 45 (Jan., 1969): 63–87.

Kennedy, William. *Texas: The Rise, Progress, and Prospects of the Republic of Texas.* Reprint from 2nd ed. Fort Worth, Texas: Molyneaux Craftsmen, Inc., 1925.

Kimball, John P., comp. *Laws and Decrees of the State of Coahuila and Texas.* Houston: Secretary of State, 1839.

Kuykendall, J. H., ed. "Reminiscences of Barzillai Kuykendall," *Quarterly of the Texas State Historical Association* 6 (Apr., 1903): 311–30.

———. "Reminiscences of Capt. Gibson Kuykendall," *Quarterly of the Texas State Historical Association* 7 (July, 1903): 29–64.

Lathrop, Barnes F. *Migration into East Texas, 1835–1860: A Study from the United States Census.* Austin: Texas State Historical Association, 1949.

McAlister, J. "The Reorganization of the Army of New Spain, 1763–1767." *Hispanic American Historical Review* 30 (Feb., 1953): 1–32.

Bibliography

McClintock, William A. "Journal of a Trip through Texas and Northern Mexico in 1846–1847," *Southwestern Historical Quarterly* 34 (1930–31): 20–37, 141–58, 231–56.

MacLachlan, Colin M. *Criminal Justice in Eighteenth Century Mexico: A Study of the Tribunal of the Acordada.* Berkeley: University of California Press, 1974.

Mexico. Archivo General de la Nación. México, D.F., México.

Miller, Thomas Lloyd. *The Public Lands of Texas, 1519–1970.* Norman: University of Oklahoma Press, 1972.

Montejano, David. *Anglos and Mexicans in the Making of Texas, 1836–1986.* Austin: University of Texas Press, 1987.

Moorhead, Max L. *The Apache Frontier: Jacobo Ugarte and Spanish-Indian Relations in Northern New Spain, 1769–1791.* Norman: University of Oklahoma Press, 1968.

Morfí, Juan Agustín. *Viaje de Indios y diario del Nuevo México con una introducción bibliográfica y anotaciones por Vito Alessio Robles.* 2nd ed. México: Antigua Librería Robredo, 1935.

Myers, Sandra L. *The Ranch in Spanish Texas, 1691–1800.* University of Texas at El Paso Social Science Series, no. 2. El Paso: Texas Western Press, 1969.

Nance, Joseph Milton. *After San Jacinto: The Texas-Mexican Frontier, 1836–1841.* Austin: University of Texas Press, 1963.

Newcomb, W. W., Jr. *The Indians of Texas, from Prehistoric to Modern Times.* Austin: University of Texas Press, 1961.

Nixon, Patrick Ireland. *Medical Story of Early Texas, 1528–1853.* San Antonio: Mollie Bennett Lupe Memorial Fund, 1946.

Novisima Recopilación de las leyes de España. 6 vols. Madrid: Impresa de Madrid, 1805.

Nuestra Señora del Refugio de la Bahía Mission. "Record Book." Refugio, Texas.

Nueva Recopilación de las leyes de España. Madrid: Imprenta Real, 1772.

O'Connor, Kathryn Stoner. *The Presidio La Bahía del Espíritu Santo de Zuñiga, 1721 to 1846.* Austin: Von Boeckmann-Jones Co., 1966.

Patch, Joseph Dorst. *The Concentration of General Zachary Taylor's Army at Corpus Christi, Texas.* Corpus Christi, Texas: Mission Printing, 1962.

Pierce, Frank Cushman. *Texas' Last Frontier: A Brief History of the Lower Rio Grande Valley.* Menasha, Wisconsin: Collegiate Press, 1917.

Pierce, Gerald S. *Texas under Arms: The Camps, Posts, and Military Towns of the Republic of Texas, 1836–1846.* Austin: Encino Press, 1969.

Pomeroy, Earl S. *The Territories and the United States, 1861–1890: Studies in Colonial Administration.* Seattle: University of Washington Press, 1947.

Poyo, Gerald E., and Gilberto M. Hinojosa, eds. *Tejano Origins in Eighteenth-Century San Antonio.* Austin: University of Texas Press, 1991.

Prieto, Alejandro. *Historia, geografía, y estadística del estado de Tamaulipas.* México: Escalerillas, 1873.

Ramsdell, Charles, Jr. "Spanish Goliad," MSS. Barker Texas History Center. University of Texas at Austin.

Rather, Ethel Zivley. "DeWitt's Colony." *Quarterly of the Texas State Historical Association* 8 (Oct., 1904): 95–191.

Refugio County. Deed Records. County Clerk's Office. Refugio, Texas.

Richardson, Rupert Norval, Ernest Wallace, and Adrian N. Anderson. *Texas: The Lone Star State*. 3rd ed. Englewood Cliffs, N.J.: Prentice Hall, 1970.

Rodriguez, J. M. *Rodriguez Memoirs of Early Texas*. San Antonio: Passing Show Printing Co., 1913.

Rowe, Edna. "The Disturbances at Anahuac in 1832." *Southwestern Historical Quarterly* 6 (Apr., 1903): 265–99.

Rubio, Abel G. *Stolen Heritage: A Mexican-American's Rediscovery of His Family's Lost Land Grant*. Austin: Eakin Press, 1986.

San Antonio. "Minutes of the City Council of the City of San Antonio, 1815–35" (transcript). Translated and transcribed and typed by Texas Works Progress Administration. Office of the City Clerk. San Antonio, Texas.

San Antonio. San Fernando Archives. San Fernando Cathedral. San Antonio, Texas.

Sánchez, José María. "A Trip to Texas in 1828," translated by Carlos Eduardo Castañeda. *Southwestern Historical Quarterly* 29 (1925–26): 249–95.

San Felipe de Austin. Miscellaneous Papers, Barker Texas History Center. University of Texas at Austin.

San Miguel, Guadalupe, Jr. *"Let All of them Take Heed": Mexican Americans and the Campaign for Educational Equality in Texas, 1910–1981*. Austin: University of Texas Press, 1987.

Santamaría, Francisco J. *Diccionario de Mejicanismos*. 2nd ed. Méjico: Editorial Porrua, 1974.

Santos, Richard. "A Preliminary Survey of the San Fernando Archives." *Texas Libraries* 28 (Winter, 1966–67): 152–72.

Sayles, John, and Henry Sayles. *Early Laws of Texas*. 3 vols. 2nd ed. St. Louis: The Gilbert Book Co., 1891.

Scott, Florence Johnson. *Historical Heritage of the Lower Rio Grande*. Waco: Texian Press, 1966.

Sibley, Marilyn McAdams. *The Port of Houston: A History*. Austin: University of Texas Press, 1968.

Spain. Archivo General de las Indias (transcripts). Audencia de Guadalajara. Barker Texas History Center. University of Texas at Austin.

Spencer, Rafael Aguáyo, comp. *Obras de D. Lucas Alamán: Documentos Diversos*. 4 vols. México: Editorial Jus, 1947.

Stambaugh, J. Lee, and Lillian J. Stambaugh. *The Lower Rio Grande Valley of Texas*. San Antonio: Naylor Company, 1954.

Tamaulipas. "Governación: Decreto Número 73." Ciudad Victoria, Nov. 13, 1828. Salce Arredondo Imprints. Nettie Lee Benson Latin American Collection. University of Texas at Austin.

Taylor, Paul S. "Historical Note on Dimmit County, Texas." *Southwestern Historical Quarterly* 24 (Oct., 1930): 79–90.

———. *An American-Mexican Frontier, Nueces County, Texas*. Chapel Hill: University of North Carolina Press, 1934.

Taylor, Virginia H., ed. and trans. *The Letters of Antonio Martínez: Last Spanish Governor of Texas, 1817–1822*. Austin: Texas State Library, 1957.

Texas. Béxar Archives. Barker Texas History Center. University of Texas at Austin.

Texas. General Land Office. Spanish Archives. 42 vols. and supplements. Austin, Texas.

Texas. Nacogdoches Archives. Texas State Library. Austin, Texas.

Texas, Republic of *Journals of the Fourth Congress of the Republic of Texas, 1839–1840 to Which Are Added the Relief Laws*, vol. 1, *The Senate Journal.* Austin: Von Boeckmann-Jones Co., n.d.

Texas General Land Office. *Abstract of All Original Texas Land Titles Comprising Grants and Locations to August 31, 1942.* 8 vols. Austin: State of Texas, 1942.

————. "J. de Cordova's Map of the State of Texas, 1849" (K-4-11).

————. *Maps of All Texas Counties.* Tulsa, Oklahoma: Wolf & Bennett, n.d.

————. *Spanish Archives.* James R. Miller and W. H. Bourland, "Report of James R. Miller and W. H. Bourland, Commissioners to Investigate Land Titles West of the Nueces" (*MS*, 1854).

Thompson, Jerry Don. *Sabers on the Rio Grande.* Austin: Presidial Press, 1974.

Thonhoff, Robert H. *The First Ranch in Texas.* Southwest Texas Heritage Series, no. 1 (March, 1968).

Index

acequia systems, 38, 53
Acosta, Juan Ysidro, 32
Adaesaños, 18. *See also* Nacogdoches
Ahumada, Mateo, 82
Alamán, Lucas, 51, 98, 127
Alamo, founded, 8, 80
Alarcón, Don Martín de, 8
alcalde, 27, 28, 39–40, 41
Aldrete, José de Jesús, 16
Almonte, Juan N., 67
Almy, Leon R., 114
Amangual, Francisco, 10, 80
Anáhuac, fort, 7
annexation, 119
arancel, 40–41
arbitrios, 68
Archer, Branch T., 89
Arciniega, Gregorio, 115
Arciniega, Miguel, 69, 96, 115
asesor general, 41, 43
Austin, J. E. B., 111
Austin, John, 129
Austin, Moses, 7
Austin, Stephen F.: and Anglo-Tejano con-
flict, 123; appointment of, 105; arrested,
134; and civil code, 72; and cotton
industry, 115; and defense, 87; as
empresario, 47; at San Felipe convention, 130; and slavery, 110; as state deputy, 126
Austin's Colony. *See* San Felipe de Austin
ayuntamiento, 26–27, 28; duties of, 36–38;
elections to, 31, 35

Balmaceda, José María, 11, 126, 131
Bastrop, Baron de, 35, 102; and defense,
87; legislative agenda of, 105, 106, 107,

108; and provincial deputation, 96; as
state deputy, 101
Bayou Pierre, 29
Béjar. *See* Béxar
Benavides, Placido, 15
Benton, Thomas Hart, 42, 119
Béxar: ayuntamiento of, 33, 125; education
in, 60, 63; juez de campo of, 78; and
memoria, 131; round-ups in, 68
Béxar-Goliad region, 5
Blanco, Victor, 114
Boca de Leones, 10
Bolton, Herbert E., 6
Bowie, James, 114
Bradburn, John Davis, 128
Burnet, David G., 128, 133
Bustamante, Anastacio, 84

caballada, 80
calpulli, 28, 46
Cameron, John, 128
Campos, Juan Vicente, 107, 111
Canary Island settlers, 9, 28
Carlos Rancho, 15
Castañeda, Juan de, 96, 100
Castellanos, Nicolás, 29
Cavasos family, 17
Chambers, Thomas Jefferson, 43, 135
Chaves, Francisco Xavier, 11
cholera epidemic, 50
Chriesman, Horatio, 129
Coahuila y Texas, 98–101, 102; colonization
law of, 107, 108; districts in, 105; elec-
tions in, 103; homestead law of, 120
Cobián, José María, 16
Código de las Siete Leyes constitucionales, 43,
135

colonization laws, 34, 106–108, 122
comisario, 39, 46
comisión de escuelas, 58
Committee of Piety, 59
common lands, 47
communications, 65
community, sense of, 46
compañía volante, 9, 79, 80–82
Concepción, Mission, 9, 53
conciliation: as legal principle, 40, 41
Constitution, Coahuila y Texas, 58, 111
Constitution of 1812, Spanish, 3, 30, 76, 93
Constitution of 1824, Mexican, 135
Consultation of 1835, 44
Córdova, Vicente, 86, 138
Córdova family, 20
cotton, 115
Cuellar, Jesús, 90

Decree No. 272, on pre-emption land
    grants, 118
de Croix, Teodoro, 68–69, 79, 93
de la Garza, Carlos, 15, 86, 138. *See also*
    Carlos Rancho
de la Garza, Felipe, 96
de la Garza, Refugio, 49, 94
de Leon, Alonzo, 66
de Leon, Fernando, 137
de León, Martín, 15, 85
department chief, 104
Department of Texas, 104–105
de Soto, José Martinez, 28
despoblado, 5, 65, 69, 73
de Torres, Patricio, 32
de Valle, Santiago, 107
de Veramendi, Juan Martín, 49
DeWitt, Green, 24, 122, 123
Díaz, José Salvador, 42
Dill, James, 19, 29
Domenech, Abbé Emmanuel, 71
Durst, John, 135

Eastern Interior Provinces, 93, 94, 96
Echevarrí, José Antonio, 95
economic enterprise, 114–15
education, public, 58–64
Edwards, Haden, 109
Eldee family, 20
elections, 35–36, 94, 97, 103
Elizondo, Dionisio, 111, 134
empresario, 47
entertainment, 48
entradas, 66
Escandón, José de, 10, 66

fandango, 48
federalism, Mexican, 120
Ferdinand VII of Spain, 3, 30
Flores, Gaspar, 85, 99, 101
Flores, Salvador, 86
flying squadron. *See* compañía volante
Fontán family, 20
Fredonian Rebellion, 30
frontera, 4, 5–6, 9–11, 19, 25, 26, 65–66, 82,
    119

Gama y Fonseca, José Antonio, 59
García, José Antonio, 82
García, Luciano, 96
García Dávila, Pedro, 84
General Consultation of Texas, 1835, 89
Giles, Bascom, 119
Goliad, 15, 32; abandoned, 138; ayunta-
    miento of, 33; cholera epidemic in, 50;
    education in, 60; juez de campo of, 78;
    and memoria, 132
Gómez Farías, Valentín, 134, 135
Gómez Pedraza, Manuel, 134
Gonzales, 34–35
González, Rafael, 82
Guadalupe de Jesús Victoria, 15
Guerrero, Vicente, 114
Guerrero (warship), 48
Gutiérrez-Magee expedition, 19

Haden Edwards Rebellion, 109
Harris, Lewis Birdsall, 72
Harrison, Jonas, 119, 131
Hays, John C., 90
headright system, 118–19
Hernández, Manuel, 19
Hewetson, James, 122
Hidalgo, Miguel, 3
Hidalgo, Salvador, 29
holidays, 48
hombres buenos, 40, 41
horses, 71–72
Houston, Sam, 90, 91, 133
Huizar, Bruno, 59

Ibarvo, José Ignacio, 32
Indians: Cherokee, 109; Comanche, 6;
    Karankawas, 85; Lipan, 6; Tawakoni, 85
irrigation, 51, 52–54. *See also* acequia
    systems
Isabella of Castilla, 74
Iturbide, Agustín de, 4, 87, 95

jefe politico, 30
Jesús y Jaen settlement, 7

Jones, Oliver, 135
Jones, Randall, 88
judicial system, 40–43, 44
juez de campo, 39, 65, 73, 74, 77–78
junta de sanidad, 38, 48, 54
junta gubernativa, 94
junta patriotica, 48

King, W. H., 89
Kuykendall, Abner, 88, 89
Kuykendall, Gibson, 88
Kuykendall, Robert 88

La Bahía: cattle at, 66. *See also* Goliad
LaBahía del Espíritu Santo, Presidio, 14, 123
Lamar, Mirabeau B., 45, 62
land grants, 97, 118–19
Laredo, 22, 26; charter of, 28; cholera epidemic in, 50; education in, 60; first American election in, 45; Indian invasions of, 82
law and order, 38
Law of April 6, 1830, 15, 127, 131
legal traditions, 27
liberal reforms, 3, 76
livestock husbandry, 68–71; regulation of, 72–73
local government, 25–45
López, Gaspar, 96
López de Herrera, Vicente, 118
López family, 20
Loreto, Mission, 14

McCulloch, Ben, 72
Madero, Francisco, 114
Manchola, Rafael Antonio, 16, 83; and DeWitt, 123; offices of, 123; at San Felipe convention, 129; as state deputy, 126
Martinez, Andrés, 45
Martinez, Antonio, 30, 87, 94
Maverick, Samuel A., 55, 57
Maynes, Francisco, 49
Menchaca, José Antonio, 11, 15
mercader, 69
Mesta, 75–76
mesteñas, 67–68
mestizaje, 5, 8, 9, 10, 11, 23
Mexía, José Antonio, 129
Michelí, Don Vicente, 20
Mier, José Servando Teresa de, 98
Mier y Terán, Manuel de, 51, 85, 125
military, on Texas frontier, 5, 6, 13; reorganization of, 82–86
militia, 83–90
Miller and Bourland Report, 118

Monclova, 10, 134
Monterrey, 94
mortality rates, 11–13, 16
Muldoon, Miguel, 122
mules, 72
municipal charters, 32–33, 34
municipality, 25–26, 33. *See also* local government
Músquiz, Manuel, 126–27
Músquiz, Ramón, 33; appointment of, 105; during epidemic, 49; as political chief, 117, 133; and provincial deputation, 96; at San Felipe convention, 130

Nacogdoches, 5, 29; ayuntamiento of, 33; education in, 63; evacuation of, 141; founded, 18; *junta piadosa* of, 59
Navarro, José Antonio, 115, 116
Navarro, Luciano, 125
Neighbors, Robert S., 55
New Regulations of Presidios, 18
Norris, Samuel, 30, 32

O'Connor family, 20
Organic Law, 44
oxen, 72

Palafox, 22, 29, 119
Parras, 10, 28
patriotic events, 48
Perry, J. F., 42
Piedras, José de las, 124, 129
plan de arbitrios, 36
Plan de Casa Mata, 95, 96
Plan de Cuernavaca, 135
Plan de Jalapa, 85, 125–26
Plan de Veracruz, 128–29
Pobedano, Enrique, 16
porción, 23, 51
Power, James, 122
Pre-Emption Act, 119
presidial amalgamation, 7, 8, 11, 15
Procela, Luis, 19, 30
Procela, Pedro, 19, 30
propios, 34, 36, 47
Provincial Deputation, Texas, 96–100
pueblo water rights, 47, 55, 57
Punto de Lampazos, 10

Querétaro, 10

Ramón, Domingo, 8, 14
Ramos Arizpe, Miguel, 6, 67, 93–94, 97, 99
ranches, 15; in Nacogdoches region, 19; along Río Grande, 22–23; along San Antonio River, 16

ranching, 65–66, 71; along Río Grande, 5, 21–22, 138–39
Recopilación, 27–28, 39; homestead protection, 120; on mesteñas, 68; on ranching, 71
Recopilación de las leyes de los reinos de las Indias, 27
Refugio, Mission, 14
regidor, 28, 39
Río Grande: ranching frontier on, 5, 21–22, 138–39
Rodriguez, Ambrosio, 131
Rodriguez, Mariano, 86
Rodriquez, Fernando, 100
ronda, 38
Rosario, Mission, 14
Ross, James, 88
Rubí Marques de, 6, 19

Sabriego, Manuel, 138
Salinas, José María, 49
Salinas, Juan José, 60
San Antonio de Béxar, Presidio de, 8
Sánchez, José María, 11
Sánchez, Nemesio, 82
Sánchez, Nicasio, 85
Sandoval, José, 100
San Esteben community, 28
San Felipe Convention, 61, 63, 89, 129
San Felipe de Austin, 24, 33
San Fernando, 9, 53
San Francisco de Espada, Mission, 9, 29, 53, 59
sanitation, 50, 53
San José, Mission, 9, 29, 53
San Juan, Mission, 9, 29, 53
San Marcos de Neve settlement, 7
Santa Anna, Antonio Lopez de, 128
Santa Fe, N.Mex., 81
Santa Hermandad, 74
San Telésforo settlement, 7
Saucedo, José Antonio, 59, 72, 96–98, 104
schools, 63, 64
Seguin, José Erasmo, 29; as alcalde, 30; in national Congress, 97–99, 110, 121; and new municipalities, 35; in provincial deputation, 101
Seguin, Juan (of Nacogdoches), 29–30
Seguin, Juan N.: and ayuntamiento, 125; and Béxar convention, 131; commissioned, 90; as elector, 94; family of, 97; and militia, 86; as political chief, 133; and resistance to Anglos, 137
Sepúlveda, José Antonio, 19, 109
settlement efforts, 6–7, 22, 66
Simms family, 20

slavery, 109–10, 111, 115–18
Smith, Henry, 90
Stuart, James, 82
sumaria, 40
syndico, 39
syndico procurador, 30, 38, 39

Taylor, Zachary, 91
taxes, 68–69
Tejanas, 10, 13; and community property, 121; as contributors, 59; regional costumes of, 48
Tenoxtitlán, fort, 7
Terán, fort, 7, 19
territorial limits, 120
Texas Provisional Governing Junta, 96
Texas Ranger, 90–91
Tijerina, José Antonio, 114
Tijerina family, 17
Tlascalan settlers, 9–10, 28, 80
Tolle v. Correth, 57
Travieso, Vicente, 77
Trespalacios, José Felix, 47, 87, 95
Trinidad de Salcedo settlement, 7

Urdiñola, Francisco de, 10

Valero, Mission San Antonio de, 8
Vásquez, Encarnación, 30
Vásquez, José Antonio, 135
vecindario, 46
Vehlein, Joseph, 128
Velásquez, Miguel, 75
Victoria, Guadalupe, 114
Victoria, 15, 34, 50
Viesca, Agustín, 114, 117, 134, 136
Viesca, José María, 33, 69, 88, 111, 114, 117; as state deputy, 104, 107, 134
Viesca political faction, 114, 118, 126
Villareal, Enrique, 86

Waco, 55
water law, 50–57
Wharton, William H., 129, 133
Williams, John A., 130

Ybarbo, Antonio Gil, 19
Ybarbo family, 17, 32
Yoakum, Henderson, 101
Yorkinos, 114

Zacatecas, 136
Zambrano, Juan Manuel, 94, 96
Zaragoza, Ignacio, 15
Zavala, Lorenzo de, 114, 128
Zepeda, Victoriano, 59